James Carr offers a much-needed foray into the lives of Muslims in Ireland as they attempt to negotiate their place in the face of popular Islamophobic racism and the simultaneous state denial of its existence. As Carr himself declares, anti-Muslim racism is both un-researched and un-theorised in the Irish context. Thus, he leads the way in illuminating how Islamophobia plays out at the level of a quintessential neo-liberal state. Far from simply a critique, the book also offers an empirical and theoretical foundation from which to challenge exclusionary sentiments, practices and policies.

Professor Barbara Perry, *University of Ontario Institute of Technology, Canada*

Drawing upon results from his own extensive fieldwork, James Carr provides fascinating new insights into the forms and impacts of anti-Muslim racism in contemporary societies. Utilising international perspectives coupled with a case study of Ireland, his excellent and perceptive analysis of this damaging social phenomenon will be of immense value to students, academics and practitioners alike.

Mr Jon Garland, *University of Surrey, UK*

This text is as timely as it is unique. Deconstructing with clarity the sometimes dichotomous relationship between Islamophobia and anti-Muslim racism, Carr's study offers a number of new critical insights into a still embryonic field of inquiry. While focusing on the Irish context – a geographical area that to date has been somewhat overlooked in existing studies – the analyses underpinning and informing this book have a much wider relevance especially those framed by theories of neoliberalism. Without doubt, this book deserves to be widely read.

Dr Chris Allen, *University of Birmingham, UK*

Experiences of Islamophobia

Since 9/11 interest in Islamophobia has steadily increased – as have the number of academic publications discussing the phenomenon. However, theoretical expositions have dominated the field. Lived experiences of Islamophobia, by contrast, have received little attention. In recognition of the importance of addressing this imbalance, this book provides theoretically-informed analyses alongside everyday testimonies of anti-Muslim racism, set comparatively in an international context.

Carr argues that the failure of the neoliberal state to collect data on anti-Muslim racism highlights the perpetuation of 'race' blindness within governance. Not only does this mean that the salience of racism is denied in the lives of those who experience it, but this also enables the state to absolve itself from challenging the issue and providing the necessary supports to Muslim communities.

Offering original empirical research and theoretical engagement with the concept of 'race'-blind neoliberal governance, this book will appeal to students and scholars across the social sciences, in addition to policymakers and activists working in this topical area.

James Carr is based in the Department of Sociology, University of Limerick, Ireland.

Routledge Research in Race and Ethnicity

1 **Racial Discrimination**
Institutional patterns and politics
Masoud Kamali

2 **Black Masculinity and Sexual Politics**
Anthony J. Lemelle, Jr.

3 **Represent**
Art and identity among the black upper-middle class
Patricia A. Banks

4 **Blackness and Transatlantic Irish Identity**
Celtic soul brothers
Lauren Onkey

5 **Music, Difference and the Residue of Race**
Jo Haynes

6 **Black Citizenship and Authenticity in the Civil Rights Movement**
Randolph Hohle

7 **Migrants and Race in the US**
Territorial racism and the alien/outside
Philip Kretsedemas

8 **The Black Professional Middle Class**
Race, class, and community in the post-civil rights era
Eric S. Brown

9 **Race and Class Distinctions Within Black Communities**
A racial-caste-in-class
Paul Camy Mocombe, Carol Tomlin and Cecile Wright

10 **Making Diaspora in a Global City**
South Asian youth cultures in London
Helen Kim

11 **A Moral Economy of Whiteness**
Four frames of racializing discourse
Steve Garner

12 **Race and the Origins of American Neoliberalism**
Randolph Hohle

13 **Experiences of Islamophobia**
Living with racism in the neoliberal era
James Carr

Experiences of Islamophobia
Living with racism in the neoliberal era

James Carr

LONDON AND NEW YORK

First published 2016
by Routledge
2 Park Square, Milton Park, Abingdon, Oxon OX14 4RN

and by Routledge
711 Third Avenue, New York, NY 10017

First issued in paperback 2017

Routledge is an imprint of the Taylor & Francis Group, an informa business

© 2016 James Carr

The right of James Carr to be identified as author of this work has been asserted by him in accordance with sections 77 and 78 of the Copyright, Designs and Patents Act 1988.

All rights reserved. No part of this book may be reprinted or reproduced or utilised in any form or by any electronic, mechanical, or other means, now known or hereafter invented, including photocopying and recording, or in any information storage or retrieval system, without permission in writing from the publishers.

Trademark notice: Product or corporate names may be trademarks or registered trademarks, and are used only for identification and explanation without intent to infringe.

British Library Cataloguing in Publication Data
A catalogue record for this book is available from the British Library

Library of Congress Cataloging-in-Publication Data
Carr, James (Sociologist)
Experiences of islamophobia : living with racism in the neoliberal era / James Carr.
  pages cm. – (Routledge research in race and ethnicity)
  Includes bibliographical references.
  1. Islamophobia. 2. Neoliberalism. I. Title.
  BP52.C37 2016
  305.6'97–dc23   2015012294

ISBN 13: 978-1-138-48487-0 (pbk)
ISBN 13: 978-1-138-85175-7 (hbk)

Typeset in Times New Roman
by Wearset Ltd, Boldon, Tyne and Wear

For my four shining stars – let's light up the darkness!

Contents

	Acknowledgements	xii
1	**Introduction**	1
	Introduction 1	
	Anti-Muslim racism in the neoliberal era 2	
	'Truth' and rational government 4	
	Theorising 'race' and racism-*lessness 6*	
	Anti-Muslim racism and the neoliberal state 8	
	Chapter outline 11	
2	**Conducting 'race' in a neoliberal world**	15
	Introduction 15	
	Sovereign and disciplinary power 16	
	Disciplinary power and the norm 17	
	Governmentality 18	
	'Truth' 19	
	Neoliberalism as a regime of 'truth' 21	
	The 'truth' of neoliberal governmentality 21	
	'Race', racism and the post-racial neoliberal 'moment' 26	
	Resisting 'racelessness' and anti-Muslim racism 29	
	Discussion and conclusion 31	
3	**De-constructing Islamophobia**	33
	Introduction 33	
	Defining Islamophobia 34	
	Defining racism 36	
	Defining anti-Muslim racism as anti-Muslim racism *37*	
	Neoliberalism and efficient racialised 'truths' of the Muslim as 'other' 44	
	Discussion and conclusion 53	

4 Measuring anti-Muslim racism: Ireland and abroad 55
Introduction 55
Recording racism: Ireland and the international context 56
Alternative and complementary data on racism 64
Encouraging reporting 67
Discussion and conclusion 70

5 Conducting hearts and minds: anti-Muslim racism in a neoliberal state 74
Introduction 74
Anti-Muslim racism in Ireland 74
Hegemonic Irishness 76
Neoliberal Irishness 77
Suspect communities 82
Suspicious communities 86
Religious identifiability and 'selective (in)visibility' 88
'Liberating' the oppressed 92
Discussion and conclusion: 'day in and day out' 96

6 Neoliberal governmentalities of 'care': rhetoric and anti-Muslim racism in Ireland 99
Introduction 99
The neoliberal (non)racial republic 99
The smiling face of Janus: the Irish state and anti-racism 101
Janus turns: the Irish state and rhetorical anti-racism 104
Discussion and conclusion 112

7 Janus turned: (counter)productive policing 114
Introduction 114
(Not) reporting racism in Ireland 114
Discussion and conclusion 130

8 Opportunities for positive change in the recording and reporting of anti-Muslim racism in neoliberal Ireland 133
Introduction 133
Neoliberal governmentality: 'truths' and rationalities 133
Neoliberal Ireland and anti-Muslim racism 135
'A lot of talk ... not much action' 139
Resisting anti-Muslim racism in the neoliberal era 140
Learning from best practice: recording of anti-Muslim racism 145
Conclusion 147

Appendix 1: methodology 151
Mixed methods research 151
Accessing the knowledges of anti-Muslim racism 151
Understanding the impact of 'reality' 152
Building trust with Muslim communities in Ireland 153
Hearing all voices 154
Positionality 155
Sampling methods: respondent driven sampling 157
Snowball sampling 158
Purposive sampling 159
Phase one: self-completion questionnaire 159
Phase two: discussions with a purpose 160

Appendix 2: hate mail sent to Muslim communities in Dublin, November 2013 162

Bibliography 163
Index 191

Acknowledgements

Permissions

Carr, J. (2011) 'Regulating Islamophobia: The Need for Collecting Disaggregated Data on Racism in Ireland', *Journal of Muslim Minority Affairs*; Special Issue on Islam in Ireland, 31(4), 574–593. Copyright © Institute of Muslim Minority Affairs, reprinted by permission of Taylor and Francis Ltd, www.tandfonline.com on behalf of Institute of Muslim Minority Affairs.

Carr, J. and Haynes, A. (2013) 'A Clash of Racialisations: The Policing of "Race" and of Anti-Muslim Racism in Ireland', *Critical Sociology*, published online July 2013, 1–20. Copyright © The Authors 2013, reprinted by permission of Sage.

Parts of this book originally appeared in Carr, J. (2014) *Experiences of Anti-Muslim Racism in Ireland*, Hate and Hostility Research Group, University of Limerick.

Parts of this book originally appeared in Carr, J. (2013) 'Communicating "Truth": Challenging Islamophobia', in Ternés, A. (ed.) *Communication: Breakdowns and Breakthroughs*, first published by Interdisciplinary Press.

Acknowledgement of funding

The research conducted for this book was funded by an Irish Research Council Postgraduate Scholarship 2010–2013.

1 Introduction

Introduction

Before I started the research upon which this book is based I knew very little about Islam and of Muslim communities in Ireland; less still about their experiences of Islamophobia, or anti-Muslim racism as I prefer to call it for reasons that will become clear later. However, as a student of sociology, I was keenly aware of the discourses surrounding the so-called 'global war on terror'. I also understood that these discourses would have a profound effect on Muslim communities the world over but was unsure how. I set about searching for evidence of anti-Muslim racism in the Irish context only to discover that very little information was available at the level of the state. I subsequently studied the international horizon to find a pattern emerging wherein very little official data were available on this phenomenon, an incredibly relevant phenomenon given the ongoing discourses of terror.

The limited, qualitative insight that was available, then provided by the now defunct National Consultative Committee on Interculturalism (2013) evidenced various incidents of anti-Muslim hostility in Ireland. These ranged from instances of verbal abuse and jibes of 'Osama Bin Laden' and 'London bomber', to reports of physical assault. However, as a sociologist I wanted to discover how prevalent anti-Muslim racism is in Ireland; to understand at a deeper level how it manifests; and how it is lived by Muslim men and women in their daily lives. Given the lack of data on this phenomenon it was also necessary to understand why this lacuna in evidence existed: whether it was due to a 'blindness' on the part of the state toward this phenomenon; because people were not reporting it, if so why not; or was anti-Muslim racism really a problem at all. If the problem lay with the practices of the state what were its underpinnings; were they ideologically informed or just an oversight on the part of an Irish State perceived as homogenous? This book addresses these questions and is based on original empirical research on the issue of anti-Muslim racism in Ireland and the state's approach to this phenomenon. The arguments made below derive from extensive fieldwork with Muslim communities in Ireland; representatives of non-governmental organisations and retired police officers; and an evaluation of international best practice in the area of recording racism. The fieldwork here was conducted in Ireland but, as will be demonstrated, the findings resonate far beyond into the broader international context both in terms of the experiences of anti-Muslim racism and their resonance, and also in the responses of nation states in the neoliberal era.

Anti-Muslim racism in the neoliberal era

Consistently and repeatedly throughout the last decade, international research has demonstrated inadequate data collection vis-à-vis anti-Muslim racism. This paucity of data has resulted in consistent and repeated calls for better data collection on this phenomenon (Allen and Nielsen 2002; European Union Agency for Fundamental Rights 2012; European Union Monitoring Centre for Racism and Xenophobia 2006; Organisation for Security and Cooperation in Europe 2011; 2012). Such calls for improved data collection are set in a context wherein anti-Muslim racism continues to affect Muslim communities across the globe and as Muslim communities continue to grow in societies where Muslims have historically been in the minority (see for example Ameli *et al.* 2012; Pew Research 2011; Poynting and Noble 2004; Zempi and Chakraborti 2014).

The past three decades have witnessed strong growth amongst Muslim communities across Europe. Accounting for about 30,000,000 people in 1990, the figure reached 44,000,000 in 2010 and is projected to rise to just shy of 60,000,000 by the year 2030, almost 10 per cent of the population. Notably, Ireland's Muslim population is expected to increase threefold between 2010 and 2030, the largest increase in any European state (Pew Research 2011). Despite their number and myriad diversity, Muslim communities are frequently presented in popular Western discourses as alien and incompatible with a presumed homogenous West (Gest 2010). Almost 20 years ago, the Runnymede Trust, a UK based non-governmental organisation, published a seminal report entitled *Islamophobia: A Challenge for us all* (Runnymede Trust 1997). As the date of publication indicates, this report was compiled in an era far removed from the events of September 2001, demonstrating that anti-Muslim sentiment is not just a recent phenomenon. Indeed, there is a history of constructing Muslims as 'other' in the Western public perception that spans centuries. Events such as the Islamic Revolution in Iran in 1979 and the Salman Rushdie fatwa affair in the UK have added to these historic 'truths' to colour the image of all Muslim communities as the outgroup in the West (Abbas 2011; Said 2003).

Today, notions of idealised culture fill the space where 'race' could once reside unimpeded but is today taboo (Lentin and Titley 2011). Political groups of various hues call for a return to mythicised 'cultural purity' and for the protection of national values (Fekete 2009, p. 3; Vakil 2014). 'Re-imagined European national identities – pristine cultural paragons like 'Britishness, *fraternité* and *hispanidad*' are invoked in the face of an alleged 'failed' multiculturalism and failures of integration (Gest 2010, p. 7). Muslim communities are frequently cast collectively as a group who 'fail' to meet the standards of belonging in liberal societies. Markers of Muslimness, visual signifiers of identity, particularly the hijab and niqab, are utilised to demonstrate the alleged failure of Muslim communities to integrate (as if no Muslim person was ever born and raised in the West) as a group that want to live apart (Brown and Saeed 2014; Lentin and Titley 2011).

Across Europe, policies have been enacted that impact directly upon Muslim communities and their ability to manifest their faith. Prohibitions on the wearing of the hijab, niqab and/or burqa are in place in France and Belgium as well as certain German Lander and parts of Spain (BBC News 2014; Mock and Lichfield 2010). Switzerland has imposed a ban on the building of minarets as the result of a referendum called by right-wing groups who proclaimed they were saving their 'occidental Christian heritage' (Baumann 2009). Far-right groups the length and breadth of Europe have called for stringent measures to be taken against Muslim communities including the closure of mosques and curbs on immigration. These calls invoke racialised discourses of Muslims as 'other', not only a threat to our values but our security (Hafez 2014; Hellyer 2009; Human Rights First 2014; Saul 2014).

In addition to these discourses of cultural incompatibility, Muslim communities are also in the cross-hairs of international discourses of security, radicalisation and the fear of home-grown terrorism, heightened again in the era of ISIS (Neumann 2014; Kundnani 2014). In the contemporary context, Muslim has almost become synonymous with 'suspect'. Hickman *et al.* (2011) detail the manner in which Muslim communities are today a prime 'suspect community', subjected to securitisation practices that operate on Muslimness as a marker of threat. Evidence of increased security towards Muslim communities is rich across the West (Fekete 2009; Human Rights First 2014; Kundnani 2014). More recently the figure of the 'foreign fighter', the 'radical', has taken centre stage in these discourses (Brown and Saeed 2014; International Centre for the Study of Radicalisation 2014; Kundnani 2014). 'Bearded men, veiled women, converts' are presented to us as fitting the profile of 'suspect' subject (Brown and Saeed 2014, p. 2). This despite the seeming impossibility of nation state security bodies successfully profiling 'terrorist' behaviour (Human Rights Watch 2014). Nonetheless, as Fekete (2009, p. 103) argues: 'European intelligence services have promoted the view that young Muslims are increasingly receptive to radicalisation' (see also Human Rights First 2014). While it cannot be denied that a small minority of those who have engaged in terrorist acts have been 'home grown', Muslim communities are presented as an enemy within and this has real effects on the lives of ordinary Muslim men, women and children (Fekete 2009).

Despite the aforementioned paucity of official data on anti-Muslim racism, research from across the West clearly demonstrates the effect of racialised discourses, policies and practices on Muslim communities. Allen and Nielsen (2002) note the manner in which anti-Muslim racism manifests across Europe in the post 9–11 climate with Muslim women singled out due to their religious identifiability. Poynting and Noble (2004) evidence the presence of anti-Muslim racism in Australia and the manner in which it intersects with 'traditional' racisms and xenophobia. Ameli *et al.* (2011) illustrate anti-Muslim racism in

4 *Introduction*

France while the Open Society Institute (2011) elucidates the manner in which French Muslim women negotiate their lives and racism while wearing the veil; all in an era where in France 'popular and radical anti-Muslim rhetoric, supported by inflammatory discourse in segments of the media but also by public figures, has started to become normal' (Open Society Institute 2012, p. 85). Discourses of an alleged incompatibility between Islam and the West proliferated in the aftermath of the attacks on the offices of Charlie Hebdo and a kosher supermarket in Paris. These discourses were simplistic to say the least, lacking in nuance and any recognition of the diversity of Muslim communities in France and indeed worldwide (Allen 2010; Fekete 2015; Hassan 2015; Ramadan 2015; Younge 2015). Evidence indicates that these discourses were accompanied by a rise in anti-Muslim hostility on Muslim communities in France (Tell MAMA 2015a). In addition to the research findings below, members of Muslim communities in the Irish context have reported increased experiences of anti-Muslim racism with direct reference being made to the rise of ISIS and the brutal murders of Western hostages (Meagher 2014). In the UK, Muslim communities have had to live with the increased levels of anti-Muslim racism in the aftermath of the brutal murder of Fusilier Drummer Lee Rigby in Woolwich, London, and revelations of child sex abuse in the North of England, associated with South-Asian men but generalised to all Muslims (Feldman and Littler 2014; Tell MAMA 2015b).

The evidence of anti-Muslim racism presented here and later in this book is very clear: Muslim communities are living with a distinct form of racism that targets them on the basis of their Muslimness. This evidence behoves a state response; that is, of course, if the state sees itself responsible for 'caring' for racism in an era that espouses 'self-governance and self-reliance' (Thompson 2007). To understand the role of the state in the neoliberal era, and indeed some of the broader findings that emerged in this research, I draw on the work of Michel Foucault among others.

'Truth' and rational government

At this point I want to emphasise that although I came to this study from a predominantly Foucauldian perspective, I was always intent on remaining true to the voices of participants as shared through their narratives, their knowledges (Foucault 1980a). The theoretical framework deployed in this study is underpinned by the work of Michel Foucault and those who have developed his insights in the period since his untimely death in 1984. I must state at the outset that my use of Foucault's work presents what may be perceived as an optimistic reading of his work. This is understandable and I acknowledge the tensions between my reading of Foucault's work openly. After all, Foucault (1998) clearly presents the calculative, manipulative manner in which society can be organised by those in authority. Foucault (1998) argues of the regulation of the social body in the interests of government, with society increasingly at the centre of efforts of state administration and regulation. In the era of neoliberal hegemony these process of governmental regulation take on a marketised lens evidenced through discourses of efficiencies, performance indicators and self-reliance (Gray 2013; Thompson 2007). In the contemporary context, governmental intervention in the social is delimited by its perceived utility to the advancement of neoliberal ends (Donzelot 2008; Foucault 2010; Giroux 2008).

A range of Foucauldian concepts are utilised during this study: the work of Michel Foucault allows for rich theoretical insight to be gained on the relationship between power and dominant discourses; the manner in which these discursive formations are formed and deployed as 'truth'; how these 'truths' are utilised to legitimise rationalities of government of the state and the government of the self, at the expense of competing discourses. Foucault (1980) argued that 'truth' is contingent and related to power; in every society there is a 'regime of truth'. Dean (2010a) argues that neoliberalism is the dominant regime of 'truth', or as he puts it, a 'regime of double truths' of our time (see also Harvey 2005). Adopting a Foucauldian lens can reveal the role that power can play in discursive constructions of 'truth'. Thus I utilise a Foucauldian approach here to understand how global constructions of 'truth' position Muslims as 'other' in the public perception. At a more local level I also apply a Foucauldian discursive perspective to understand the character of historic and contemporary constructions of national belonging, using Ireland as an example, which can easily translate to other contexts albeit with obvious localised dimensions. The interrogation of given 'truths' and their relationship to power enables the analysis conducted in this study to move from the purely empirical to allow for a more theoretical understanding of anti-Muslim racism to emerge.

Foucauldian thought on government reveals the manner in which governmental rationalities inform the conduct of the state and that of personal behaviour (Foucault 1991). Combining Foucauldian insights on the dominant regime of 'truth' (or double 'truths') with those derived from the field of governmentality studies allows for a deeper theorisation of anti-Muslim racism and state responses to this phenomenon. In particular, this alignment of Foucauldian thought makes it possible to reveal the relationship between the dominant legitimising discourses ('truths') and the rationalities of government. The application of a Foucauldian perspective reveals the connection between dominant regimes of 'truth', their impact on governmental rationalities, but also the manner in which conduct is conducted, with dominant 'truths' becoming imbibed as popular mentalities or common sense (Dean 2010).

Foucault's theoretical insights provided a platform for this study to theorise anti-Muslim racism and state responses to this phenomenon. However, one of the reasons that I was attracted to the work of Foucault (hence my positive reading of his work), lies in the manner in which he stresses the possibility for resistance; in particular, his concepts of 'counter conduct[s]' (Foucault 1998, p. 95); and *'insurrections of subjugated knowledges'* (Foucault 1980a, p. 81; emphasis his). Thus, while this book refers to the role of dominant regimes of 'truth' and presents the lived realities of anti-Muslim racism, Foucault's work also offers the possibility for change, for resistance. This is vital in the context of a study such as this which endeavours to identify opportunities for change in the manner in which anti-Muslim racism can be challenged by the state. Overall, the Foucauldian perspective adopted in this study allows for a sensitive theorisation of anti-Muslim racism, drawing on the Irish experience, and state responses to this phenomenon and their ideological underpinnings; all the while remaining true to the overarching aim of this research – to challenge anti-Muslim racism.

Theorising 'race' and *racism*-lessness

The originality of this study means that it breaks ground not only empirically but also theoretically. At a general level, the first theoretical contribution of this book is the theorisation of anti-Muslim racism qua anti-Muslim racism within the Irish context; Ireland as discussed below is presented here as an exemplar neoliberal state. Despite previous empirical research conducted in relation to Muslim communities, anti-Muslim racism is under-researched empirically and theoretically. The theoretical contributions of this research are grounded in rich primary data, remaining close to the voices and experiences of participants but also endeavouring to move beyond the empirical in order to develop a deeper understanding of this phenomenon. In addition to Foucault, various distinct and intersecting theoretical perspectives also inform this study and shed light on anti-Muslim racism in the contemporary context. These include perspectives on the concept of Islamophobia; neoliberalism and its relationship with racism; racialisation and the role of the nation state; and the field of governmentality studies.

Multifarious valuable contributions have been made on the subject of Islamophobia from a range of perspectives (Allen 2010; Bunzl 2005; Cesari 2011; Dunn *et al.* 2007; Fekete 2009; Halliday 2003; Kumar 2012; Modood and Meer 2010; Riley-Smith 2010; Schiffer and Wagner 2011; Sheehi 2011; Vakil 2010; inter alia). For example Allen's (2010) interrogation of the term Islamophobia provides deep processual insights on this phenomenon and the manner in which ideas of Muslimness inform exclusionary practices. Likewise, Kumar (2012) relates the role neoliberalism can play in constructing Muslims as 'other'. Pertinent theorisations for this study on the topic of neoliberalism and its role in contemporary racism also derive from a broad range of contributors (Davis 2007; Donzelot 2008; Foucault 2010; Giroux 2008; Goldberg 2002, 2009; Lentin and Lentin 2006; Lentin and Titley 2012; inter alia). These studies demonstrate the manner in which neoliberalism denies the salience of 'race' and racism in the contemporary context and the impact this has on whether or not racism qua racism is recognised as a specific phenomenon. These insights are particularly pertinent to and indeed frame the argument being made in this book vis-à-vis the neoliberal state. Various insights also enable a theorisation of the nation state and the role it plays in the maintenance of nation, defining who belongs or who is 'othered' (Balibar and Wallerstein 1991; Essed 2001; Fanning 2012; Foucault 2003; Garner 2009; Goldberg 2002, 2009; Omi and Winant 2001). Finally, the dominant theoretical strand that informs this research, as noted above, derives from the work of Michel Foucault and also what Dean (2010a) refers to as the field of governmentality studies (Dean 2010, 2010a; Foucault 1991; Gray 2011; Lemke 2001; Miller and Rose 2008; Rose *et al.* 2006).

The utility of the aforementioned perspectives in isolation is undeniable. For example, theories of racialisation, belonging and the creation of nation such as those provided by Fanning (2012) and Garner (2009) are vital if exclusionary practices that delimit national belonging are to be understood in Ireland and beyond (see also Goldstone 2002; Guerin 2002; Lentin 2002; Lentin and McVeigh 2006; Ní Chathain 2011; Ní Shuinéar 2002). Research in Greece (Triandafyllidou and Gropas 2009), the Netherlands (van Nieuwkerk 2004) and in Australia (Poynting and Noble 2004) for example demonstrates the manner in which Muslimness can be juxtaposed with historic imaginings of belonging. These studies provide a historically informed and nationally contingent lens to understand anti-Muslim racism in Ireland which also applies to other contexts. Indeed, the fact that anti-Muslim racism is an international phenomenon implies the presence of global racialised constructions of Muslim as 'other' (see for example Allen and Nielsen 2002; Giroux 2008; Goldberg 2009; Kumar 2012; Poynting and Noble 2004). Thus, framed in this light, it is clear that Muslim communities in Ireland, and other nation states, may face exclusion for not fitting within nationally imagined 'norms' of belonging, and/or on the basis of being perceived as a member of a globalised, negatively racialised grouping. In other words, and by way of example, a Muslim person in Ireland may face racism on the basis of their global racialised identity and/or for being perceived as outside of traditional conceptions of who belongs in Ireland. This denotes a relationship between racialising discourses at the global and national levels which impact upon individual experiences of anti-Muslim racism. Theoretically then, I argue that to understand the 'othering' of Muslim communities, and indeed how contemporary notions of national belonging are constructed, requires a theoretical synthesis and sensitivity that is cognisant of multiple processes of racialisation and 'truths' of belonging.

In the chapters that follow I will also theorise the underlying processes that inform governmental rationalities in the recognition, or lack thereof, of anti-Muslim racism in the neoliberal state, with a particular focus on the role of the police. There is some literature on the recording and reporting of racism in the Irish context. However, this literature is predominantly empirical and lacks a theorisation beyond the immediate experience (Clarke 2013; European Union Agency for Fundamental Rights 2009; Lynch 2011; Taylor 2010). Indeed, there is a complete absence of theoretical insight and knowledge in relation to the related issues of reporting (by victims) and recording (by the state) of anti-Muslim racism as a distinct manifestation of racist practice. I argue that to fully understand the stance of the Irish State towards anti-Muslim racism, it is necessary to draw on a number of theoretical perspectives that emphasise the connection between hegemonic global discourses and local practices of government. The work of Foucault (1991) and Goldberg (2002, 2009; see also Lentin and Titley 2012; Roberts and Mahtani 2010; Thompson 2007) is particularly insightful in this regard; as are the contributions of those scholars within the field of governmentality studies (Dean 2010, 2010a; Miller and Rose 2008; Rose *et al.* 2006). Goldberg (2002, 2009) and Lentin and Titley (2012) theorise the manner in which states deny the salience of 'race' in an era of post-racialism. This blindness towards 'race' denies the lived experiences of racism, allowing the state to absent itself from any responsibility towards caring for those who are targeted through racist exclusionary practices. It is argued here that this blindness has neoliberal rationalities at its core which direct the attitude of government and 'conduct the conduct' of neoliberalised individuals.

Anti-Muslim racism and the neoliberal state

Ireland, as will be argued throughout this study is held here as an exemplar neoliberal state; a state wherein neoliberalism has become core to the rationalities of government, at the level of the state and permeating into governance of the self. That is not to say that everyone in Ireland is neoliberal but that in Ireland as abroad, as Harvey argues:

> Neoliberalism ... has become hegemonic as a mode of discourse. It has pervasive effects on ways of thought where it has become incorporated into the common-sense way many of us interpret, live in, and understand the world.
> (2005, p. 3)

I do of course recognise and indeed evidence below the distinctness in terms of contexts, politics and histories of different states. The influences of colonialism and counter colonialism in the Irish context and its influence on historically based notions of belonging in Ireland; or the manner in which the murder of Stephen Lawrence catalysed the UK Government to challenge 'race' hate (this is not to say that arguably racist state practices persist; see, for example, Peachy 2014). Like Harvey (2005) and Thompson (2007), I do contend that neoliberalism is the dominant source of discourses and 'truths' of how to be in our time. Neoliberalism informs how nation states recognise and react (or not) to 'race' and broader forms of hate and exclusion. As will be demonstrated below, internalised neoliberal ideals also direct the manner in which those who have been subjected to anti-Muslim racism feel they should react when they experience hostility. After all, in the neoliberal "society of individuals' all the messes into which one can get are assumed to be self-made' (Zygmunt Bauman, cited in Giroux 2008, p. 591). As such, in this era of neoliberal 'responsibilisation' (Thompson 2007), it is up to each of us to manage our own experiences of racism.

According to the most recent census conducted in 2011 (Central Statistics Office 2012), there are just under 50,000 Muslim men and women in Ireland. These communities are incredibly diverse and derive from over 40 different nationalities. Existing research conducted with Muslim communities to date also reveals that various religious traditions or aspects of Islam are also represented in Ireland. These are made up primarily by a Sunni majority but there is also a considerable Shi'a presence, numbering approximately 10 per cent of the total population, and a small Ahmadiyya community (Scharbrodt and Sakaranaho 2011). To date, academic studies on Islamic communities in Ireland have included important contributions in terms of: comparative international research on Muslims and multiculturalism (Sakaranaho 2006); civil integration of Muslim communities in Ireland (Ciciora 2010); historical and contemporary dynamics of Muslim communities in the Irish context (Flynn 2006; Scharbrodt 2011, 2012), the experiences of Muslim women in Ireland including Irish female reverts to Islam (Shanneik 2011); global influences on Muslim communities in Ireland (Khan 2011); Islam and the Irish education system (Hogan, 2011); Islamic finance in Ireland (Richardson 2011); and a history of Islam in Ireland authored by Oliver Scharbrodt and colleagues at University College Cork. An obvious lacuna remains on the topic of Islamophobia or as I prefer and will argue for later, anti-Muslim racism.

The empirical research conducted for this study is the first to engage specifically and extensively with anti-Muslim racism in Ireland and contributes to studies from across the globe that have provided insights into the levels and the lived experiences of this phenomenon (Allen and Nielsen 2002; Ameli *et al.* 2012; Dwyer *et al.* 2008; European Network Against Racism 2013; European Union Monitoring Centre for Racism and Xenophobia 2006, 2006a; Hussain and Bagguley 2012; Open Society Institute 2011; Poynting and Noble 2004; Sheridan 2006; van der Valk 2012; Zempi and Chakraborti 2014). In doing so, this research provides an original and unique evidence base of anti-Muslim racism in Ireland: providing heretofore unavailable insights on how pervasive this phenomenon may be lived among Muslim communities; the nuances in terms of how it manifests in the Irish context; is it reported or not and why; how it is approached by the State; and how the Irish experience compares internationally.

The now outdated Irish National Action Plan against Racism (Department of Justice Equality and Law Reform 2005) specifically referred to Islamophobia and the need for official data on all forms of racism in Ireland. However, there remains a severe paucity of data on anti-Muslim racism in Ireland. The limited official statistical data that are available on racism are not disaggregated to allow levels of anti-Muslim racism as a specific phenomenon to be revealed (Office of the Minister for the Promotion of Migrant Integration 2015). To date only two surveys have been conducted by state agencies that have enquired into the experiences of Muslim communities and the topic of discrimination (McGinnity *et al.* 2012; Russell *et al.* 2008). Thus experiences of anti-Muslim racism in Ireland remain undocumented, making the research presented here all the more urgent.

In addition to providing original insights into anti-Muslim racism, the various research methods deployed in this study also interrogate the effect of the state's failure to recognise this phenomenon – its racism blindness. Walsh (2009) argues that different communities need to have their distinct policing needs recognised.

This study reveals the impact of the non-recognition of anti-Muslim racism at the level of the neoliberal Irish State, focusing in particular on the Irish police service – An Garda Síochána – and, to a lesser extent, the Central Statistics Office vis-à-vis recording practices. National and international studies have demonstrated the negative effects that poor policing practices can have on those who experience racism qua racism, frequently discouraging those vulnerable to such hostility or discrimination from ever making a report of their experience to the police (Browne 2008; European Union Agency for Fundamental Rights 2009a; Lynch 2011; Poynting and Noble 2004). In addition to revealing insights and understandings of anti-Muslim racism, this book also investigates and illuminates perceptions towards, and practices of, reporting racism to the state among Muslim communities in Ireland. I argue that these findings, like the themes of anti-Muslim racism that are elaborated below, albeit influenced by their location in the Irish context, are equally transferable abroad. One of the most striking aspects of undertaking this research was the similarities, evidenced below, between experiences and responses to anti-Muslim racism in Ireland and those reported in other national contexts.

The fact that anti-Muslim racism is not officially recognised in Ireland, as in other nation states (see Organisation for Security and Cooperation in Europe 2015), means that it is currently impossible for the State to construct policies that could effectively challenge this phenomenon. Moreover, the lack of data on anti-Muslim racism allows the State to absent itself from its responsibility in this area, to remain blind. International experience demonstrates that data on anti-Muslim racism are vital if we are to challenge this phenomenon through informed policies. Scholars in the UK and Irish contexts (including Allen (2011a, 2012), Hickman (1998), King-O'Riain (2007), Moore and Hickman (2012)) have made repeated calls for official data on minority communities. These scholars make the case that the provision of official data could go some way to challenging the experiences of exclusionary practices as lived by vulnerable minorities. The need for official data on anti-Muslim hostility and discrimination in the UK, as argued by Allen (2011a, 2012), is also a view held within Muslim communities. This was underscored during an interview I conducted with one British participant who has been a member of various UK based Muslim NGOs for the last number of years and an advocate of getting 'Islamophobic crimes' recorded by the London Metropolitan Police. From his perspective, data are:

> [V]ery fundamental, I don't think we can achieve any of the change unless we have data that are reliable I think for the last ten years we've just been talking anecdotally [about anti-Muslim racism] … and it's become a political football people use it for political purposes, you have ministers [who] will make comments at particular time [that] Islamophobia is really bad, but we know it's bad [but] … there's nothing happening and I think … just going by how other hate crimes have been dealt with, my experience is … that when they have good datasets it actually helps in first of all policing it, but secondly, actually people taking the issue seriously and dealing with it

... having proper legislation ... because the phenomena we are facing is [sic] not going to go away in the next ten years, I don't think so if you look at the media reporting it's still very negative against Muslims, it is creating Muslims in a particular stereotype in a particular persona which encourages further normalisation of Islamophobia or anti-Muslim hatred ... I think data is ... not the be all and end all don't get me wrong, but it's an important step.

In terms of policy relevance this study presents an evidence base from which it is possible to argue in favour of the recognition and collection of data on anti-Muslim racism as a distinct form of racist activity. This in turn can inform the creation and implementation of policies that can effectively challenge anti-Muslim racism in Ireland. Furthermore, the collection and collation of data on anti-Muslim racism can also provide a platform from which civil society, including Muslim communities themselves, can also challenge this phenomenon. In arguing for change – applicable to Ireland and also the broader international context – examples of best practice in terms of capturing data on anti-Muslim racism (and other forms of hate) are evaluated below. Insights are drawn from four States which have been cited as 'best in class' in relation to capturing data on racist activity in the EU, namely the UK, Finland, Sweden, and the Netherlands (European Union Agency for Fundamental Rights 2012). This is not to say these states are perfect as the comments above demonstrate. However, as I will argue below, each of these States provides important insights on practices that, if deployed, could be used to challenge anti-Muslim racism and encourage those targeted to report their experiences.

Chapter outline

There are eight chapters in this book. Chapter 2 presents and elaborates the theoretical framework that underpins this study, which is premised on the work of Michel Foucault and later Foucauldian theorists. I start this chapter by tracing the development of Foucault's theories of the art of government and the relationship between 'truth' and power (Foucault 1980, 1991). I contend that Foucault's concept of governmentality is particularly useful as an analytical tool to interrogate the manner in which our conduct is conducted in the social through the 'rationalities and techniques' of government (Rose *et al.* 2006, p. 99). As noted above, Foucauldian theories of government allow for incisive analyses into the way power permeates society penetrating the population and the interactions between individuals. I argue that, in the contemporary era, neoliberalism as the dominant 'regime of truth' (Foucault 1980, p. 131) or 'regime of double truths' informs the rationalities and techniques of government at the level of the state and the self (Dean 2010a, p. 10). I contend that 'race' and racism are at the core of contemporary neoliberal forms of governmentality and the rationalities associated with this form of government. However, while 'race' and racism play a central role in neoliberal governmentality, the part they play is obfuscated in the arguments of how to govern the state and the self and the need to bring freedom to those who do not conform to the neoliberal norm (Goldberg 2009; Lentin and Titley 2012). In sum, the work of Michel Foucault allows research such as this the opportunity to go beyond the lived immediate experience of racist incidents in order to understand how neoliberal 'truths' inform and underpin 'lived' racism and the rationalities of government vis-à-vis challenging anti-Muslim racism.

While in Chapter 2 I establish the role of neoliberalism as the dominant regime of 'truth' and its effect on governmental rationalities, in Chapter 3 I turn specifically to the concept of Islamophobia. I argue that the term Islamophobia is itself problematic and should be replaced with anti-Muslim racism. To make this argument, I draw theoretically from the concept of racialisation to emphasise the processes at play in constructing Muslims as 'other'. I review some of the debates and contributions made heretofore on the concept of Islamophobia and argue that greater utility can be gained in challenging this phenomenon if anti-Muslim racism is used in its place.

The rationale that underpins this argument lies in what I contend is the greater discursive, emotive power that anti-Muslim racism as a concept holds over the somewhat ambiguous Islamophobia. From here I present a definition of anti-Muslim racism that I argue could have greater purchase in public discourses and thus allow a challenge to be made to this normalised form of racism. I argue that Islamophobia as a concept is not fit for purpose if that purpose is challenging the racism experienced by Muslim men, women and children. Moreover, I contend that the term Islamophobia actually allows experiences of anti-Muslim hostility and discrimination to continue unchallenged, obfuscating the experiences of Muslim communities behind a veil of conceptual ambiguity and fitting the neoliberal zeitgeist of 'race' and racism blindness (Goldberg 2009). This has to change if those of us in a position to potentially influence public policy are to be effective and true to those about whose experiences we theorise.

Chapter 4 is the last of a tripartite literature review and focuses specifically on the manner in which the neoliberal Irish State records or fails to record data on racism, focusing in particular on anti-Muslim racism. The evaluation undertaken in this chapter is set in a comparative context to other European Union Member States that have been described as having the best in class procedures in terms of recording multifarious forms of racism. Although Chapter 4 is primarily empirical, I also develop the theoretical arguments made in preceding chapters, particularly in relation to the non-recognition or blindness toward 'race' in the neoliberal context. Indeed, this chapter exposes the manner in which the Irish State as an exemplar of neoliberal governmentality does the bare minimum to counter pernicious social phenomena such as racism. This chapter also fulfils an important function in this book as it provides the empirical bedrock from which recommendations can be made vis-à-vis how states, Ireland or otherwise, could recognise and record anti-Muslim racism.

In Chapter 5 I present heretofore unknown insights into anti-Muslim racism in Ireland derived from the quantitative and qualitative phases of this study. The findings revealed in this chapter provide a platform from which an understanding of anti-Muslim racism in Ireland can emerge, based on the local, 'subjugated knowledges' (Foucault 1980a, p. 81) of Muslim communities.¹ Throughout this chapter, the knowledges of Muslim men and women provide the basis for the further theorisation of anti-Muslim racism in Ireland and its relationship with the global context. This includes issues such as the role of historically informed notions of belonging in Ireland and the contemporary securitisation of Muslimness on the global stage, framed in a neoliberal era that valorises the individual. The importance of signifiers of Muslimness and gender on experiences of anti-Muslim racism in the Irish context is also made clear. While I do not claim to represent the experiences of all Muslim communities in Ireland, this chapter reveals the 'reality' of anti-Muslim racism in Ireland as captured through its effects.

From establishing the presence of anti-Muslim racism in Ireland in Chapter 5, in Chapters 6 and 7 I focus on the related topics of recording and reporting of anti-Muslim racism. Analyses of both quantitative data and rich narrative data provide insights on the perceptions towards and practices of reporting anti-Muslim racism by Muslim communities in Ireland. The voices of Muslim participants are added to here by retired members of An Garda Síochána and representatives of Irish based non-governmental organisations in order to get an insider perspective on state practices vis-à-vis racism. It is argued that the Irish State is disengaged when it comes to caring for those vulnerable to racism. Moreover, I contend that the Irish State, true to neoliberal rationalities of government, by not 'caring', actively encourages those who are targeted with anti-Muslim racism to either care for themselves or to seek support among privatised providers of care. I contend that this process of caring for the self continues state practices of policing the nation and challenging the maintenance of collective identities that grate against contemporary notions of what it means to belong in the neoliberal state.

The final chapter of this book presents the conclusions I have arrived at, based on the theorisation of primary data that emerged in both the quantitative and qualitative phases of this study. Here, I draw together the various strands of the argument that has developed over the course of this research. On the basis of these conclusions I proffer some recommendations in terms of opportunities for positive change in relation to the recognition of anti-Muslim racism in Ireland that also transfer to a broader international context. Importantly, these recommendations are premised on the argument that to challenge neoliberal rationalities one must meet neoliberalism on its own terms. As Thompson (2007) argues, 'since 'everyone' has become so much a part of this [neoliberal] programme, no one can escape it or stand aside from or externally criticise it'. I contend that there is a strong argument in favour of state recognition of anti-Muslim racism on neoliberal terms and that resistance can manifest even in an era where neoliberalism has assumed a hegemonic status.

More generally, by drawing on the work of Foucault and his concepts of counter conduct (1998) and subjugated knowledge (1980a), I contend that this book can be perceived as an 'insurrection of subjugated knowledges' (Foucault 1980a, p. 95) of those who live anti-Muslim racism in Ireland. To the voices of

Muslim participants can be added those of people who once represented the State, retired police officers and members of non-governmental organisations. Revealing these experiences and voices can provide a platform from which to argue for a counter conduct that can challenge anti-Muslim racism in the Irish context: turning the normalising gaze on those who engage in this phenomenon instead of Muslim communities. Given the dearth of knowledge on anti-Muslim racism in Ireland, this book is also a resource for others wishing to research this topic. Thus, in its own way, this book plays its own part in challenging the race and racism blindness of the neoliberal state. It is hoped that the arguments made below will be utilised to catalyse change and help challenge hate in all its forms, in Ireland and abroad.

Note

1 '[S]ubjugated knowledges are ... those blocs of historical knowledge which were [always have been] present but disguised within the body of functionalist and systemising theory ... which criticism ... has been able to reveal' (Foucault 1980a, p. 82). For Foucault (1980a, p. 81) there are two aspects to his concept of subjugated knowledges. First, there is that which takes the form of 'historical contents', those contents, multiplicity of histories from below, whose existence has been denied and hidden. It is through the revelation of these historical contents that criticism of hegemonic 'truths' can be contested, serving to unsettle their discursive foundations and legitimacy. Subjugated knowledges also refer to a stratification of contemporary knowledges. Here, entire knowledges are eschewed, presented as 'inadequate' or poorly defined and baseless (Foucault 1980a, p. 82).

2 Conducting 'race' in a neoliberal world

Introduction

The work of Michel Foucault and later Foucauldian thinkers provide the theoretical underpinnings for the arguments I proffer in this book. The purpose of this chapter is to sensitise the reader to the various conceptual tools that will be utilised in the theorisation of anti-Muslim hostility and discrimination, and its governance. I commence by providing a 'genealogy' of Foucault's theories of governance from the mode of the sovereign through to the contemporary art of government with its neoliberal 'regime of truth' (Foucault 1980, p. 133). According to Foucault, 'We live in an era of governmentality' (2009, p. 109). Rose *et al.* (2006, p. 99) argue that Foucault's concept of governmentality is an analytical tool that allows us to map the course of 'governmental rationalities and techniques'. As a concept for inquiry, governmentality enables us to undertake critical analyses of how our 'conduct is conducted' and the rationale(s) that undergirds this process (Sending and Neumann 2006). Utilising a Foucauldian perspective I argue that neoliberalism is the dominant 'truth' of government in the contemporary era. I contend, drawing on renowned international scholars, that racism is a central aspect of neoliberal 'truth' and attendant rationalities.

Neoliberalism denies the salience of racism, all the while utilising racist discourses in its armoury to justify the expansion of the neoliberal regime of truth at home and abroad. Foucault's work on the 'art of government' is particularly incisive in the context of this study, allowing as it does for a deeper theorisation of the government of those communities deemed 'other'. In particular, Foucault's (1991) concept of governmentality offers investigations of racisms such as these a theoretical route to go beyond the lived immediate experience of racist incidents in order to understand how neoliberal 'truths' inform the gaze of 'us' toward the 'other' and underpin 'lived' racism. In what follows, I will commence by charting the manner in which Foucault developed his theories of government before applying them to racisms in the neoliberal age.

Sovereign and disciplinary power

In the *History of Sexuality: Volume One* (1998) Michel Foucault discussed how the previous state regimes of the sovereign or prince exercised power over life by asserting power over death: 'the right to *take* life or to *let* live'. Heads of state ruled over the life chances of their populations, punitively taking the lives of those deemed a threat or deducting life on the battlefield, taking taxes and expecting loyalty in return (Foucault 1998, pp. 135–137). However, commencing in the seventeenth century, this power to 'take' started to be replaced by a power that is more calculative, a power that drives to observe, to organise and manipulate society; here, life itself replaces death as the focus of power. Life in the form of the population; its productivity and re-productivity are increasingly the centre of efforts at state administration and regulation (Foucault 1998).

Foucault (1998, p. 139) describes how this development of 'power over life' manifested and was deployed in the form of 'two poles'. The original of these two poles focused on the individualistic performative aspect of the human form: an 'anatamo-politics of the human body'. The body had become the focus of power in the classical period, a malleable 'docile' entity that could be examined and disciplined so as to create an enhanced and more productive individual (Foucault 1991b, pp. 136–138). Power now worked to increase the utility of the body while contemporaneously making the body more docile and accepting of its position vis-à-vis power relations; the body was to be trained in order to ensure the optimum use of resources, to self-manage (Foucault 1991b, pp. 138 and 170). The body was increasingly the focus of refinement through disciplinary practices of control that worked upon the minutiae of bodily functions creating in the process a more efficient and productive individual (Foucault 1991b). Institutions such as the military, the factory and the academy all operated as key conduits of these disciplinary practices of the body (Foucault 1998).

This power over the individual body was accompanied at a later time with the second pole that emerged under this new focus on power over life. Here, the population or 'species body' joins the individual body as the focus of attention. The wellbeing of the population, 'the processes of life' – rates of reproduction and life expectancy and all intervening factors – became subject to supervisory 'regulatory controls: a bio-politics of the population' (Foucault 1998, p. 139). Multifarious new processes emerged to secure power over life, heralding the birth of 'an era of bio-power' (Foucault 1998, p. 143). While the practices of disciplining the body arose in institutions such as the education system and the military, 'population control' necessitated the emergence of new inquiries and analyses of population dynamics and societal economics – '*bio-power* ... brought life ... into the realm of explicit calculations and made knowledge-power an agent of transformation' (Foucault 1998, p. 143). There began a drive to understand the population, to gain knowledge of the multifarious aspects of the populace through demographic data, immigration, rates of health and wellbeing inter alia. Statistical knowledge 'gradually reveals that the population possesses its own regularities: its death rate, its incidence of disease ... regularities of accidents' (Foucault 2009, p. 104). The knowledge gleaned from the statistical analysis of the population would serve to inform government policy and the management and manipulation of society in later forms of government (Foucault 1980; 1998; 2009).

Disciplinary power and the norm

The focus on life as opposed to power over death and deduction necessitated the creation of a 'normalising society' (Foucault 1998, p. 144). From the seventeenth century on, power aimed to increase all forms of production. This required a new formation of power that could permeate social life and the bodies of individuals (Foucault 1980). Although the methods to discipline the body manifested prior to the seventeenth century it was from this point that these 'disciplines' became a primary means of ensuring 'appropriate' behaviour (Foucault 1991b, p. 137). Unlike illicit behaviours specifically proscribed in codified laws, disciplinary power fills the space that penal laws have failed to penetrate. Whereas the codes employed by the judiciary operated through penal mechanisms and the vast accumulation of legal texts, from the eighteenth century, these mechanisms are joined by the instrument of normalisation (Foucault 1991b).

> The normalising society is ... not ... a sort of generalised disciplinary society whose ... institutions have swarmed and ... taken over everything ... the normalising society is a society in which the norm of discipline and the norm of regulation intersect.
> (Foucault 2003, p. 253)

The norm becomes the standard to be attained, that to which individuals must aspire, and upon which others base their judgements. It operates concomitantly and thus efficiently on the level of the individual and society: 'the norm ... can be applied to both a body one wishes to discipline and a population one wishes to regularise' (Foucault 2003, p. 253). Normalising power directs how individuals are to behave and distinguishes between those who conform and those who do not, those who belong and those who do not. Society is constructed upon 'degrees of normality' in a hierarchical distribution of the social (Foucault 1991b, pp. 183–184). Disciplinary power penalises abnormality and non-conformance to prescribed norms, failure to meet the norm results in sanction. In such cases one must be rehabilitated to conform to the norm, to be like the normal 'us' (Foucault 1991b). The disciplines operate through the penetrative power of the norm and the associated processes of normalisation, defining what is good or indeed bad behaviour, what belongs and what does not. The power of the norm judges all in a constant process of comparison setting apart those who fail to meet the desired standard as 'abnormal' (Foucault 1991b).

Counter to the extravagant displays of the will of the sovereign, disciplinary power operates as a more 'simple', subtle and unnoticed method through the form of a ubiquitous surveillance that crosscuts society in the form of the norm

(Foucault 1991b). The art of this surveillance lies in the manner in which it operates overtly but also discreetly: it mechanistically and systemically penetrates the entire population; all are subjects of disciplinary power; all are subjects of constant supervision; all spaces and those therein are constantly open to a 'network of gazes' (Foucault 1991b, pp. 171 and 176–177). This panoptic surveillance operates continuously, and those who are subject to it are always aware of their position in the gaze. This awareness encourages self-regulation of behaviour to ensure conformity and the acceptance of personal responsibility for one's actions (Foucault 1991b). It is the knowledge of being under observation that 'maintains the disciplined in his [sic] subjection' (Foucault 1991b, p. 187). This socially diffused observation acts as a calculative, resourceful means of ensuring the effect of power, efficiently managing more with less through 'power of mind over mind' (Foucault 1991b, p. 206).

Governmentality

The development of the disciplinary practices discussed thus far was matched by a concomitant and increasing preponderance of inquiry into the most effective forms of government. Foucault (1991b) argues that the issue of theorising governance 'explode[d] in the sixteenth century' with discourses proliferating on the problematic of how, and by what methods, one should govern. Taking Machiavelli's treatise on government, *The Prince*, as a focal point of reference, Foucault (1991) engages in a comparison with the then developing literature on the question of what are the best means to govern.

For Machiavelli, the work of governance for the sovereign involves securing his/her possession, namely the territory which they have come to appropriate. The nature of this appropriation means that there is but a tenuous link between the sovereign and the state, acquired as it is through inheritance or conquest, thus the prince stands in a position of externality to the state. Governance for the sovereign focuses only on ensuring the retention of his/her acquired possession, which is constantly under threat both from within and without. The sovereign has little regard for the inhabitants or the territory in which they dwell, save for the role they may play in maintaining what she has come to appropriate (Foucault 1991; 2009). However, 'from the eighteenth century government also begins to take responsibility for people's conduct, to conduct people' (Foucault 2009a, p. 197).

Contrary to the overarching externality of the power of the sovereign, the 'art of government' involves continuity between government and the population; it seeks to invest itself in and through society (Foucault 1991, p. 91). While the sovereign was attentive toward her property, securing it as her possession, the art of government is concerned with 'the relationships of man with things', including the wellbeing, productivity and prosperity of the population and the environment (Foucault 1991, pp. 92–95 see also Dean 2010). Under sovereign forms of governance, the law operated so as to ensure that the crown retained her possession: the territory of the state. The art of government focuses instead upon utilising tactical means to ensure particular ends are met. The aim of government is to manage to meet these ends (Foucault 1991).

The growth of the population in the eighteenth century, concomitant with increases in the level of capital, provided the art of government an opportunity to develop (Foucault 1991). Now, management of the population and the economy in a modern sense take precedence in their own right, with the statistical knowledge developed in earlier forms of rule playing a central role (Foucault 1991). Equipped with this access to knowledge, population management becomes the focus of governmental tactics through overt campaigns that encourage certain desired behaviours; for example, the aim to increase the uptake of particular vaccinations, or more covert strategies which aim to meet a specific end. While the populace itself is subject to these campaigns it may be unaware of what is being done to it (Foucault 1991). 'The population is the subject of needs, of aspirations but it is also the object in the hands of the government, of what it wants, but ignorant of what is being done to it' (Foucault 1991, p. 100). Incorporating disciplinary practices, governmental tactics now operate on the 'consciousness of the individual[s]' that constitute the population (Foucault 1991, p. 100); 'the exercise of power is a 'conduct of conducts' and a management of possibilities' (Foucault 2000, p. 341).

The 'normalising society' is a fundamental aspect of the conduct of conduct given its position at the point intersection between discipline and regulation (Foucault 2003). Governmentality is an efficient form of regulation in that the targets of government, informed by various rationalities, self-govern (Dean 2010, p. 193; Foucault 1984). Government works indirectly, conducting individuals through disciplinary techniques and regulating the population through apparatuses of security that control epidemics, mortality, birth rates, perceptions of how to be a good citizen inter alia (Dean 2010; McNay 2009). Power through both technologies of discipline and technologies of regulation efficiently succeeds in covering the whole space that lies between individual bodies and the body of the population (Donzelot 2008; Foucault 2003).

'Truth'

The construction of 'truth' is fundamental to the formation of the norms so crucial for conducting individuals and the population through the 'diffuse production of consent' (Goldberg 2002, p. 106). According to Foucault (1991c, p. 79) the 'problem [we need to understand] is ... how men govern [themselves and others] by the production of truth'. Foucault (1980) does not speak of truth in some idealised sense, something which can be proven to be true and accepted or false and rejected. There exists in every society a 'regime of truth' (Foucault 1980, p. 131): that is, the particular, dominant discursive formations that operate in the social and are accepted to be the 'truth'. For Foucault 'truth' functioned as a tool to support and sustain how people act in the social. 'Truth' has a utility in getting people to reach the desired ends of conduct; thus it is 'truth' that needs to take centre stage when critically engaging political practice (Foucault 1991c, p. 79).

Foucault (1980) proffered that there are particular characteristics of what is accepted as 'truth'. First of all there is a constant appeal to what is held as 'truth' to in order to direct certain social, economic or political ends, 'truth' as the mainspring of rationale action; what we consider as 'truth' is produced by particular 'scientific discourses and institutions' that are deemed as legitimate sources and custodians of knowledge; finally, emanating from the aforementioned sources inter alia, 'truth' production invests throughout society, mediated by select institutions such as the academy and the media (Foucault 1980, pp. 131–132). 'Truth' or more accurately 'truth production' is a field of ongoing contestation. 'There is a battle "for truth" ... not "on behalf of truth" but about the status of truth and the economic and political role it plays' (Foucault 1980, p. 132). The aim in this battle is not to obtain 'truth' in some absolute, idealised sense. Instead the goal should be to break the hegemonic hold of the dominant regime of 'truth' (Dean 2010; Foucault 1980, p. 133).

The dominant regime of 'truth' is a field of discursive constructs that are derived from authoritative institutional settings. This 'truth' informs 'mentalities of government' (Dean 2010, p. 25) which refer to:

> [T]he way in which the thinking involved in practices of government is explicit and embedded in language and other technical instruments but it is also relatively taken for granted i.e. it is not usually open to questioning by its practitioners.
>
> (Dean 2010, p. 25)

Mentalities of how to govern derive from 'truths' whose source lies in the various locations of 'authoritative' knowledge (Dean 2010). At the institutional level these mentalities inform governmental 'regimes of practice', the 'how to' in different forms of government (Foucault 1991c, p. 75; see also Dean 2010). Foucault's (1991c) investigations of practices, denoting the everyday accepted rationale and logic behind certain actions and their resultant material reality, were based on revealing the codes that dictate how particular areas of interest should be done. For example, how one is to 'properly' carry out a medical examination is informed by and should accord with the legitimising 'true discourses' (Foucault 1991c, p. 79).

Mentalities of how to govern are not restricted to institutional regimes of practice but also extend into the social. Individuals draw from the purveyors of expert knowledge in a practice of self-government to reach a desired end; conducting their conduct in line with prescribed norms derived from 'truths' of how to behave (Dean 2010). In both the institutional setting of government and that of the individual, the role of 'truth' is central to how to govern 'correctly'. In the contemporary context, both the institutional and the individual spheres of government are dominated by a hegemonic neoliberal regime of truth or more accurately, a neoliberal 'regime of double truths' (Dean 2010a, p. 10).

Neoliberalism as a regime of 'truth'

Neoliberalism is not perceived here as a 'coherent ideology' or political rationality' (Dean 2010a, p. 11). Multifarious perspectives inform neoliberal thought, taking different forms in terms of style and governmental rationale in a diverse range of settings (Dean 2010a, pp. 4–6; Miller and Rose 2008, p. 11). Nonetheless, Dean (2010a, p. 11) warns that we should not 'underestimate the coherence of neoliberalism as a thought collective'; herein multifarious actors converse to share and debate ideas and experiences while also 'permitting the crystallisation of a consensus' (Dean 2010a, p. 6). Neoliberal regimes of 'truth' or double 'truths' emanate from this loosely organised thought collective and go on to inform the rationalities and practices of government of the self and of the state (Dean 2010a).

Neoliberalism as the dominant regime of 'truth' permeates society in the current context seeping through public, media and academic discourses 'as a powerful mode of public pedagogy' (Giroux 2008, p. 591). Mentalities of self-government and governmental practices of the population are constructed through a neoliberal 'truth' that informs how our conduct should be conducted. I discuss the effects of the neoliberal regime of 'truth' below in their contemporary manifestations. Before then it is important to underscore the Janus-faced character of this neoliberal regime of double truths. Neoliberalism as a regime of double 'truths' denotes how discourses presented as 'true' 'can be expressed differently in relation to different audiences' (Dean 2010a, p. 10). The 'truth' expressed to the public differs in content to that which is disseminated among the elites. For example, the invocation of threat from an enemy (constructed as the suspicious Muslim) within and without can inform a 'politics of fear' that legitimates military expansionism abroad and the curtailment of democratic forms and practices at home (Kumar 2012, p. 164 see also Goldberg 2009; Harvey 2005). It is important to bear this in mind in later chapters and in the following discussion on neoliberal practices of government of the self and the state.

The 'truth' of neoliberal governmentality

To quote from David Harvey

> Neoliberalism has, in short, become hegemonic as a mode of discourse. It has pervasive effects on ways of thought to the point where it has become incorporated into the common-sense way many of us interpret, live in, and understand the world.
>
> (2005, p. 3)

Likewise, Grahame Thompson argues that in the contemporary context: 'Neoliberalism has been ingested into the body-politic so thoroughly, has so become the prevailing commonsense of everyday life' (Thompson 2007). Today, neoliberalism is the dominant regime of 'truth' that invests mentalities and practices of self-government and the rationalities of various apparatuses of the state. According to McNay (2009, p. 56), Foucault believed 'neoliberalism is an exemplar of the indirect style of social control, the *conduct of conduct* that typifies [contemporary] governmental reason'. Neoliberalism as the output of a 'more or less organised thought collective' (Dean 2010a) is more than just the primacy of laisser-faire capitalism as it is often popularly conceived; it is about extending the principles of individualism and the free market into all realms of sociopolitical life. Neoliberalism is far-reaching socially, politically and culturally and involves the application of market principles to the social (Dean 2010; Foucault 2010; Lemke 2010; Oksala 2011). With neoliberal market-based principles inculcated into social mentalities and practices, people come to perceive the 'truth' of the world through the neoliberal lens that idealises individualism, self-care and competition: a Darwinian survival of the socially fittest (Giroux 2008). Neoliberal governmentality operates to ensure the dominance of neoliberal 'truth' as a model for directing conduct.

The neoliberal *weltanshauung* is not just left to happenstance but is encouraged by the state. This includes the promotion of various tenets including: an ethos of deregulation; increased private ownership; the valorisation of the entrepreneur; and the application of cost–benefit analyses from the market to the entire social sphere (Giroux 2008). The neoliberal state contra traditional liberal views, *is* interventionist; it is, according to Foucault, not less government but '*do-not-laisser-faire* government' (Foucault 2010, p. 247). Despite popular misconceptions, the neoliberal state is not smaller but instead represents a realignment of governmental objectives to regulate the populace in accordance with neoliberal rationalities (Dean 2010; Giroux 2008; Goldberg 2009). Neoliberal governmental policies and behaviours are subjected to calculative processes, viewed through a marketised lens with the aim of ensuring 'efficiencies' and meeting targets (Gray 2013). From the perspective of neoliberal mentalities:

> market rationality ... can be extended to all sorts of areas that are neither exclusively, nor even primarily, concerned with economics, such as the family ... the birth rate ... and crime and delinquency.
>
> (Dean 2010, p. 72)

Calculations of efficiency and cost–benefit analyses rule the day with governmental intervention in the social limited by its perceived calculated utility to the advancement of neoliberal ends (Donzelot 2008; Foucault 2010; Giroux 2008). The limit of social care is marked out by its ability to ensure that everyone has access to the 'game' and remains therein (Donzelot 2008, p. 130). Thus, the need for social 'mechanisms of security' that 'care' for the populace is severely undermined unless these mechanisms can empower individuals towards meeting neoliberal ends (Dean 2010, p. 179).

State recalcitrance vis-à-vis caring in the social is underpinned by neoliberal mentalities that view the market as *the best* source of solutions for problems arising in the social. The view that the state could be a mainspring for the provision of collective remedies to social problems is anathema to neoliberal mentalities that uphold individual responsibility and privatised market based solutions (Giroux 2008; Thompson 2007). The social state is hollowed out under the dogma of neoliberalism in the name of individualism and the economic, *rational* imperative (Davis 2007; Lentin and Titley 2011). 'Care' of vulnerable social groups has to happen at the lowest possible cost calculated through a rational economic grid. Criminality is also viewed through this rational grid wherein the need for intervention is calculated on a cost benefit analysis (Dean 2010; Foucault 2010).

This calculative rationality is also applied to racism wherein the need for state intervention must be premised on an economic calculus before any action will be deemed necessary. Aspects of social care that are deemed too expensive for direct state management, for tackling racism and addressing its outputs, are outsourced. There is a privatisation of previously publicly situated goods and services wherein the care of the social becomes an issue for private interests (Giroux 2008). '[T]actics of government ... allow the continual definition of what should or should not fall within the state's domain ... what is and what is not within the state's competence' (Foucault 2009, p. 109). What falls out of governmental competency is outsourced to the private world of rational, self-responsible individuals or the privatised world of philanthropic care.

Caring for the self

The absence of state care means that those who are vulnerable to racism must become rational, calculating actors. Imbued with the neoliberal mentality of self-government, they must make calculated decisions on how they should care for themselves as individuals. Neoliberalism as 'truth' and rationality heralds individualism; in the words of the late Margaret Thatcher, 'there is no such thing as society' (Thatcher 1987, cited in Dean 2010, p. 177). Instead of collective responsibility, the population is presented as a collection of 'one-man [sic] archipelagos' (Giroux 2008, p. 592). The freedom of the individual is valorised. The protection of competition and the construction, disciplining, of entrepreneurial individuals takes priority over state social protection, 'instead of the promotion of *equality*, the focus is on *inclusion*' in the competition (Gray 2013, p. 77). Through processes of 'self-regulation', individuals learn how to compete in a neoliberalised space (Lemke 2010, p. 201). Society becomes fragmented through processes that conduct individuals away from competing rationalities of social solidarity to the primacy of 'individual autonomy' which is core to the disciplinary processes of neoliberal governmentality (McNay 2009, p. 62). Neoliberal 'truths' encourage an individual conduct of self-government which is both efficient and effective from the governmental perspective: 'he [sic] is governable because he governs himself. He governs himself according to economic laws' (Donzelot 2008, p. 131); one is only 'free in specific ways' (Rose *et al.* 2006, p. 89). Economic, market based laws can be manipulated to conduct conduct; for example, if the state does not provide a service of 'care', the individual will have to meet their demand for care themselves, they will have to become calculative actors – 'freedom is a condition of subjection' (Dean 2010, p. 193).

Disciplinary practices and a norm of competition permeate as 'truths' in neoliberal mentalities. 'Neoliberal governmentality involves the shaping of "our notion of the deserving citizen" via "a regime of normalising whereby *homo-œconomicus* is the standard against which all other citizens are measured and ranked"' (Ong 1999, cited in Gray 2011, p. 95). According to Foucault (2010b, p. 226), the ideal individual in neoliberal 'society', *'homo-œconomicus'*, is one who takes action on the basis of a rational cost–benefit analysis. '*Homo-œconomicus* is … an entrepreneur of himself [*sic*]', a self-dependent, producer of his/her own satisfaction (Foucault 2010a, p. 226). The entrepreneur of the self engages in developing their own 'human capital' to make them more amenable to the vicissitudes of the marketised society (Foucault 2010a, p. 229); under the illusion that they are free to choose (that we are all free to choose), the 'free' individual calculates rationally how to take a particular course of action (Dean 2010; Gray 2013; Lemke 2010). But there is another side to the sword of neoliberal individualism.

The valorisation of choice and self-responsibility is matched by the neoliberal rationale that any failure you may have is your own fault, an output of your inadequacies (Giroux 2008; Roberts and Mahtani 2010; Thompson 2007). All failures are personal regardless of any structural bases that may underpin them, thus 'absolving the government' of responsibility for the mechanisms that maintain or could intervene to prevent social inequality (Davis 2007, p. 349). The primacy of the individual 'depoliticises social and political relations by fragmenting collective values of care, duty and obligation' (McNay 2009, p. 65). Your 'failings' are yours alone and the result of your 'faulty character' (Giroux 2008, p. 598); the most assistance one can get in an era of neoliberal governmentality is the encouragement to engage in an entrepreneurship of the self, to be responsible and to make amends for your own privatised shortfalls (Lemke 2010; McNay 2009).

Not only is one responsible for their own 'faulty character', they are also responsible for their exposure to risk thus they must engage in a form of risk management (Dean 2010). This is particularly important for those whose presence is constructed as a threat to the neoliberal order and who are targeted through 'regressive symbolic and corporeal violence' (Giroux 2008, p. 601). Racialised constructions of communities as threat operate to legitimise acts of racism against the 'othered'. However, in keeping with the neoliberal regime of double 'truths' (Dean 2010a), experiences of racism are presented as being the result of the recipients' own 'faulty character'. If one is the bearer of racialised signifiers of 'difference', they should remove them. By this 'logic', Muslim women should rationally choose not to veil if this exposes them to anti-Muslim racism. Likewise Sikh men should not wear the turban, regardless of the meaning that these signifiers of faith may have to those targeted. Moreover, if members of racialised communities are ('able' but) unwilling to minimise their risk of exposure to racism, then they should not look to the neoliberal state for assistance. Individuals who experience racism must engage in a process of self-care based on their own rational analyses. Any aid the neoliberal state may provide is superficial at best or limited on the basis of a cost benefit calculus. Faced with state inaction, individuals looking for care in response to racism (or other forms of exclusion) are conducted away from the state to report their experiences of racist practices and seek assistance in privatised providers of 'care': non-governmental organisations.

This is not by chance but the intentional output of limited state assistance that directly – through non-provision of services – and indirectly – through 'race' blindness (discussed below) – discourages those who experience racism from turning to the state to make for help. It is all part of the rationality of neoliberal government which aims to conduct individuals towards the market for care they cannot provide for themselves. It is the individual's fault that they are in the predicament that they are in, and as such, it is the individual's responsibility to seek help where it may seem forthcoming (Giroux 2008, p. 601).

Privatising care

The promotion of self-responsibility or 'responsibilisation' (Thompson 2007), self-care and the idealisation of entrepreneurship are contemporaneous with the rolling back of the state as a social actor or, more accurately, as a provider of 'care' under neoliberal rationality (Gray 2013). Non-governmental organisations (NGOs) strive to assist those left to their own devices by government and populate the spaces of care vacated by the state. Those working in the NGO sector genuinely endeavour to help those left without state support. However, this outsourcing of 'care' does not represent a break in governance but is instead an example of 'governing at a distance' (Rose *et al.* 2006, p. 89). True to neoliberal rationalities, 'this is a marketised civil society of [*forcibly?*] competing organisations all involved in the act of "governing"' (Gray 2013, p. 78 my addition). Instead of directly providing and managing the 'care' of those who need assistance, the neoliberal state outsources this 'responsibility to privately funded NGOs who may have the necessary expertise to act as an estranged arm of government' (Sending and Neumann 2006, p. 658; see also Gray 2013). This outsourcing of 'care' to the NGO sector is an example of 'indirect techniques' of managing conduct without having to take any responsibility for those who should be served by the state (Lemke 2010, p. 201). NGOs and other civil society actors have become an extension of government (Gray 2011; Sending and Neumann 2006) and fulfil the role of a caring face for the vulnerable and socially excluded.

In the case of Ireland, the manner in which the Irish State has historically engaged in social partnership can be read as an exemplar of the outsourcing of governmental care to civil society actors, cutting costs and channelling the needs of, for example, migrants. Gray (2013, p. 82) demonstrates how since the late 1980s, until recently (see Clifford 2015), Irish governmental policies have worked on the basis of partnership, inspired by earlier Catholic models of 'social activism'. This partnership model has included civil, voluntary/community and business actors engaging in and agreeing upon roadmaps for government, including in 2003 the development of a policy around, migrant integration (Gray 2013, p. 83).[2] This 'consensual' arrangement of agreeing the management of 'care' of those vulnerable to racism has been overshadowed in recent years by the intentional retreat of the Irish State in addressing the care of those who experience racism. The Irish government eviscerated the State anti-racism infrastructure in answering the call to 'austerity' required in the name of our 'patriotic duty' (Holt 2009).[3] The void left by bodies such as the National Consultative Committee on Racism and Interculturalism (NCCRI) has resulted in an enforced NGO scramble to 'care' for those left without an effective state repository of assistance.

Those who experience racism are faced with a choice in the era of outsourced governance. Take responsibility for experiences of racism yourself; in other words, fix your own faults or take up your concerns with an NGO who will at least provide some modicum of care. NGOs have at least some capacity to provide advice to those who experience racism and act as a voice with/for those vulnerable members of minority communities. These are all positive acts on the part of the NGOs and their hardworking staff. However, as iterated above, NGOs are also a means to govern at a distance (Miller and Rose 2008). NGOs fill the spaces that should be populated by the neoliberal state that does not want to 'care' for, in this case, those who experience racism; this is unless it can have some beneficial effect on the extension of neoliberal rationalities. Those who experience racism are thus conducted away from the state to care for themselves or to seek solace among privatised proprietors of 'care'.

'Race', racism and the post-racial neoliberal 'moment'

In the following chapter I will engage in arguments of racism and the importance of recognising racism for what it is and the underlying processes of racialisation. Before then, I want to draw on Foucault and other Foucauldian theorists to elaborate the role of racism in the neoliberal era. According to Foucault (2003, p. 254) under biopower, 'racism is inscribed as the basic mechanism of power as it is exercised in modern states'. The first function of racism is to divide the population to introduce 'a break into the domain of life that is under power's control: the break between what must live and what must die' (Foucault 2003, p. 254). By presenting 'races' as 'naturally distinct groups', the concept of 'race' fragments the population that is the target of power; it is 'a way of separating out groups' (Foucault 2003, p. 255). One way in which 'races' are divided is through the 'discourses of the historian' (among others, a legitimate source of 'truth') who constructs racial histories to justify and reify the power of the dominant group to 'intensify the lustre of [the hegemonic] power' (Foucault 2003a, p. 66). Secondly, racism functions in the service of the argument that the more the inferior 'other' is excluded the better the 'us' population will be as a whole in terms of vigour, health and purity (Foucault 2003). Thus 'race' is inherent to the workings of the biopower state that utilises racism in the 'exercise ... [of] sovereign power' (Foucault 2003, p. 258).

Analyses of 'race' and racism have to be cognisant of the moment they are framed within and the socio-political, historical and economic factors which bear down on this process (Davis 2007). Roberts and Mahtani (2010) argue that deployment of 'race' and the processes of racialisation are at the core of neoliberal regime of double 'truths'. 'Othered' communities are constructed along racialised lines as groups to be 'cast out' (see also Dean 2010a; Razack 2008). The racialised identity of the target subject is interwoven with beliefs and practices that are deemed antithetical to neoliberal 'ideal types' (Roberts and Mahtani 2010).

The state, in the era of neoliberal globalised hegemony and attendant labour flows, endeavours to manage and restrict the flow of 'threats' 'more or less silently racially perceived' (Goldberg 2009, p. 332). While some 'others' may be classed as resource-*ful* and therefore welcome in the state, more are constructed as risky populations in terms of a 'drain' on welfare or as the bearer of identities that are contrarian to the neoliberal norm of individualism, as a threat to 'our' security, 'our ways' (Goldberg 2009; Gray 2011; Razack 2008). The term 'race' may never be explicitly mentioned, instead a 'muted racism' persists (Davis 2007) with terms such as 'non-national' and 'citizenship tourism' implying the presence of an 'other'. Racialised constructions of the 'other' remain central to the management of bodies and the rationale for the expansion of neoliberalism as a regime of truths (Goldberg 2009; Kumar 2012).

Curiously however, 'race' and racism ostensibly speak contrary to the neoliberal rhetoric of meritocratic success and are therefore denied through the logics of 'race' blindness and the constructed illusion of a 'raceless' society (Davis 2007; Lentin and Titley 2011). Under neoliberal rationality, one's identity is not an impediment to success; it is their willingness to develop their human capital, to become entrepreneurs of the self that is the determining factor for success. It follows that failure to participate in the neoliberal economy is the result of personal failure in terms of self-development, and not emblematic of institutional barriers (Davis 2007). According to Goldberg (2009) racial neoliberalism is characterised by the implicit and subtle invocation of 'race' and racialising processes abroad discussed further below. Domestically, these processes are matched by notions of racelessness and the restriction of 'race' as an issue for the private sphere, the effect being to evacuate the state for addressing racism as hostility and discrimination. The welfare of the 'other' is a matter for the self, as well as NGOs and charities in the 'business' of caring for those exposed to racism (Goldberg 2009).

Racelessness is an 'explicit conception of state governmentality under globalising neoliberal conditions' (Goldberg 2009, p. 30). Neoliberalism denies the role of 'race' by emphasising socio-political 'race' blindness (Davis 2007). The effect of 'race' blind perspectives and practices is to restrict investment in policies that would target racially informed inequalities (Davis 2007). Instead of recognising the importance of 'race' and associated practices of exclusion, the 'diversity agenda' is the policy *de jour*, the effect of which is to attenuate policies that could specifically challenge racism (Davis 2007, pp. 349–350).[4]

But then that is the point. The denial of the import of 'race' and racialised identities in the neoliberal state operates to maintain the power of the dominant 'in-group' when faced with claims for recognition and inclusion within increasingly diverse societies. In this context, the state presents itself as a neutral arbiter and champion of diversity, but in reality the substance or lack therein of its policies continue to perpetuate the wont of the dominant racial group and its management of the 'other' (Goldberg 2002; Kaya 2011; Lentin and Titley 2011). Thus 'the neoliberal state exacerbates inequality [by] further privileging the already privileged' (Goldberg 2009, p. 332), precisely because 'race' is denied as a factor in social inequality (Davis 2007).

The institutional failure to cater for the whole of society limits full access to society and stratifies ones' ability to 'compete', it exposes and makes vulnerable (Carmichael and Hamilton 1967). However, neoliberal states have to maintain a façade of 'care'. After all, 'we [states] are all competing for talent and labour power and must seek to make ourselves attractive in certain areas' (Office of the Minister for Integration 2008, p. 34). States must present themselves as an attractive destination for corporations to invest, and also to lure those resource-*ful* immigrants. Part of this attraction lies in the pretence that states meet the requirements of international human rights instruments such as the United Nations Convention on the Elimination of All forms of Racial Discrimination, the European Union Framework Decision on Combating Racism and Xenophobia, inter alia. The aforementioned 'diversity agenda' is part of this 'keeping up of appearances'.

By prioritising diversity instead of effectively challenging racism,

> a state may licence racist expression within its jurisdiction simply by turning a blind eye, by doing little or nothing to prevent or contest it, by having no restricting rules or codes or failing to enforce those on its books.
> (Goldberg 2002, p. 144)

Essentially by doing little or nothing to challenge racially motivated hostility and/or discrimination the state outsources racism to those 'would be' police of the 'other'. The elision of 'race' and racism from official discourses and planning in combination with racialised constructions of 'other' de facto legitimises those who would engage in racist acts without the fear of negative sanction. Thus the 'other' is conducted by the 'rightfully' deserving population and racial regulation is outsourced in the name of constructing the neoliberal nation, to make them like 'us'. All the while, as noted above, by not recognising racism as a problem that should lie firmly in the purview of state care (unless of course caring for racism could benefit the aims of the neoliberal rationality) the neoliberal state also outsources the 'care' of those who cannot care for themselves to privately funded NGOs whose jobs it is to manage the flow of those subjected to governmental policies that exclude (Goldberg 2009). The limits of intervention are marked out by their utility in truly neoliberal terms. The neoliberal state outsources racism and concomitantly the 'care' for those who experience racist practices, perfectly efficient neoliberal conduct of conduct.

As I have argued, neoliberalism is not a purely market based phenomenon but a broader political and cultural project. There is a need to go beyond stating that neoliberalism is the dominant mode of being to understanding the attendant regimes of 'truth' that are created and disseminated and that enable the hegemony of the neoliberal regime of 'truth' to pertain (Giroux 2008). As Oksala (2011, p. 480) argues, neoliberalism is a 'comprehensive political project that sees the market as the model for the state and for the overall organisation of society'. The primacy of individual freedom and choice, as purveyors of neoliberal thought would have us believe, is the best route to attaining a successful society. Mesmerised by our freedom, we are encouraged through racialised constructions of the 'other' to rally in-step behind the territorial and corporeal expansion of 'our' neoliberal common-sense, chiming with classic racialised rhetoric, to those that have not developed enough to truly be 'free'. Neoliberalism does not just deny 'race', it utilises it as 'truth' as I will demonstrate in the following chapter with reference to the racialisation of Muslim communities.

Resisting 'racelessness' and anti-Muslim racism

Foucault's work, peeling back the skin of governance, exposes the manner in which we are conducted and the role that dominant constructions of 'truth' and associated norms play in this government. However, Foucault's work not only reveals the darkness but also the persistence of embers and indeed flames that can vitalise hope in the face of neoliberal governmentality. Foucault (2000, pp. 344–345) argued that power manifests as 'action on the action of others'. Power is ubiquitous, but over time it has increasingly had the state as its locus, not because the state creates power but because it has *attempted* to appropriate power. But power relations are part of a series of mutable processes that permeate the entirety of society and all groups therein (Foucault 2000). Power can operate socially in the form of the norm, acting as a type of ubiquitous societal surveillance wherein certain social acts and traits are approved, others deemed deviant and consequently subject to sanction and marginalisation; judged, as they are in a 'field of comparison' (Foucault 1991, pp. 180–184). However, when power arises freedom does not just wither; when power manifests it does so necessarily in the presence of freedom (Foucault 1998; 2000).

Foucault (2009, pp. 194–195) identifies the manner in which governance in the form of the 'pastorate'[5] that endeavoured to conduct societal behaviour gave birth to movements that attempted to resist forms of governance of conduct. These efforts of resistance against conduct were attempts to redefine how people were governed (Foucault 2009). The manner in which people have been conducted has faced resistance across history. A central aspect of these resistances has been the challenge they have laid down to how people are conducted and by whom (Foucault 2009). Foucault (2009, pp. 197–199) describes how the 'pastorate' as the conductor of society was replaced in the seventeenth and eighteenth centuries by government in a more contemporary sense, functioning through the machinations and processes of governmentality as detailed above. The goal remains to 'conduct people', but whereas resistance to pastoral power had a religious core, 'conflicts of conduct' now had an inherent political tone. These conflicts remain centred on challenges to forms of governance of conduct, by how and by whom, and the 'pursuit of a different form of conduct' (Foucault 2009, pp. 197–199). Foucault (2009, p. 201) labelled movements of resistance to being conducted and challenges to particular forms of 'truth', as 'counter-conduct[s] ... struggle[s] against the process implemented for conducting others'.

Dean (2010) argues that government that relies on self-regulation, as in neoliberal governmentality, de facto leaves open a space for agency and resistance. The concept of conducting conduct through governance necessarily denotes that people are thinking actors. Thus, while the practices of governance may endeavour to manage freedom they do not appropriate or control it. Individual actors retain their agency in thought and in practice thus raising the possibility of doing otherwise than conducted (Dean 2010). Furthermore, it is worth noting that counter conduct does not necessarily mean a will to completely change the state-government dynamic; it may instead mean a redirecting of government policy, changing how one is governed (Dean 2010). This, I contend, is possible even in the face of hegemonic neoliberal governmentality.

As noted, neoliberal 'truth' is the hegemonic discourse of our time, 'incorporated into ... [our] common-sense', our mentalities (Harvey 2005, p. 41), framing our actions and interactions. There is a need to change how we are conducted. There is a need for a new knowledge, a new 'truth' to challenge constructions of the 'other' and the attendant experiences of racism. The focus of this book is the racialisation of Muslims as 'other' and lived anti-Muslim racism, however the arguments made can also apply to other racisms. It is argued here that change can be catalysed, at least in part, through the provision of disaggregated statistical data on racist behaviour that specifically recognises and details anti-Muslim racism. Here, the technologies that manipulate society can be utilised to ameliorate the position of those subjected to racism by informing anti-racism policies thus increasing their efficacy. Paul Iganski (2008, p. 87) argues, that measures employed to tackle racist behaviour 'provide an important declaratory purpose aimed at individuals who might offend'; serving to de-normalise and thus deter racisms including those targeted towards Muslim communities by changing the 'production of truth' (Foucault 2000a, pp. 131–132); de-normalising anti-Muslim racism, turning the 'network of gazes' on those who engage in hostility and discriminatory behaviour towards Muslim communities (Foucault 1991b, p. 171). The collection of statistical data on anti-Muslim racism is an important step in challenging this 'truth'.

Statistical data are core to practices of governmentality in the contemporary state allowing for more efficient policy outcomes (Ghatak 2008). Counter to the utilisation of statistical insight, the absence of data collection on experiences of racism by the state supports the neoliberal perspective outlined above that 'race' is something that is a private concern. Goldberg (2009) demonstrates the manner in which neoliberal actors have sought the curtailment of data collection on racism and the de facto legitimisation of this phenomenon in what he refers to as the 'protection of private racial discrimination initiative'. 'Racial neoliberalism involves the commitment to remove any explicit articulation or expression from the public sphere – in government and by government – of racial arrangement' (Kapoor 2013, p. 1034). I am not the first to argue for the collection of data at the level of the state on the position of minority communities with the aim of challenging exclusion. Precedent exists wherein challenges to the management of vulnerable groups by themselves, counter conducts, have taken place with specific reference to the collection of data. Representatives of the Traveller Community in Ireland, and indeed the Irish community in the UK, in the form of the census, underscore the manner in which the excluded 'other' has sought inclusion through the collection of official data. This inclusion, it is argued, can help inform measures to ameliorate experiences of discrimination (Hickman 1998; King-O'Riain 2007; Moore and Hickman 2010). To challenge anti-Muslim racism, the argument proffered in this book will meet neoliberalism head-on, insidious as it may be, on the basis of cost–benefit analysis.

Discussion and conclusion

The purpose of this chapter was to examine and elaborate on the theoretical premise upon which the argument proffered in this book is framed. I started by recounting of the progress of governance from the sovereign before moving to the form of neoliberal governmental rationalities that seem to overwhelm in the contemporary context. Foucault's theory of governmentality allows for an incisive analysis into the way power permeates society, penetrating the population and the interactions between individuals. As I have argued above, neoliberalism is a regime of 'truth'; moreover, a regime of double 'truths' that informs mentalities and associated practices of how to rationally govern in both the institutional setting and that of the self. Neoliberal government is an outsourced government, operating on the individualised body and the population as a whole, acting as conduct on conduct. As individuals, we are disciplined to accept our atomised status and social solidarity is eschewed; what is important is that the individual accepts responsibility for their own success by being an entrepreneur of the self while also 'accepting' that any failings are theirs and theirs alone. Neoliberal state intervention in 'caring', for example, for those who experience racial exclusion, reaches its paltry zenith in its rhetoric of diversity. 'Race' 'care' no longer matters to the state, if it ever did. Instead this 'care' is outsourced to the self or privately-funded NGOs who act as an extension of government. However, the neoliberal state utilises racism as a means to govern the conduct of society and by denying the salience of racism outsources the policing of the 'other'.

Racism plays a vital role in maintaining the hegemonic status quo. Neoliberal policies of 'race' blindness deny the salience of racism in the lives of racialised groups. Experiencing racism is perceived as the fault of the individual – it is your fault that you have not developed your 'human capital' – obfuscating the role that racialised inequalities play in maintaining the privilege of the dominant group at home. But neoliberalism is not satisfied with just maintaining things the way they are, neoliberalism is voracious in its wont for expansion at home and abroad and racism is a vital mechanism deployed in conducting conduct to meet these ends. Abroad, the 'other' is constructed as a threat to our ways, so much so that we must engage in pre-emptive action to secure our 'interests'. In the domestic sphere, neoliberalism utilises 'race' in its endeavours to create a population that is a collective of individuals.

Collective racialised identities deemed antithetical to neoliberal individualism become the target of discourses which aim to fragment these collectivities to make them more like 'us'. These racialised collectivities are to be reformed under a new neoliberal unitary collectivity of individuals, held together by discourses of nation and national histories of who we are. The self-racialised guise of 'nation' acts as a holding device, a glue for a collectivity of individuals who have inculcated neoliberalism as 'truth' and are the benchmark to be met by the 'othered'. Yet there remains hope that a challenge can be put down to the neoliberal state on its own terms that it should act against racism. In the following chapter I will theoretically unpack the concept of anti-Muslim racism, also known as Islamophobia, and elaborate on how racialised discourses are recruited and deployed for the expansion of the neoliberal regime of 'truth'.

Notes

1 From a Foucauldian perspective, the concept of ideology is problematic. Ideology denotes the existence and recognition of competing 'truth' claims but does not help studies such as this which endeavour to identify *how* various 'truths' operate in a given context (Foucault 1980).
2 Government and the social partners agree[d] on the desirability for the development of a comprehensive policy framework on migration.... This would incorporate issues that properly fall to government ... it will also incorporate issues on which government will consult with the social partners – specifically, economic migration ... integration ... racism and interculturalism.
(Department of the Taoiseach 2003, p. 26)
3 In 2008 the Irish government embarked upon a policy of austerity that targeted key strands of the Irish equality sector. Funding to the semi-state agency the NCCRI was cut completely and the body had to close, with it went the only means to gather information multifarious forms of racism. Furthermore, bodies such as the Equality Authority and the Irish Human Rights Commission were effectively emasculated through budgetary cuts that seriously impacted their ability to function (see Carr 2011; Carr and Haynes 2013). In November 2014, a new, rationalised equality and human rights body: the Irish Human Rights and Equality Commission commenced operations subsuming the functions of the Equality Authority and the Irish Human Rights Commission see www.ihrec.ie/about/ for more. See also Equality and Rights Alliance (2014) for a critique of some of the issues facing the new Commission.
4 An Garda Síochána (2013) is one exemplar of this diversity agenda. The website of the Garda Racial, Intercultural and Diversity Office is replete with the term diversity but hardly mentions racism as an issue, if at all.
5 Pastoral power is not a relationship of the sovereign to the state in a territorial sense. It is imbued instead with religious connotations: the head of state/sovereign is the shepherd of her flock, an intermediary between God and the people, a manager of souls (Foucault 2009b, pp. 123–129).

3 De-constructing Islamophobia

Introduction

In the previous chapter I established how neoliberalism as a regime of double 'truths' (Dean 2010a) denies the salience of 'race' as a meaningful category while contemporaneously outsourcing the 'care' for experiences of racism to the self or privately funded 'carers'. I also outlined the manner in which neoliberalism as a regime of double truths instrumentally constructs 'race' as a means to further neoliberal ends: utilising racialised constructions as discursive tools to justify the expansion of the neoliberal rationalities at home and abroad in an era of 'racelessness'. This chapter will interrogate and unpack the concept of Islamophobia itself, and, in so doing, argue for its replacement. In what follows I will adumbrate some of the heretofore key discussions vis-à-vis definitions of Islamophobia thus laying the groundwork for the subsequent argument in favour of the use of the term 'anti-Muslim racism'. Before this, I will first engage with debates on the character of racism qua racism in order to support the argument to follow. In particular, I will draw on the work of Miles and Brown (2003) whose definition of racism as ideology is particularly useful. However, I will develop the manner which Miles and Brown (2003) define racism so that it is less about the presence of phenotypical characteristics and more about the construction of the 'other' through processes of racialisation. Where appropriate I will draw on historical and contemporary examples of racialisation that operate in the absence of a phenotype, using the Irish experience as a critical example. From here I will move to define anti-Muslim racism.

I contend that the term 'anti-Muslim racism' has a greater utility in challenging this eponymous phenomenon than Islamophobia. In particular, I place an emphasis on the emotional resonance that the word racism can conjure in public 'common sense'. The definition I proffer below will also provide the platform from which the overall argument of this book can be developed: namely that anti-Muslim racism as a distinct form of racism needs to be recognised and enumerated as such if it is to be countered. Recognition of anti-Muslim racism is vital if we are to raise subjugated knowledges of Muslim communities to public attention; thus creating a new 'truth' that elucidates the lived experiences of

Muslim men and women. I conclude this chapter by elaborating an argument for the hope of resistance to neoliberal 'truths' of the 'other'.

Defining Islamophobia

Chris Allen (2010) argues that the concept of Islamophobia has been poorly defined historically both in terms of what this phenomenon actually is and how it should be addressed. One particularly important definition is that of the Runnymede Trust whose 1997 report: *Islamophobia: a challenge for us all* is described by Allen (2010, pp. 54–55) as a 'landmark in the establishment and development of Islamophobia both as phenomenon and as a concept'. Islamophobia is defined by the Trust as a 'shorthand way of referring to dread or hatred of Islam and, therefore, to fear or dislike of all or most Muslims' (Runnymede Trust 1997, p. 1). The Trust presented Islamophobia as a dichotomous model of 'open' and 'closed' views, the latter of which being associated with Islamophobic sentiments as detailed in the following:

1. Islam is viewed as a 'monolithic bloc, static and unresponsive'.
2. Islam as 'other', a value system separate to and alien from Western ideals.
3. Islam as atavistic, misogynistic, barbarous and inferior to the West.
4. Islam as an aggressor and threat towards the West.
5. Islam as a (the only) religion used instrumentally for political gain.
6. Islamic critiques of Western practices are ignored or rejected.
7. Discrimination and exclusion of Muslims and Islam is deemed legitimate.
8. Islamophobia as the norm, acceptable.

(Runnymede Trust 1997, p. 5)

Unquestionably, the Runnymede Trust report has been of tremendous significance to the study of this phenomenon and continues to inform how Islamophobia is defined (see Cincotta 2011). However, for the most part it has been utilised uncritically, with questions remaining over the manner in which Islamophobia is defined (Allen 2010). Allen (2010) argues that there are inherent flaws in the definition of Islamophobia as proffered by the Runnymede Trust (1997) and its reliance on a dualistic model of 'open' and 'closed' views.

Garner (2010) argues that the Runnymede Trust dualistic paradigm of Islamophobia fails to recognise the divergent range of opinions that may exist outside of any purely open or closed view. According to Allen (2010), the Runnymede Trust model operates on a premise wherein Islamophobia (closed views) must be contrasted with Islamophilia (open views), whereby one is either in one camp or the other. This simple dichotomous perspective is very problematic. Just because a person is Muslim with particularly held views does not mean that they are, nor should they be, insulated from any criticisms pointed towards them; nor does it mean that such critiques are inherently Islamophobic. However, if a Muslim group or individual does not match up with the expectations of the essentialised 'good' Muslim, it does not legitimate prejudice and discrimination against them on the basis of their Muslim identity. 'No hierarchy or victim, based upon adherence to essentialised or in-essentialised norms must be established' (Allen 2010, p. 79).

This leads to a final criticism of the Runnymede (1997) report which is that it fails to distinguish between 'race' and religion. Indeed, the report conflates racial or ethnic markers with aspects of religious identities. A lack of clarity of what exactly is Islamophobia, as distinct from what may be another form of racism, for example, provides oxygen for arguments against the existence of specifically anti-Muslim phenomena (see, for example, Malik 2005; Harris, cited in Vale 2014). This underscores the need for clarity of definition, and that research that argues the presence of anti-Muslim racism does so firmly premised on an evidentiary base that focuses on one's Muslim-*ness* in experiences of hostility and/or discrimination for it to be classed as anti-Muslim (Allen 2010; Halliday 2003, p. 163; Zempi and Chakraborti 2014).

Despite the invaluable nature of the academic debates present in the discourse of Islamophobia, what needs to remain central to the discussions and definitions of this phenomenon is the effect it has on real people. Indeed, Miles and Brown (2003, p. 165) argue that what is pertinent for the discussion of Islamophobia is not the issue of 'closed views' in isolation but how these closed views when manifest, relate to and combine with racism resulting in 'exclusionary practices, exclusionary discourses and hostility' (Miles and Brown 2003, p. 165). What is required is a nuanced definition that informs and pays attention to the historical, ideological and processual aspects of Islamophobia. As Meer and Modood (2010) argue, the conceptual frameworks that look to explicate and define what Islamophobia actually is must: (a) include both the historical and contemporary discourse of the West/Islam opposition; (b) separate legitimate criticism of Islam from racialised rhetoric; and (c) draw from the legacy of racism debates and its conceptual tools and relate these to defining Islamophobia.

Thus a definition that encompasses and is more sensitive to exclusionary practices while encapsulating the ideological, racialised and affective aspects of Islamophobia is required. This is provided by Chris Allen who posits that

> Islamophobia is an ideology, similar in theory, function and purpose to racism and other similar phenomena, that sustains and perpetuates negatively evaluated meaning about Muslims and Islam ... shaping and determining understanding, perceptions and attitudes in the social consensus.... As a consequence, exclusionary practices – practices that disadvantage, prejudice or discriminate against Muslims and Islam in social, economic and political spheres ensue, including the subjection to violence.
>
> (2010, p. 190)

I will return to this definition later. What is crucial to note in Allen's (2010, p. 170) definition for now is the manner in which it reveals the processes that underpin anti-Muslim sentiment and their contingent character. In the current socio-political milieu, ideologically driven images present Islam and Muslims as the 'problem', associated historically with repeated, albeit temporally contingent, thematic assertions on the nature of their faith and their identity. Muslims are framed as the prime 'other' and this works to legitimate particular responses and exclusionary practices to the perceived Muslim 'problem' (Allen 2010).

These exclusionary practices, as reported by the Runnymede Trust (1997, p. 12) in what it terms as 'aspects of Islamophobia', include: social exclusion; violence; prejudice; and discrimination. Islamophobia as a lived phenomenon has taken multifarious forms including verbal and physical assaults; attacks on property; the application of negative stereotypes through both media and political discourses; discriminatory institutional and employment practice; ignorance of the socio-economic situations of Muslims; and denial of religious freedoms (Muir and Smith 2004). Yet something remains that is troubling in the term Islamophobia itself that leads me away from using it. It is this problem to which I turn my attention below, that is, the utility of the label Islamophobia itself in challenging this phenomenon.

Defining racism

Racism as defined here draws on the work of Miles and Brown (2003) but is developed in a manner which provides the basis for a conceptual perspective on racism that is not premised solely on phenotypical differentiation. The aim here is to provide a definition of racism that can encapsulate a variety of *racisms* and has the ability to shed light on the experiences of those who experience these phenomena. I contend here that the experiences of anti-Muslim hostility and discrimination, demonstrated later, which are not restricted to phenotype, evidence a particular form of racism based on the identification, real or perceived, of Muslimness. I agree with McVeigh's (2002) argument that perceiving racism through a dominant phenotypically derived black/white binary serves to subordinate racisms as experienced by other communities undifferentiated by phenotype. Instead, by recognising and isolating distinct racisms, deeper analytical insights can be gained on how these phenomena manifest and who they affect (Guerin 2002; Meer and Modood 2010). I argue that taking anti-Muslim racism as a distinct manifestation of racist belief and practice can allow for deeper and more thorough analyses of how this phenomenon is lived. Moreover, the use of the term *racism* has the potential to raise a popular discussion (not just an academic debate) that may be useful in countering this phenomenon, a point I return to below. I first want to elaborate on the conceptual definition of racism as presented by Miles and Brown (2003).

Miles and Brown (2003, p. 103) argue that 'racism is ... a representational form which, by designating human collectivities ... functions as an ideology of inclusion and exclusion.' As an ideological formation, racism results in disadvantage or 'exclusionary practices' for those constructed as 'other' (Miles and Brown 2003, p. 103). Racism 'presumes a process of racialisation'; that is, racism is contingent upon processes of signification where meaning is attached to 'markers' of the 'self' or the 'other', defining who belongs and who does not (Dunn *et al.* 2007; Miles and Brown 2003). The process of auto-racialisation (Miles and Brown 2003, p. 85) refers to the creation of an idealised 'us'; evidenced in the Irish context wherein belonging has come to be premised on notions of whiteness and Catholic-ness inter alia (Connolly 2006; Fanning 2012; Garner 2009; Lentin and McVeigh 2006 Ní Chatain 2011; Tracey 2000). Conversely the concept of hetero-racialisation (Miles and Brown 2003, p. 85) refers to the process of constructing the 'other' to legitimise one's own social position.

There is a wealth of evidence of these processes in the Irish context, for example, whether in relation to British constructs of the atavistic Irish during colonial rule; in more contemporary Irish constructions of members of domestic 'others' including members of the Traveller Community, Protestant communities (read British); Ireland's Jewry; and diverse immigrant groups (Fanning 2012; Garner 2009; Ignatiev 1995; Lentin 2002; McVeigh 2002, 2007; Ní Chatain 2011; Ní Shúinéar 2002). It is worth underscoring at this point that very many of those who have been constructed as the 'other' in Ireland have been so defined in the absence of any phenotypical difference. Instead, it is the presumed absence of markers of idealised Irishness which have been implicated in setting the 'other' apart (Fanning 2012; Fanning *et al.* 2011; Garner 2009, 2010; Lentin 2002, 2006; MacGréil 1977; McVeigh 2002, 2007; Ní Chatháin 2011; Ní Shúinéar 2002; Power *et al.* 2012; Rolston and Shannon 2002; Tracey 2000).

The process of racialisation stresses the point that '"races" are socially imagined rather than biological realities' (Miles and Brown 2003, p. 89; see also Kundnani 2014). Yet, while racism is premised on processes of racialisation, it is made distinct from these processes through the infusion of an 'explicitly negative evaluative component' (Miles and Brown 2003, p. 104). The combined construction of the 'other' and the infused negative evaluative component inform racist practices and beliefs resulting in exclusionary practices that can manifest as experiences of hostility and discrimination (Miles and Brown 2003). The manner in which Miles and Brown (2003) define racism as an ideology has particular utility in that it demonstrates the presence of underlying processes of racialisation and also how the outputs of these processes (exclusionary practices) underpin manifest lived experiences of hostility and discrimination.

Defining anti-Muslim racism as anti-Muslim *racism*

Although acknowledging the manner in which Muslimness can intersect with phenotype, Miles and Brown (2003, p. 163) do not define Islamophobia as a form of racism:

> The alleged distinctiveness of the Muslim is not usually regarded as biological or somatic.... However, it does interact with racism ... there was a quasi-racialisation of the Muslim (as 'Saracen', 'Turk' or 'Moor') in the Middle Ages.

For Miles and Brown (2003) Muslims can only experience racism when they are targeted on the basis of phenotype; for them, Islamophobia then is not racism but something else. But racism is not just about phenotypical difference but the 'deeper and more complex matrices of power and signification' (McVeigh 2002, p. 150). To restate the point made above by Miles and Brown (2003, p. 89) '"races" are socially imagined' and as such this acknowledgement of the constructed character of racial categories calls into question the reliance on phenotypical difference in defining a phenomenon as racism (see also Meer and Modood 2010; Kundnani 2014; Rana 2007; Semati 2010). Meer and Modood (2010, p. 77) argue that the 'racialisation of a group is not the invocation of a biology but a radical "otherness" and the perception and treatment of individuals in terms of physical appearance and descent'.

I contend here that this treatment of the 'other' on the basis of appearance and descent need not be restricted to phenotype. Indeed, Miles (1982, cited in Meer and Modood 2010, p. 75) has previously stated that those engaged in the study of 'race', racism and racialisation 'must not restrict the application of the concept of racialisation to situations where people distinguish one another by reference to skin colour'. It has been argued elsewhere that 'anti-Muslim sentiment' operates concomitantly on various markers of difference employed to define 'otherness' including 'race, culture and belonging' (Meer and Modood 2010, p. 83). Cultural identities can act as a proxy for 'race', yet the function remains the same: to maintain or indeed fortify the prevailing position of the dominant group in a given society along racialised lines (Semati 2010). Cultural identity presented as innate and immutable has played a key role in the development of racialised discourses, drawing on religious and broader identifiers of culturally defined 'otherness' (Kundnani 2014; Rana 2007, p. 149; Semati 2010). Semati (2010, p. 265) argues that there has been, among some theorists at least, a move in the manner in which racism is theorised from one purely based on phenotype and biology to that which invokes cultural markers which are symbolic of the 'other' and essentialised cultural inherentisms: 'racism[s] without races' (Balibar 1991, cited in Semati 2010, p. 266).

According to Meer and Modood (2010, p. 78), 'cultural racism builds on biological racism' wherein cultural difference operates in concert with phenotype to legitimise exclusionary practices. Dunn et al. (2007, p. 567) place an emphasis on the manner in which the 'two logics' of these racisms resonate not only in how they manifest but also in the manner that they are subject to processes of racialisation. For Dunn et al. (2007, p. 567) 'anti-Islamic racism' is premised on processes of racialisation that operate on the religious and the cultural as opposed to biological; thus Muslim communities can experience racism without the required invocation of racial difference as preferred by Miles and Brown (2003). Instead, anti-Muslim sentiment can operate 'upon certain markers of culture ... a racialisation process, but without "race"' (Dunn et al. 2007, p. 583). Rana (2007, p. 159) also argues in favour of an inclusive concept of racism that not only holds space for 'race' but also for 'racialised religion'.

Indeed, 'modern' racism, based on phenotype and biology has antecedents in earlier religiously derived constructions of the 'other' (Dunn et al. 2007; Meer and Modood 2010). Religion as a means of defining the 'other' informed early formations of 'race'; from the eighteenth century this process became secularised with the development of 'scientific' arguments about racial group difference (Rana 2007). This assertion has obvious implications for constructing cultural racisms as 'new' given the historical precedent of such experiences in various contexts (Barker 1981; Garner 2010; Guerin 2002; Hickman 1998; Mac an Ghaill 1999; Rana 2007). I argue that cultural identifications, including those associated with religion, can act as a proxy for 'race' in order to define the 'other' and preserve 'extant racial hegemonies' (Semati 2010, p. 266). In the Irish context, racialisation of the 'other' as evidenced in the experiences of Ireland's Jewish, Protestant and Traveller communities has invoked religious difference as a means of constructing a racial out-group (Fanning 2012; Lentin 2002). MacGréil's (1977) seminal research on prejudicial attitudes in Ireland in the late 1970s demonstrated clear evidence of anti-Semitic sentiment in the Irish context, informed by racialised international stereotypes of the Jewish 'other' (see also Fanning 2012; Lentin 2002). This is not peculiar to Ireland as Meer and Modood (2010, p. 77) point out, in the European context 'non-Christian religious minorities ... undergo processes of racialisation where the "otherness" ... that is appealed to is connected to a cultural and racial otherness'. It is their religious identity, then, that can set them apart from 'real' Europeans who are presumed to be homogenously Christian.

Following Garner (2010, p. 159) I argue that exclusionary practices premised on the racialisation of groups, based on culture and/or phenotype, 'are two sides of the same phenomenon' which have become interwoven in recent decades. Specifically in relation to Islamophobia, Garner (2010, p. 173) notes:

> Islamophobia illustrates the intertwined nature of the physical and the cultural in recurring formations of 'race' and racism ... racism utilises ideas drawn from both biological and cultural domains.

Counter to these arguments, Miles and Brown (2003) insist that for a group to be racialised there is a requirement for some phenotypical or somatic distinctiveness. Yet they also state that Muslim communities may find themselves 'excluded from the nation', 'not really belonging', premised on perceived 'cultural incompatibility' and a 'blood theory of nationality combined with a racialisation of the Muslim'; the Muslim whose religion and culture are held as being outside of national traditions (Miles and Brown 2003, p. 167). In the Irish context, the negatively racialised figure of the Muslim lies outside of 'traditional' notions of belonging that emphasise Catholic-ness as atomic in Irish identity (Tracey 2000). What is striking in the language used by Miles and Brown above (2003) is the manner in which essentialised, naturalised, innate differences are evident in the terms they use to describe Muslimness constructed as outside of the nation, culturally incompatible and outside of the national blood line. Miles and Brown also state that:

> The Muslim will always be regarded as practicing irrespective of whether or not this is the case for any individual. As the representative of a different civilisation, the Muslim will be regarded as having a fundamentally different mindset, or even engaged in a clash of civilisations ... an enemy within.
>
> (Miles and Brown 2003, p. 167)

Miles and Brown (2003) clearly demonstrate the manner in which racialising processes and the invocation of negative evaluation can actually operate on non-phenotypically derived markers of the 'other'; thus satisfying the criteria for racism as proffered by Miles and Brown (2003) without the required presence of 'race' qua 'race' that they insist upon elsewhere, instead the racialised religious identity is clearly to the fore.

I argue that the term racism as a discursive tool can enable broader recognition and analyses of the true character of the processes by which Muslim peoples' outsider status is constructed, legitimised and lived. In using the term racism I do not for one moment suggest that Muslims form a single, unique 'race' but emphasise processes of socio-political construction and lived experiences of racialised groups (Kundnani 2014; Richardson 2009). Furthermore, given the complex character of racisms and the manner in which different bases for exclusion may intersect (Crenshaw 1991), I am of course aware that a Muslim person may experience racism on the basis of their racial identification, their racialised religious identity or their ethnicity, independently or contemporaneously (see for example Poynting and Noble 2004). What I want to emphasise here, and throughout this text, drawing in part on the authors above, is that a Muslim person may experience anti-Muslim hostility and/or discrimination on the basis of racialised constructions of their faith and given the synonymy with other manifestations of racism it should be classed as such. As Miles and Brown (2003, p. 165) argue, Islamophobia resonates with racism qua racism not only in terms of the processes of racialisation noted above, but also in the manifestation of 'exclusionary practices, exclusionary discourses and hostility' directed toward Muslims constructed as a homogenous 'other' group. However, I also agree with Allen (2010) that it is fundamental that a specifically anti-Muslim element must be in evidence in order for it to merit being called anti-Muslim racism (Allen 2010).

Recent cases of racism in the Irish context can be usefully deployed to further clarify my argument. In early November 2013, a *halal* shop in the Tallaght suburban area of Dublin, *Al-Minnah Foods*, was vandalised with significant damage and loss incurred, including some theft. The racist aspect of this incident was clear in the graffiti daubed on the walls which included the terms 'NIGGRS OUT' [sic] and 'PAKIS OUT' (O'Carroll 2013). The Director of *Al-Minnah*, an Algerian man, reported to the press that he had experienced racism in the past but nothing on this scale. In this incident it is clear that a *halal* store, an outlet to supply the dietary requirements of local Muslim communities, was targeted. However, the terms daubed on the walls did not refer specifically to Muslimness, making it somewhat problematic to claim that this was anti-Muslim racism as opposed to racism based on phenotype. However, it could also be argued, given the fact that the outlet serves local Muslim people, that Muslimness did figure in the motivation for the vandalism. Arguably, the 'otherness' associated with Muslimness may result in the use of terms such as 'Paki' or 'Nigger', at times interchangeably with for example 'terrorist' or 'bin Laden' (see Brown 2006 for examples from the UK context). I will return to this in later chapters.

Another incident, also in Dublin in November 2013, underscores the manner in which Muslim communities in Ireland can be targeted regardless of phenotype, with Muslimness racialised as outside of Irishness. Here, a number of Dublin-based Muslim organisations, community groups and schools were the target of a hate mail campaign (Islamic Foundation of Ireland 2014). The language used in the letter was telling as the following quotes demonstrate, written in capitals as in the original (see Appendix 2):

> WE ARE THE DEFENDERS OF IRELAND AND WE TAKE OFFENCE OF [sic] MUSLIMS IN OUR COUNTRY ... WE ARE READY AS THE TRUE HOLDERS OF THE IRISH PEOPLES [sic] HERITAGE AND HISTORY TO USE WHATEVER POWERS WE NEED TO STOP YOU THE MUSLIM PEOPLE WHO HAVE NO RIGHT TO BE ON OUR ISLAND.

> MUSLIMS HAVE NO RIGHT TO REMAIN IN IRELAND, THE IRISH PEOPLE ARE NOT HAPPY WITH YOUR PRESENCE IN THIS COUNTRY WHICH BELONGS TO THE TRUE IRISH PEOPLE.

> WE WILL DEFEND OUR CULTURE AT ANY COST, WE WILL DEFEND OUR CHRISTIAN FAITH AT ANY COST AND WILL ATTACK ANY MUSLIM OR PERSON WE FEEL IS MUSLIM.

> PEOPLE WHO HAVE BEEN MADE A CITIZEN [e.g. naturalised] ARE NOT IRISH, THEY HAVENT PLAID [sic] ANY PART OF OUR HISTORY, THEY WERE NOT HERE IN THE 1920'S [sic], 1916 OR EVENTS SUCH AS THE FAMINE.

Clearly, then, in the words of the perpetrators of this campaign and others, Muslimness is something that is incompatible with 'true' Irishness. The threats made in this letter refer to those that the perpetrators deem as 'Muslim or person they feel is Muslim'. The reference here to phenotype is notable by its absence. Instead, people may be singled out on the basis of being identified as Muslim, presumably based on what Allen and Nielsen (2002, p. 8) refer to as 'visual identifiers' of Muslimness – the hijab or long beard, for example – religious signifiers which are deemed un-Irish. The above examples demonstrate that members of Muslim communities may be targeted on what appears to be racism qua racism without the reference to Muslimness; or, as the latter example demonstrates, Muslim communities may be targeted purely on the basis of their Muslim identity which is racialised as anathema to Irishness; or, indeed, through the intersection of racial, religious and ethno-national identities.

Cole (1998, p. 40) argues that it is often difficult to make a distinction between either biological or cultural racism which may at times operate in conjunction. Instead of viewing racism as 'pre-eminently biological or pre-eminently cultural ... racism might be more accurately described as a matrix of biological and cultural racism'; a continuum of racism so to speak with polar opposites 'based purely on biology ... or purely on culture' (Cole 1998, pp. 39–40). Cole's (1998) matrix suggestion can be usefully employed to describe the experiences of racism that members of Muslim communities may be exposed to, acknowledging the issue of intersectionality of racisms. On the biological extreme, members of Muslim communities may experience racism based on phenotype; at the other end, experiences of racism that specifically target Muslimness; with biology, culture and religious identity becoming more or less amplified along the way.

Arguably, anti-Muslim racism in a 'pure' sense, drawing on Cole's (1998) model above, would sit at the cultural end of the continuum, thus fitting the argument proffered by Meer and Modood (2010) of Islamophobia as a form of cultural racism. However, I find this claim of cultural racism problematic vis-à-vis Muslim communities. I acknowledge that a broadly recognised ethnic group such as the Traveller Community in Ireland can experience a distinct cultural racism (Guerin 2002). However, this assertion of cultural racism to Muslim communities is inappropriate given Muslim cultural diversity and instead can in itself have an essentialising effect. Thus, I agree with Allen (2010) that utilising the term cultural racism for religious groups derived from multifarious cultural backgrounds serves only to further homogenise Muslims and is counterproductive to efforts that wish to dispel the constructed image of Muslims and Islam as a monolithic community, stripping Muslim communities of their internal diversity and presenting and reinforcing a homogenous identity – premised on notions of an essentialised Muslimness.

However, although I do not employ the term cultural racism in relation to Muslim communities, I do want to retain use of the term racism to explain the underlying processes and experiences of hostility and discrimination experienced by Muslim communities in Ireland, premised on their Muslimness. The rationale for utilising the term anti-Muslim *racism* is twofold. First, the term racism has greater utility due to the manner in which this term can alert us to the underlying processes of racialisation that inform contemporary perceptions of Muslimness and Islam. Second, I also argue for the use of the term racism, given the resonance that this term may have in popular discourse, or 'common sense'; a resonance that I contend is much greater than which can be offered by the neologism Islamophobia.

This is no doubt an area for further research and is certainly an area for debate. Vakil (2010, p. 36) argues that the term Islamophobia has an established 'international currency' as a conceptual term and as such should be utilised to refer to the experiences of hostility and discrimination lived by Muslim communities. Likewise, Garner (2010, p. 173) argues that there is a strong case to use Islamophobia as a conceptual term – even though Garner, as referred to above, perceives this phenomenon as racism. Miles and Brown (2003, p. 166) make an important point in arguing that Islamophobia is also used and understood by Muslims themselves and I acknowledge the primacy of Muslim voices. Zempi and Chakraborti (2014, p. 49) in their research with Muslim communities state that:

> [P]articipants were familiar with the term 'Islamophobia' and had a relatively good understanding of what the term meant – that is, hostility towards Islam and Muslims. A couple of participants had not heard of the term before but it became apparent that they had nonetheless experienced incidents that could be described as Islamophobic.

Interesting, here, is not so much that some of the participants understood the term Islamophobia while others had not heard of it, but *what* they understood. Do they understand Islamophobia as just hostility towards Islam and Muslims? Or as something more complex that includes an understanding of the underlying processes that construct Muslims as 'other'. As stated throughout this chapter I argue for the use of the term anti-Muslim racism as it underscores that it is racialised Muslimness, replete with references that often invoke Islam as a source of 'otherness', that is being targeted; furthermore, in using the term racism, a space is created for critical reflection on the processes of racialisation that inform anti-Muslim hostility and discrimination; finally, it is also argued here that the inclusion of the term racism as a discursive tool can gain greater traction in popular discourses given its established legacy and help challenge this phenomenon. According to Miles and Brown

> [R]acism has an everyday use and many everyday meanings. During the past fifty years or so, it has become a key idea in daily discourse as well as in sociological theory.... The concept of racism is also *heavily negatively loaded, morally and politically*. Thus, to claim that someone has expressed a racist opinion is to denounce them as immoral and unworthy.
>
> (2003, p. 3, emphasis mine)

In the post-World War II era, discourses around 'race' premised on racial pseudo-science, although not eliminated, have become subject to negative sanction in the public and political arena (Cole 1998; Garner 2010). Indeed, there exists a shared view that racist acts or beliefs should be treated with condemnation (Miles and Brown 2003). Indeed, the negative evaluation afforded to the term racism is easily recognisable in the manner in which far right political groupings such as the English Defence League deny being racist – 'Not racist, Not violent, Not silent' (English Defence League 2014) – and instead try to argue that they are simply protecting their own, assumed homogenous, culture (Allen 2010a; Barker 1981; Britain First 2014).

Islamophobia, I argue, on the other hand, does not carry the same negatively loaded connotations to the broader public 'common sense'. Criticisms of the term Islamophobia based on the problematic use of the term 'phobia' are not new and I will not linger on these here (Richardson 2009). However, it is worth considering to what extent racialised constructions of Muslim communities do, as is their intent, create an element of fear (perceived legitimate) in those who are exposed to the predominant racialised 'truths' of Muslimness that permeate media, public and political discourses further demonstrated below (see also Allen 2010a; Frost 2008, 2008a; Inspired by Muhammad 2013). If these discourses are to be challenged as racialised constructs, I contend that they need to be exposed for what they are as opposed to the fear they may incur. While the concept of Islamophobia may hold a certain discursive traction, it remains shrouded in ambiguity, failing to communicate the experiences of racism as lived by Muslim individuals and communities, fitting all too easily within the postracial context of 'race' denial (Goldberg 2009).

I contend that the term anti-Muslim racism can gain a stronger purchase in the public mind-set capitalising on the established foothold that the term racism already has. As a 'linguistic sign' (Allen 2010, p. 149), racism connotes a particular meaning, one that resonates in the 'common sense', and in doing so may raise a broader consciousness of the phenomenon and 'alert the next generation to the dangers of all forms of racism' (Cole 1998, p. 45), challenging the dominant racialised 'truth' (Mac an Ghaill 1999). The call for the use of the term anti-Muslim racism is to not only better identify this phenomenon but to also lay a foundation from which to challenge it and associated ongoing processes of racialisation.

Neoliberalism and efficient racialised 'truths' of the Muslim as 'other'

According to Lentin (2008) the political longevity of racist ideologies is built on their ability to employ/deploy various 'logics' over time and space. Historically, 'race' has denoted phenotype yet the designation of a 'racial group is always socially rather than biologically based' (Bonilla-Silva 1997, p. 469; see also Goldberg 2009; Kundnani 2014). Racist ideologies are dynamic as are the racialised groups targeted and the manner in which they are evaluated and attributed positive or negative characteristics (Miles and Brown 2003). In the contemporary era, Muslim communities are constructed as 'other' through historically informed racialised discourses that espouse assertions of Muslim homogeneity, inferiority, misogyny, atavism and incompatibility with presumed homogenous 'Western values'. Muslim identities and symbols of Islam are frequently presented as synonymous with terrorism, fundamentalism, repression of women and extremism (Allen 2010, 2010b; Dunn *et al.* 2007; Garner 2010; Runnymede Trust 1997).

There are differing views on the genealogy of anti-Muslim sentiment. Allen (2010) synopsises multifarious perspectives on the phenomenon's development.

The least convincing argument presents anti-Muslim sentiment as a phenomenon that is purely born of our times, unrelated to and thus ignoring any historic formulations (Allen 2010). Alternative perspectives posit that contemporary anti-Muslim sentiments are part of an ongoing historical antipathy between the West and Islam, manifesting itself today in the manner it did then – a view devoid of any sensitivity to contextual fluctuations (Allen 2010). It is interesting to note the manner in which Muslim communities, at times at least, have been constructed as a racialised 'other' historically. This is exemplified in the orders of Pope Urban in his invocation for the First Crusade in 1095, describing the 'Turk' as 'an accursed race, a race utterly alienated from God' (cited in Armstrong 1988, p. 3). Sayyid (2010) argues that the manner in which anti-Muslim sentiment manifests itself is mutable and temporally contingent. It may be inherent in certain Western discourses, but it operates in periods of greater or lesser intensity, amplified during particular periods, such as the aftermath of the terrorist atrocities of the last decade (Allen 2010; Halliday 2003). Similarly, Muir and Smith (2004) argue that the anti-Muslim sentiment of the Crusades differed in its motivations to that of the *Reconquista* which was in turn different from the anti-Muslim feelings directed towards the Ottoman Empire (Muir and Smith 2004). Anti-Muslim sentiment, then, is not a new phenomenon, simply a product of the September 11 terrorist atrocities; there is a history of 'othering' Islam in the West to meet differing ends (Esposito 2011; Iqbal 2010; Said 2003).

In the contemporary, global, neoliberal era Muslimness is presented as the problematic identity *par excellence*. Muslim communities are portrayed as atavistic and illiberal; neoliberalism, encoded as democracy, is to be brought to the 'other' through conflicts and practices of surveillance that operate under the guise of liberation. It is a form of what Goldberg (2002, 2009) refers to as historic racism, wherein it is the aim of the West to help those who are underdeveloped at home and abroad to become like the 'advanced' and 'free' us. Countries targeted abroad (normally those with resources to exploit), and cultural communities at home, are portrayed as the last bastions of atavism that need 'our' help to (neo)liberalise. To build legitimacy for such expansionism, discursive racialised constructions are continually and opportunistically invoked to justify the neoliberal incursion into the world of the uncivilised 'other' (Goldberg 2009; Kumar 2012).

Muslims and Islam are created as the enemy, an imminent threat to 'us' and our freedoms. Central to the discursive constructions of Muslims as 'other' are racialised assertions of the alleged temporally and spatially immutable, monolithic, character of Muslimness with its attendant misogyny, barbarism, atavism and hapless self-governance. These characteristics are deemed inherent in the faith of Islam and, by association, all Muslim people despite myriad subjectivities present in global Muslim majority and minority societies (Kumar 2012; Runnymede Trust 1997). Through repeated governmental discourses, policies and practices, constructions of the Muslim 'other' as enemy take root in the social common sense, 'shaping and determining understanding, perceptions and attitudes in the social consensus' (Allen 2010, p. 190; see also Allen 2010a). Once rooted, they thrive and spread throughout society, where discursive repetition by private individuals reinforces the governmental conduct of conduct.

Double truths of problematic communities

The neoliberal regime of double truths (Dean 2010a, p. 10) engages in the racialised construction of Muslim as a threatening 'other' in order to generate consensus among those being conducted for its expansionist campaigns. Kaya (2011, p. 24) argues that anti-Muslim sentiment is an organising, discursive instrument that permeates the institutions of state and the populace and can be seen 'as a distinctive feature of modern governmentality'. The contemporary racialised construction of Muslim as 'other' is a central aspect of the so-called 'global war on terror'. It is an amorphous discursive tool that invokes fear and legitimates the expansion of neoliberal hegemony (Cole 2011). According to Kumar (2012, p. 164) such discourses are part of a 'politics of fear ... to justify war and continued violations of civil liberties domestically'. As Kumar (2012) points out, the conflict is not just 'over there' but discursively brought back to the West wherein we must be ever vigilant in the face of ever emerging 'home-grown' threats to our security. Our gaze, motivated by fear, is directed towards the Muslim other. As terrorism is presented as inherent in racialised Muslimness it is argued that it is only a matter of time before a Muslim person will engage in violence (Kumar 2012; see also Kundnani 2014). It does not matter where you are born and raised: if you are Muslim then you are perceived through the neoliberal 'truth' as part of a putatively extant 'Islamic' threat (Cole 2011).

Policy measures in the post-9/11 era have formed around 'discourses of suspicion' racialising Muslim communities as 'suspect' regardless of any evidentiary base (Hickman *et al.* 2011, p. 11). The revised UK government's *Prevent* (Home Office UK 2011) policy, a component of UK strategy to 'prevent' the inculcation of extremist ideals and radicalisation, is one case in point. Despite claiming that it is not singling out any particular faith, the *Prevent* (Home Office UK 2011) document focuses disproportionately on Muslim communities as a source of threat. Kundnani (2011) details the manner in which funding for the *Prevent* strategy for the periods 2008/2009 and 2010/2011 was directed to areas with a greater Muslim population; the higher the number of Muslims the higher the level of *Prevent* funding. This correlation between the distribution of funding and the numbers of Muslim residents sends a clear message that it is Muslim communities that are the main suspects in this war on radicalisation and that all Muslim communities are to be deemed 'suspect' (Spalek 2011).

This phenomenon of securitisation is not confined to the UK; Muslim communities have been religiously profiled and constructed as 'suspect' across the EU and in the USA in the post-9/11 era (Fekete 2009, pp. 47–52; Kundnani 2014). By mid-2002, the German government had amassed information on 6,000,000 people, singling out more than 20,000 as 'suspect' on the basis that they had ties to any Muslim-majority state and were aged 18 and 24 years old and had no criminal record (Fekete 2009). In Italy, in 2003, the government indicated that it would be implementing a policy of surveillance on mosques, based on the need to monitor the 'wagers of Holy War' (Pisanu, cited in Fekete 2009, p. 69). Confidential material obtained by the Associated Press (2014) details the manner in which Muslim communities in New York and New Jersey were profiled on the basis of their religious identity. Here, Muslim-owned businesses, mosques, political groups and student organisations were infiltrated and subjected to covert surveillance by members of the New York Police Department, despite a lack of any evidence being present that connected these groups to criminality (Associated Press 2014).

Fekete (2009, p. 103) argues: 'European [and US] intelligence services have promoted the view that young Muslims are increasingly receptive to radicalisation'. Constructed as 'passive pawns' in the hands of charismatic 'evil Imams' who encourage 'extremist' behaviour (Brown 2008, p. 477), theories of radicalisation present Muslim communities as hyper-vulnerable to becoming 'home grown' terror threats (Human Rights Watch 2014). While only barely acknowledging broader socio-economic factors (Jones 2013; Kundnani 2014), these theories locate proclivities towards radicalisation and eventual terrorism as directly connected to ones faith in Islam, an argument that is eschewed by both Jones (2013) and Roy (2008). Yet despite the impossibility of successfully profiling 'terrorist' behaviour (Human Rights Watch 2014), 'bearded men [and] veiled women' are subjected to an ethno-religious profiling and presented to us as *the* 'suspect' subject (Brown and Saeed 2014, p. 2).

The year 2014 saw the figure of the 'foreign fighter' take centre stage in these discourses of radicalisation, amplified due to the conflicts in Syria and Iraq and the presence therein of the so-called Islamic State of Iraq and the Levant (ISIL). Radicalised abroad, the figure of the returning 'foreign fighter' allegedly poses such a risk to our security that calls have been made for the implementation of draconian legislative responses (Hussain 2014; Maher and Neumann 2014). These calls have been made on the presumption that those who travel to participate in international conflicts are doing so to fight and also undertake training in order to commit terrorist acts upon their return to the West.

However, travelling to an international conflict does not mean that one will wish to engage in terrorism upon their return. Indeed, those within the area of security studies acknowledge that multiple motivations may underpin a person's decision to travel to international conflicts and that 'it is wrong to think of them [foreign fighters] as a homogenous group' (Maher and Neumann 2014); moreover

> [t]he only authoritative study of the issue, based on nearly one thousand jihadist returnees from previous conflicts showed that one in nine former fighters subsequently became involved in terrorist activity. This does leave a majority who do not wish to become involved with terrorism, for whatever reason.
>
> (Maher and Neumann 2014)

Media reports and biographical accounts demonstrate that a small number of Irish Muslims have travelled to foreign conflicts (Kilpatrick and Farrell 2014; Najjair 2013). State security policies and media discourses are clear on the alleged threat of returning radicalised foreign fighters (Department of Justice and Equality 2014a; Lally and Kelly 2014; Ryan 2015). Concomitantly, members of Muslim communities in the Irish context have reported increased experiences of anti-Muslim racism with direct reference being made to the rise of ISIL and the brutal murders of Western hostages (Meagher 2014). Correlation does not mean causation, however discourses and related policies of securitisation, such as those outlined above, communicate to broader society that it is Muslim identities that are problematic identities, untrustworthy and threatening, and therefore require surveillance. By locating Muslim communities as the domain of 'extremism' and 'radicalisation', policies that aim to counter terrorist activity set Muslims apart as a suspect group against whom hostility becomes socially acceptable (Allen 2010a; Hickman *et al.* 2011; Kundnani 2014). Neoliberal mentalities of governance and discourses around radicalisation and the 'global war on terror' position the figure of the Muslim as threatening in the public common sense, exaggerating the constructed threat to further justify military expeditions abroad; concomitantly legitimising restrictions on civil liberties and creating a social climate that is hostile to Muslim men, but particularly Muslim women.

Saving Muslim women

Sheehi (2011, p. 90) argues that Muslim 'women, both as agents and as a symbol, have played a central role in justifying' discourses of the 'war on terror'. Muslim women are described as 'subjugated, oppressed ... little more than slaves' in need of salvation (Kumar 2012, p. 44). Support in the USA for military action in Afghanistan was garnered from across multifarious female political figures and feminist organisations under the banner that 'the fight against terrorism is also a fight for the rights and dignity of women' (Kumar 2012, p. 45; see also Goldberg 2002). Operating under a 'veil' of gender equality, this racialised theme easily gains a foothold that resonates powerfully throughout public discourse and perception. Muslim women are constructed as in need of protection from their 'hyper-patriarchal men', so much so that people from the West must intervene to secure their freedom (Razack 2008, p. 4). All the while persistent patriarchal practices in the West are denied (Sheehi 2011; van der Valk 2012).

In a manner that resembles the racialised practices of securitisation, the negative tropes associated with Muslim women utilised to garner support for military action abroad have also been invoked to legitimate governmental techniques of population management in the West. Central to these racialised discourses of the oppressed Muslim woman is the hijab, an item frequently targeted in governmental efforts to manage the freedom of Muslim bodies (Kumar 2012). According to Allen and Nielsen (2002, p. 36), the hijab is 'highly visible' in Western societies, a symbol embellished with negative racialised misconceptions of what is perceived to be the second class role of women in Islamic communities.

The issue of women's rights and governmental techniques of controlling Muslim women's bodies in the West were first signalled in the *Chador* case in France culminating eventually, in 2004, in a ban on the hijab in public schools (Lentin 2008; Open Society Institute 2011). The prohibition of the hijab has, in turn, served to legitimise further restrictions on the rights of Muslims and increase anti-Muslim sentiment (European Monitoring Centre on Racism and Xenophobia 2006a). Prohibitions on wearing the hijab to work in public institutions in Germany soon seeped into private employment, making it difficult for those Muslim women who choose to veil to find an occupation (European Monitoring Centre on Racism and Xenophobia 2006a). In 2011, the French government banned the wearing of face coverings in public spaces. The absence (subjugation) of Muslim women's voices and their knowledges from debates on their liberation is profoundly notable (Kumar 2012; Open Society Institute 2011).

Neoliberal discourses present the Muslim body as a spectacle of how we are supposedly *not* to live, with the Muslim woman as critical exemplar. The veiled female Muslim is the anti-thesis of the neoliberal idealised subject citizen. She represents the 'non-citizen ... trapped within group based identities' (Razack 2008, p. 166). Muslim identifiers exemplify group or collective affiliation contrary to the neoliberal goal of making the aforementioned 'rational' individuals, 'one-man [sic] archipelagos' (Giroux 2008, p. 592; see also Goldberg 2009, p. 163). From the neoliberal perspective, experiences of anti-Muslim racism are simply resultant from the reticence of the Muslim individual, male and/or female, to be more like 'us'. Neo-liberal processes of individuation demand the breaking of collective ties deemed contrarian to the ideological goal and security of an individualised society wherein self-reliance and responsibility (and fault) are prioritised over notions of social solidarity (Gray 2011; Razack 2008). Communicated through discourses of rescuing Muslim women, negative governmental sanctions are accepted as the correct 'truth' and inform the public gaze. Policing the 'other' is outsourced to society *en masse*, to those who draw from racialised governmental practices to legitimate their acts of liberating Muslim women, making 'other' those who fail to meet the neoliberal ideal, like 'us', through 'regressive symbolic and corporeal violence' (Giroux 2008, p. 601).

There is somewhat of a contradiction in the manner in which Muslim women are perceived in governmental practices. As I have argued, Muslim women are constructed as the unwitting victims of hyper-patriarchal men; however, Muslim women are also constructed as a civilising influence on their barbarous male co-religionists (Allen 2014; Brown 2008). In relation to the latter, Muslim women are presented as the 'missing link' in government-led counter-radicalisation strategies (Brown 2008, p. 472). In the UK context, it is argued that, as the bearers of the moderate Islam, 'Muslim women will civilise and liberalise British Islam and Muslim communities' (Brown 2008, p. 473). The participation of Muslim women in the mosque is constructed as an effective counter measure to radicalising male influences; having benefitted the most from integration and embracing 'our values' of equality, the inclusion of Muslim women will 'de-radicalise' the mosque (Brown 2008, p. 481). In the family it is argued that maternal Muslim women can act as a conduit through which 'moderate Islam' can be taught to future generations currently vulnerable to being radicalised by charismatic clerics (Brown 2008).

The gender lines are clear, Muslim women, despite their diversity, are presented as moderating influences; Muslim men, on the other hand, are portrayed as misogynistic, backward 'fanatic radicals' (Brown 2008, p. 475). The seeming contradiction in the manner in which Muslim women are constructed comes full circle here. Despite the political agency of Muslim women evidenced in ongoing grassroots efforts at increased community inclusion, policies of governmental support for women's participation replay Orientalist style racialised imagery that Muslim women do need to be saved. Indeed, instead of helping Muslim women, these interventions in reality may actually be counterproductive and serve to build distrust amongst Muslim communities (Brown 2008). Muslim women's groups may welcome governmental support; for government, however, discourses of inclusion and ameliorating the position of Muslim women are arguably only secondary to the instrumental goal of policing a suspect community (Brown 2008).

While the anti-Muslim sun shines...

Bonnilla-Silva (1997, p. 475) argues that 'after a society becomes racialised, racialisation develops a life of its own'. Informed and legitimised by state actors, diverse groups utilise the 'other' to achieve their own ends, at the same time fulfilling their role in the government of hearts and minds. Key protagonists in the outsourced policing are political groups across Europe and abroad that, seizing the opportunity, have utilised the governmental projection of Muslim individuals and communities to further their ambitions while affirming the position of Muslims as 'other'.

The past 20 years have seen right wing political groups increase in prominence across Europe. These groups are united by their 'ethno-nationalist xenophobia', manifesting itself as opposition to immigration and political initiatives involved in promoting multiculturalism (Rydgren 2008, pp. 737–739; see also Gündüz 2010). Anti-Muslim racism is rife in European, broadly right wing, political groups such as Britain First, the British National Party, the English Defence League (EDL); the Golden Dawn group in Greece, the French Front National, and the Lega Nord in Italy; the German grouping 'Patriotic Europeans Against the Islamisation of the West' (PEGIDA) etc., all of which overtly and vociferously invoke anti-Muslim rhetoric (Allen 2010, 2011; Britain First 2014; Cesari 2011, pp. 31–32; English Defence League 2011; Iordanou 2013; Spiegel 2014).

Capitalising on state policies of securitisation and the alleged threat that Muslim communities pose to our liberal ways, anti-Muslim racism has 'passed the dinner-table test' (Batty 2011; see also Allen 2013) enabling otherwise marginalised groups to run more mainstream political campaigns on distinctly racist platforms. Discourses traditionally used to target immigrants and Europe's Jewry are deployed against Muslims, often employing Islamophobic tropes instrumentally to increase party profile (Cesari 2011). The recent growth in the public acceptability of ideologically informed anti-Muslim sentiment has predominantly been to the benefit of far right political groups, providing them with an opportunity to propagate their Islamophobic views, giving them a platform to raise their own political capital (Cesari 2011). Allen (2010, p. 88) argues that in the aftermath of the attacks in New York in 2001 and London in 2005 groups such as 'the BNP ... used the climate to acquire social and political legitimacy', capitalising on discourses of 'fear and threat'.

The public common sense, informed by hegemonic neoliberal discursive constructions of 'truth', is fertile ground for anti-Muslim discourses to be further sown to the benefit of otherwise marginal political parties. This is not lost on those would-be legitimate political groups who recycle tropes of racialised Muslimness in order to make political capital: 'We should be positioning ourselves to take advantage for our own political ends of the growing wave of public hostility to Islam currently being whipped up by the mass media' (Nick Griffin, cited in Allen 2010, p. 92). Moreover, the international discourses of fear (Allen 2010) employed by governmental discourses of securitisation and of those parties aiming to make political capital in one jurisdiction easily permeate into other international contexts in an era of ubiquitous global media coverage.

Purveyors of racialised 'truths'

Allen (2010, p. 99), argues that the media play a pivotal role in 'communicating and disseminating ideas and meanings about Muslims and Islam', discourses that are replete with stereotypical images. The process of transmitting meaning through the recurrent use of stereotypical imagery serves to normatively position Islam and Muslims as the 'other' in Western discourses, regularly conflating the faith of Islam with terms such as fundamentalist or terrorist (Allen 2010; Baker 2010). Zones of neoliberal pedagogy such as the media connect the individual to the rationality of state in the interests of the neoliberal project (Giroux 2008, p. 591). This is not denying individual agency with regard to how people receive and 'decode' media messages (Allen and Nielsen 2002; Hussain 2000). Nonetheless, as Lewis *et al.* (2011, p. 42) state 'journalism specifically seeks to persuade its audience that a particular version of events is ... "true"'.

In 2006, the Greater London Authority commissioned research into the manner in which the press represented Muslims and their faith in a 'normal week', that is, a week devoid of anything that may unduly influence the level of coverage afforded to Muslim issues. The findings of this analysis demonstrated that stories involving Muslims had increased by 270 per cent when compared to a 1996 study. Further, over 90 per cent of coverage negatively represented Muslims/Islam, while half referred directly/specifically to Muslims/Islam as threatening (Allen 2010, p. 99). Similarly, Lewis *et al.* (2011, pp. 42–46) conducted an analysis of images of discourse on the manner in which the British print media represent Muslims and their faith between the years of 2000 and 2008, encompassing 974 articles, focusing on 'everyday' news coverage of Muslims. Lewis *et al.* (2011, pp. 46–48) identify what they describe as the three most 'common "news hooks"' in Muslim related reports in the British print media. These include '"terrorism, or the war on terror", "religious or cultural issues" and "Muslim extremism"'. When combined, these categories accounted for 69 per cent of the all stories related to Muslims.

In the Irish context, media actors have played their part in the discursive chorus that stereotypically characterises all Muslims as terrorist fundamentalists through sensationalist reportage depicting Muslim communities in Ireland as the 'enemy within', fuelling what Cole (2011, p. 128) refers internationally to as the perception of Muslims as the 'green menace'. Past headlines include 'Fascist fundamentalism is rife among young Irish Muslims', 'The green jihadis' published in 2006 (see National Consultative Committee on Racism and Interculturalism 2007, pp. 1–2) and 'Al Qaeda's Irish Terror Cell: Jihad fanatics hiding out amongst us' (McElgunn 2011). Exposure to repeated pathologising depictions of Muslims and Islam increases the likelihood that these representations will be internalised as 'truths', leaving an indelible mark on those reading such constructions, a point starkly demonstrated in recent research in the UK (Allen 2010, p. 99).[1]

Proposed definition for anti-Muslim racism

The insights adumbrated above and in the previous chapter illuminate the theoretical and the practical aspects of anti-Muslim racism on which I base the definition that I now propose. This definition draws from the theoretical premise of this study to inform the empirical aspects of the research, the findings of which are discussed in the chapters that follow. It is indebted to the literature of the key scholars discussed above, particularly Allen (2010) and Miles and Brown (2003). The definition I offer adds to their theorisation an emphasis on the role of the global neoliberal regime of 'truth', which through processes of anti-Muslim racialisation justifies a *telos* of expansion at home and abroad. It is operational in that its key aspects can be observed through various research methods deployed in the empirical aspects of this study, which reveal how anti-Muslim racism is experienced by those who are targeted by it.

Anti-Muslim racism

Anti-Muslim racism has been utilised by various regimes of 'truth' across history. Manifesting itself differently over time, it is today maintained through hegemonic neoliberal discourses that racialise Muslim communities as 'other'. Despite their myriad diversity, Muslims are racialised as a homogenous threat in the 'Western common sense' to legitimate neoliberal expansionist campaigns at home and abroad. Through neoliberal racializing – 'truths' that operate on signifiers of Muslimness, at times intersecting with 'race' and gender inter alia – Muslim individuals and communities are subjected to exclusionary practices resulting from specifically anti-Muslim racism, manifesting itself as discriminatory practices in accessing goods, employment and services, and/or acts of hostility be they verbal physical and/or emotional.

Islamophobia as defined by Allen (2010) as a coherent set of ideas utilised to legitimate the exclusion of Muslim men and women in and of itself can be defined as ideology in its own right. However, I argue in addition that Islamophobia is not in itself the mainspring for processes of anti-Muslim racialisation. There is, as I have presented above, a temporally contingent overarching regime of 'truth' at play that utilises and further enhances the racialisation of Muslimness to further its own ends. Thus while I agree that Islamophobia can be perceived as an ideology, I contend that it is more appropriately framed as a tool that has historically been utilised by multifarious hegemonic regimes of 'truth' and the rationalities they deploy to suit their ends. These global regimes of 'truth', neoliberal in the contemporary era utilise Muslimness as a symbolic mechanism to legitimate their claims to domination and proliferate tropes of how to be.

Discussion and conclusion

The purpose of this chapter is to engage with the topic of Islamophobia and present an argument for its replacement with the concept of anti-Muslim racism. There is a view that Islamophobia, as a term, has gained such a degree of purchase in public discourse that we should carry on using it, for to change it would somehow be counterproductive. However, I argue that Islamophobia as a concept is not fit for purpose if that purpose is challenging the racism experienced by Muslim men and women. To persevere with what I consider an inadequate label – Islamophobia – would be to continue to do a disservice to those men and women of the Muslim faith (as well as those perceived as Muslim) who experience verbal abuse, have their hijabs torn from their heads or have bottles thrown at them from afar because they 'look like bin Laden'. History is benighted by the experiences of those who have been negatively racialised and experienced racism, thus the term racism itself already has a foothold in the realities of the 'you and I' so much so that it immediately communicates exclusion on the basis of identity.

Attaching the term 'racism' to the contemporary experiences of Muslim men and women can lay a foundation upon which a challenge to anti-Muslim sentiment can be built, upon which a new 'truth' can be founded. Islamophobia does the opposite to that which is intended by utilising anti-Muslim racism. Resonating with neoliberal claims of racelessness, Islamophobia serves to obfuscate and deny the 'truth' of how Muslim men and women are constructed and treated in the contemporary era. Neoliberalism is the dominant regime of 'truth' that pervades our time, assuming a hegemonic position and filling the social 'common sense' with constructions of Muslims as 'other' utilising symbolic forms associated with Islam to denote difference and legitimate expansion at home and abroad. One of the central themes of neoliberal governmentality and racial neoliberalism is the denial of 'race' as a point of salience in social outcomes. The ambiguity inherent in Islamophobia matches the denial of 'race' as elaborated in the previous chapter as a tool for governing the racialised. Deploying anti-Muslim racism in place of Islamophobia can allow for greater understanding and a challenge to this pervasive neoliberal 'race' denial to be catalysed.

As argued in the previous chapter, a key part of this challenge lies in engaging in a counter conduct to change the way we are managed by neoliberal governmentalities and their nuances in the neoliberal state. There is a need for anti-Muslim racism to be recognised as a particular phenomenon internationally, including in Ireland.[2] For example, statistical knowledge could demonstrate clearly the levels of racism against Muslims in Irish society if it is collected correctly and steps are taken to build trust and encourage reporting of racism among Muslim communities. In doing so, the knowledge provided by such means can allow for the creation of effective policies vital for the 'truth' of experiences of Muslims living in Ireland, policies that will challenge the norm of racism and religious-cultural prejudice.

The recognition of anti-Muslim racism, starting with efficient data collection by the state, can go some way to informing policies which aim to de-normalise and deter racisms directed against Muslim communities. The importance of this will be made abundantly clear in the later chapters that describe the visceral realities of anti-Muslim racism. The following chapter will evaluate the manner in which the Irish State currently engages with (fails to address!) anti-Muslim racism in comparison with practical examples of international best practice, delimiting the boundaries of what an effective counter conduct could achieve and what an alternative (recognition of) response to anti-Muslim racism could look like.

Notes

1 A 2010, YouGov opinion poll of UK adults (Inspired by Muhammed 2013) demonstrated that almost 60 per cent of respondents cited television news as their primary source of information about Islam, while 41 per cent cited the print media. Nearly two thirds of respondents stated that they 'did not know very much about Islam', 17 per cent knowing nothing at all. Almost 70 per cent claimed they believed Islam was repressive of women; almost 60 per cent associated Islam with 'extremism'; while half associated Islam with terrorism.
2 See the European Agency for Fundamental Rights (2012) 'Making Hate Crime Visible in the European Union: Acknowledging victims' rights', available online at http://hatecrime.osce.org/what-do-we-know (accessed 8th December 2014) and the Organisation for Security and Cooperation in Europe (2014) 'Hate Crime Reporting: What do we know?' available online at http://hatecrime.osce.org/what-do-we-know (accessed 8th December 2014).

4 Measuring anti-Muslim racism
Ireland and abroad

Introduction

In 2002, a report for the European Monitoring Centre for Racism and Xenophobia stated that 'Any ... analysis of racial violence in Ireland must be prefaced by a "health warning" on the paucity of official data of this issue both in the form of crime statistics and regular national crime surveys' (National Focal Point 2002, p. 40). Six years later Nicola Carr (2008, p. 35) argued that 'it has become axiomatic to preface any discussion on aspects of the [Irish] justice system with a reference to "data deficits" which impede any meaningful analysis'. As argued above, neoliberal states are disposed to doing just the bare minimum to counter pernicious social phenomena such as racism. In turn, any limited interventions that are implemented are only done so on the premise that it is believed that they will be of some benefit to the neoliberal zeitgeist. Focusing on the recording and reporting of racism, set to an international comparative context, the evaluation presented here demonstrates that despite a potentially favourable environment for the collection of data on anti-Muslim racism inter alia, the Irish State, particularly An Garda Síochána,[1] fails to record racist and indeed broader hate crime with any degree of efficacy. Instead it tows the neoliberal line of effectively denying the salience of 'race' in the lives of the racialised. This is despite laudable statements in the now defunct National Action Plan Against Racism that not only included a recognition of 'Islamophobia' as a particular manifestation of racism but also underscored the need for data on racist incidents:

> The effective monitoring and analysis of incidents motivated by racism will provide important data to shape and focus future policing and broader intercultural strategies to where they are most needed.
> (Department for Justice Equality and Law Reform 2005, p. 79)

Although commendable, statements such as these have not made the transition into practice and thus remain what Fanning *et al.* (2011, p. 21) refer to as 'paper polices'. A review of the latest Organisation for Security and Cooperation in Europe report on hate crime demonstrates that only 11 of 57 member States are in a position to collect data in relation to hate crimes directed towards Muslims, Ireland is not among them. Indeed, the number of OSCE members that specifically recognise anti-Muslim racism in any real sense remains in the minority.[2] Nonetheless, insights are provided here from four states which have been cited as 'best in class' in relation to capturing data on racist activity in the EU, namely the UK, Finland, Sweden, and the Netherlands (European Union Agency for Fundamental Rights 2012).

At this juncture it is important to note that in Ireland racial discrimination in terms of accessing goods and services or in the employment sphere is explicitly prohibited under Irish equality legislation (Fanning et al. 2011, p. 10). Under criminal legislation, racially motivated offences can be prosecuted in one of two ways. The first through the problematic Incitement to Hatred Act (1989) which has been under review for over ten years;[3] the second includes the processing of racist crime though other standard offence headings (NGO Alliance Against Racism 2011; Schweppe and Walsh 2008). Racism, with the exclusion of the Incitement to Hatred Act (1989) and relevant aspects of equality legislation, is not specifically defined as an offence in Ireland (Schweppe et al. 2014; Schweppe and Walsh 2008). Alternative means of sanction, such as sentence uplift for racially aggravated offences, are not provided for in statute. Although a judge may use her discretion in regards to considering a racist motivation when issuing sentences, the fact remains that 'there is little statutory guidance on how judges should sentence any given offender' (Schweppe and Walsh 2008, p. 78; see also Taylor 2010). Nonetheless, in keeping with neoliberal 'truths' of calculated intervention, by legislating against incitement offences and providing for judicial discretion in the sentencing of racist offences Ireland does just enough to comply with the minimum standards prescribed in the EU Framework Decision on Combating Racism and Xenophobia (Europa 2013).

Recording racism: Ireland and the international context

The fact that racism qua racism is not specifically proscribed in criminal legislation should not, at least technically, impede the collection and collation of data on racist activity or their utility in regards to policy. In this section I examine the extent to which the Irish State records racism, with a particular look at anti-Muslim racism. This evaluation is informed by four examples of international best practice. The four models explored here demonstrate different methods that can be used to collect data on racism, including how it manifests itself and may be recognised as the victims of these acts. The methods deployed across these models of best practice share similarities, but there are also nuanced differences in the manner in which each state records racist crimes/incidents. I draw from each of these models selectively to highlight methods that could enhance how racism is recorded in Ireland and indeed other states.

Ireland: An Garda Síochána

The Irish police service, An Garda Síochána, has been using the Police Using Leading Systems Effectively (PULSE) crime/incident recording system since

1999. PULSE operates as a centralised data platform that provides Garda management with the necessary data required to inform and amend future and current policing practices (National Focal Point 2002; National Crime Council 2004). In November 2002, An Garda Síochána commenced recording racist crime on the then relatively new PULSE system (An Garda Síochána 2012b; National Consultative Committee on Racism and Interculturalism 2002). Following the MacPherson report on the murder of Stephen Lawrence in the UK, *An Gardaí Síochána* defines a racist event as 'any incident which is perceived to be racist by the victim or any other person' (An Garda Síochána 2013; National Consultative Committee on Racism and Interculturalism 2002). According to Taylor (2010), if a reported event is classed as racist this detail is recorded in the narrative section of the PULSE system and as such racist crimes do not have a special 'tick box' or marker as in other jurisdictions. However, this is only partially correct. According to Garda Sergeant Dave McInerney,[4] head of the Garda Racial Intercultural and Diversity Office,

> [T]he procedure for taking a report of racist crime/non-crime is: the [Garda] member who the takes the report immediately logs it into the Pulse database under whatever category of crime that the offence is associated with. It is then flagged as 'motivated by racism'. A non-crime [incident] will be recorded in the attention and complaints section and also recorded as motivated by racism in the narrative.

In other words, the Garda recording a racially aggravated crime onto the PULSE system selects the relevant crime type, for example 'assault causing harm',[5] and then chooses from a drop down list of 'flags' to indicate the relevant aggravating factor. According to Sgt McInerney, this list includes the following options: 'racism, xenophobia, sectarianism, anti-Semitism and homophobia'. Anti-Muslim racism is not included.

It is important to note that non-crime incidents are recorded 'under the category of "attention and complaints" on the Pulse system' (Sgt McInerney). However PULSE does not offer a drop down menu of flags to assign to non-crime incidents. Hence the details of such incidents can only be captured in the narrative section of a crime report. This detail corroborates information provided in the limited literature available on racist crime recording procedures (see Clarke 2013; Taylor 2010). What is notable here is the capacity for members of the service to record 'non/crime' incidents on the PULSE system. Although not ideal, the examples of best practice reviewed below demonstrate that by recording incidents in the narrative, Gardaí can gain access to valuable data on potentially vulnerable communities or areas before serious crime develops.

Questions have been raised in the past in regards to racism recording practices of the Gardaí, including on the awareness of the necessity of recording racist incidents (Walsh 2009). Despite the aforementioned procedures for recording a racist crime or non-crime incident, existing research demonstrates a high level of inconsistency, a lack of understanding and discretionary practice in the manner in which racism is perceived and recorded by members of An Garda Síochána (Clarke 2013; Fanning *et al.* 2011; Taylor 2010). Indeed, the authors of the 2004 Garda Human Rights Audit (Ionann Management Consultants 2004), research that was commissioned by An Garda Síochána, criticised the manner in which the PULSE system was being used to record racism, stating that while the mechanism was available it was under-used by staff.

Participants in Clarke's (2013, p. 14) 'off the record' interviews with members of An Garda Síochána demonstrated a lack of awareness and understanding of the Macpherson definition of a racist crime/incident – for example, that the offence can be defined as racist by the victim or any other person. Moreover, Clarke's (2013, p. 14) research on the practice of recording racism among members of An Garda Síochána also demonstrated that some officers had 'different opinions as to how Racist Incidents are supposed to be recorded in the Pulse [*sic*] system'.[6] While some members stated that a racist event should only be recorded in the narrative (although some were unsure what detail should go into the narrative), others noted that a specific 'tick box' was to be used for the purposes of recording racist crime (Clarke 2013). It is clear from Clarke's (2013) findings that there is a high level of uncertainty and inconsistency among Gardaí as to how a racist crime/non-crime incident should be recorded. The use of flags as described by Sgt McInerney above is at best normative and clearly not standard practice.

The evidence of poor Garda recording practices of racist crime/non-crime is also demonstrated by the little data that are available on racism in Ireland. In early 2013, the European Network Against Racism (Ireland), a collaboration of various NGOs, established an online, independent third party reporting mechanism to allow victims of racism to report their experiences entitled iReport.ie (European Network Against Racism (Ireland) 2015). In the space of one month alone the iReport system logged 60 reports of racist experiences, including instances of anti-Muslim racism (European Network Against Racism (Ireland) 2015). During the same period, another NGO that operates a separate racism recording service, the Immigrant Council of Ireland, stated that it had received 50 reports of racist events in a ten week period from the launch of their service (Immigrant Council of Ireland 2015). These data compared to a figure of only 19 events recorded by An Garda Síochána for the first quarter of 2013 (European Network Against Racism (Ireland) 2015). This trend has continued and the numbers of racist crimes/incidents reported to ENAR (Ireland) and the Immigrant Council remain higher that those captured by the Gardaí (European Network Against Racism (Ireland) 2015a; Immigrant Council of Ireland 2015a). It is clear that either members of An Garda Síochána are not recording racism properly, or people are not reporting to the Gardaí; worse still, both instances may be true. This calls into question the organisational focus on challenging racism, I return to this point below, for now it is important to address what possible purposes could be served by ineffectively recording racism and the lack of any data on anti-Muslim racism.

Little or no official data on racism serves to deny the salience of 'race' and racism as factors in the lived reality of diverse communities in Ireland. Low levels of racist recorded crimes/incidents communicate a message to wider society that racism is not a problem; that racism is being addressed, and that the published figures are some sort of 'unavoidable' natural level. Similarly, the absence of data on anti-Muslim racism serves to deny existence of this phenomenon in Irish society. The following quote made at the 2011 United Nations Universal Periodic Review session on Ireland is telling. In response to the Iranian State's submission on the presence of anti-Muslim racism in Ireland, the Irish Ambassador to the UN, Gerard Corr stated

> There is no objective basis for this allegation; on the contrary the Irish government is absolutely committed to ensuring that any form of racism is combated in the most comprehensive possible manner. Robust mechanisms ... are in place to record complaints about racial discrimination and comprehensive anti-racism training is provided to members of our police force.

The Ambassador is correct, to a point. There is no official objective basis for the Iranian claim but this is because the Irish State does not recognise anti-Muslim racism as a specific phenomenon. The cited lack of evidence allows the State to maintain its stance of 'race' denial, and reject its responsibility toward addressing anti-Muslim racism as a lived reality. The Ambassador instead presents a façade of a caring Irish State equipped with 'robust mechanisms' and anti-racism trained police. However, the reality speaks to the contrary. The research discussed above demonstrates haphazard practices vis-à-vis the recording of racism, limited recognition of the various bases for which one may experience racism in Ireland[7] and a clear lack of Garda training in this area.

But it does not need to be like this. In what follows, I will draw from examples of international best practice to provide an understanding of how things could be improved in terms of recognising, recording and challenging racism should the Irish State choose to desist in its denial.

International best practice: 'flagging' racism

The UK, Finland, Sweden and the Netherlands form the four states that the European Union Agency for Fundamental Rights (2012, p. 8) has classed as having 'comprehensive data' in relation to racism and broader forms of hate crime. This 'best in class' category includes those states that have the capability to record 'a range of bias motivations, types or crimes and characteristics of incidents ... [furthermore, hate crime] data are always published'. There are commonalities and differences; as well as advantages and disadvantages among the approaches that these four states take vis-à-vis recording racism/hate crime. No one system is perfect (see Brå 2014; Kääriäinen and Ellonen 2008) but they all offer practical examples of how the Irish State and others could record racism, and in particular for the purposes of this study, anti-Muslim racism. To begin, I will look at the use of 'flags', markers or codes for indicating a criminal offence/non-crime incident as racist. From here I will elaborate on the potential uses of the narrative sections of crime reports as recorded by police.

In the UK, police record hate crimes and incidents in accordance with the Macpherson definition discussed above (College of Policing 2014). 'For recording purposes, the perception of the victim, or any other person is the defining factor in determining whether an incident is a hate incident, or in recognising the hostility element of a hate crime' (College of Policing 2014, p. 5) Accordingly, facility is made for the recording of racist and other forms of hate crimes and non-crime incidents to be recorded and associated with for example hate crimes/incidents flags (Clarke 2013; Engage 2012). While different recording systems may be employed across different forces, all are informed by the same national standards requirements and detailed guidance on the recording of all forms of hate crimes and incidents are provided to police (Home Office (UK) 2015; London Metropolitan Police Service 2014; National Policing Improvement Agency 2011).

Since 2007, a common definition of hate crime has been in place across the UK criminal justice system (Smith *et al.* 2012). This has resulted in the availability of recorded police data on various forms of hate crime in England, Wales, Northern Ireland and Scotland incorporating 'race', faith, sexual orientation, transgender, disability, anti-Semitism (Association of Chief Police Officers 2015; Crown Office Procurator Fiscal Services 2014). These data have been recorded by the police in England and Wales since 1 April, 2008; figures are published annually with the first tranche released in 2010 (Smith *et al.* 2012). Annual data for England, Wales and Northern Ireland are readily available on the various forms of hate crime under the categories mentioned above and accessible through the 'True vision' website operated by the Association of Chief Police Officers (2015). In addition, statistical reports specific to police recorded hate crime in England and Wales are published by the Home Office (Creese and Lader 2014). Similarly, annualised hate crime reports are also published by the Police Service of Northern Ireland (2014) and also in Scotland by the Crown Office Procurator Fiscal (2014).

However, a cursory glance reveals that data available on police recorded racism and broader hate crime in the UK are not without their own problems. Scotland is the only jurisdiction within the UK to produce disaggregated state level data on religiously aggravated hate crime recorded by the police and the nature of such offences (The Scottish Government 2014). In the other UK jurisdictions, published police recorded crime figures only include insights on religiously aggravated crime as a meta-category and are not disaggregated by faith, with the exception of anti-Semitism (Association of Chief Police Officers 2015).[8] Indeed, only a minority of police forces in England and Wales, three, specifically record anti-Muslim racism through the use of a defined 'anti-Muslim hate crime' category and are thus able to provide disaggregated data on anti-Muslim hostility/discrimination (Engage 2012; Muslim Engagement and Development 2015).

While there exists a lack of disaggregated data on anti-Muslim racism nationally, the UK government has committed itself to supporting third party initiatives such as Tell MAMA (Measuring Anti-Muslim Attacks), a service that allows Muslims to report their experiences of hostility, and monitors and provides data on anti-Muslim hate crime (HM Government 2012; Tell MAMA 2015). 'Tell MAMA' is a third party reporting service established for Muslim people who have experienced hate crime, with the stated aim of collecting data that can be used to complement hate crime data recorded by police. Reports can be made over the phone, via email or online. The aim is to collect data on incidents which can be used to inform government and police policies and challenge anti-Muslim attacks (Tell MAMA 2015). However, as I argue throughout, this outsourcing of data collection to an NGO, despite their good work, is arguably further evidence of neoliberal policies of 'care' for those who experience racism.

In Finland, in a manner similar to both Ireland and the UK, an offence is classed as racist if it is perceived as such by the victim, the police or any other 'involved party' (Niemi 2011, p. 115). Unlike Ireland, racism and broader forms of hate crime such as those targeting religious identity, disability and sexual orientation are defined as aggravating factors in Finnish legislation (Niemi 2011). Police in Finland have been recording suspected racist crimes since 1997 through the use of a unique racist flag or 'code' (Kääriäinen and Ellonen 2008). As is the case in the UK, the use of this racism code is not mandatory. Instead, police officers are only guided to use the code as and when required (Niemi 2011; Peutere 2009). When used, the racism code allows an opportunity for the compilation of statistical data on racist offences. Only racially aggravated offences can be captured in this manner. Finnish police have not received instructions to enter a classification for broader hate motivations (Niemi 2011; Peutere 2009). Thus there is no systematic process for the recording of the other diverse bases of racism and hate crime through the use of specific flags or codes. Arguably, as a result, problems persist in terms of consistency of recording practices by police officers (Kääriäinen and Ellonen 2008). Nonetheless, data on broader forms of hate crime can be retrieved through the use of specific search terms applied to crime report narratives as discussed further below. Data on hate crime are published annually by the Police College of Finland (Niemi 2011; Sahramäki et al. 2014).

Like Ireland, Sweden does not have a legal designation of what constitutes a hate offence as a specific form of crime (Brå 2011, 2015a).[9] Notwithstanding, in 2008 a space was created on the police Rational Reporting Routine (RAR) system to facilitate the marking of whether or not an offence contained a suspected hate motivation. The use of this marker is mandatory and must be completed by all police recording a suspected hate motivated offence (Brå 2011, 2014). This approach may have benefits in and of itself; for example, the process of having to mark a crime as a suspected hate offence may serve to alert police officers to the potential that the event was indeed motivated by bias (Klingspor 2008). However, it must be noted that despite being mandatory it is not always utilised by individual officers (Brå 2011, 2014). Given the inconsistencies in police recording of hate crime, data on the issue are also collated separately by sampling all police reported crime and reviewing the contents of the report. The data that are generated are then estimated to the level of the population (Brå 2014). Reports on police recorded hate crime in Sweden provide valuable insights on hate crime targeting sexual orientation, ethnicity or nationality, gender identity, and religious identity – including Islamophobia (Brå 2015, 2015a; Peutere 2009).[10]

There are some caveats. Sweden, like the UK, does not have a single national police force as present in Ireland for example. Thus, while the use of the hate crime marker in Sweden may be mandatory, there is 'no unified national instruction' on how this should be implemented (Peutere 2009, p. 17). This lack of instruction could arguably be the reason why the procedure has been used inadequately or indeed inappropriately as noted, with some offences recorded as being motivated by hate when this was not the case; consequently, police may actually over record levels of hate crime (Brå 2011, 2014; Peutere 2009). Clearly, then, there is a need to explicitly define what constitutes a racist hate crime if it is to be coded or flagged correctly by the relevant police officer (Peutere 2009, p. 105). The inconsistencies evidenced above underscore the importance of all police officers being cognisant of the potential for any crime/incident being hate motivated and the reasons why data on such events are important for policing (Klingspor 2008; Sahramäki et al. 2014).

In the Netherlands, police are 'required to register and investigate all complaints of discrimination' (Human Rights First 2013). The Dutch definition of discrimination is broad and includes 'criminal offences aggravated by discriminatory behaviour' (van Donselaar and Rodrigues 2008, p. 163). Dutch police have been recording 'criminal discrimination' since 2008 across 25 different forces (European Union Agency for Fundamental Rights 2012, pp. 34 and 41). According to Dinsbach et al. (2009, p. 25) the criminal discrimination flag was introduced in response to a poor history of recording discriminatory offences. There are eight parent 'flag' categories of bias motivation each with their own sub-categories. For example, the label 'religion/belief' includes subheadings of Muslim, Christian, no faith etc. Of the 27 EU states listed in the EUFRA report, the Dutch provide the most comprehensive array of bases for recording hate crime – including Islamophobia (European Union Agency for Fundamental Rights 2012, p. 35). Moreover, the Dutch model also accounts for the intersectionality of identities in experiences of hate crime. Any one recorded criminal incident can be recorded across a range of bias motivations thus accounting for the intersection of multiple characteristics e.g. religion and gender (European Union Agency for Fundamental Rights 2012; van Donselaar and Rodrigues 2008).

The use of a racist hate crime flag has clear benefits. Utilised properly, the use of a hate crime/incident flag can provide a very efficient means to compile statistical data that can identify who the targets of racist hate crime and non-crime events are – including anti-Muslim racism – as demonstrated by the Dutch and Swedish models above (Niemi 2011; Peutere 2009). However, the mere existence of a racism flag or code does not mean it will be used or used correctly (Peutere 2009). Police may forget to use the code or fail to realise the statistical importance of flagging events as hate motivated (Peutere 2009). The Swedish model of mandatory recording, while problematic, has the ability to remind police to be conscious of the presence of racism/hate when attending a crime. Nonetheless, the Swedish model also demonstrates that police need to understand what constitutes a racist/hate crime and the importance of recording these events. Clearly then, there is a need for the explicit definition of what constitutes a racist crime/non-crime incident. Police must understand why and when they should mark a crime/non-crime incident as hate motivated. Clarke's (2013) research clearly demonstrates how this understanding is lacking in the Irish context. It is imperative that the implementation of diverse categories of hate crime is followed up with appropriate training of police staff. This should be easier to implement in the Irish context than in the UK or Sweden, given the unified character of An Garda Síochána as a force. Admittedly, the goal of perfect recording practices or racist hate crime/non-crime incidents by police through the use of flags or codes may be somewhat of a chimera. As this is the case, I will now discuss an important complementary means to capture data on racism.

Identifying racism through narrative reports

The utility of police recorded data on crime lies in their ability to provide insights into trends of criminality, how crime manifests itself, and where and what communities are exposed to this activity (Home Office 2011). In the Swedish context, Brå (2011) clearly indicate that the purpose of the hate crime statistics they produce is to reveal insights into hate crime in Sweden in order to inform policy. Moreover, hate crime reports in Sweden provide more than just statistical data on levels of criminality but also deeper contextual information (Brå 2011, 2014). To access this detail requires more than the use of markers or 'flags'. The rich insights provided on hate crime in both Sweden and Finland also derive from the application of specific search terms to the narrative detail of specified reported crimes (Brå 2012a, 2014; Niemi 2011; Peutere 2009).[11]

During an analysis of hate crime in Sweden in 2010, 400,000 narrative reports were searched with almost 380 search terms yielding over 30,000 instances of crime to be coded manually by researchers (Brå 2011). When applying search terms to narrative reports in order to identify whether or not specific groups are being particularly targeted it is important to use contemporary, relevant search terms (Peutere 2009). Peutere's (2009) research on hate crime in Finland recommended the inclusion of specific searches for religiously aggravated offences to allow for a 'more comprehensive collection of incidents motivated by, for instance, Islamophobia or anti-Semitism'. The list of search terms used by the Brå is updated annually in order to remain contextually relevant. For example, the search terms used in identifying Islamophobic hate crimes include contemporary essentialised referents such as 'Taliban' 'terrorist' and/or '9/11' (Brå 2011, 2012; Peutere 2009).

There are clear advantages in the application of search terms to police recorded narratives. Firstly, in pure statistical terms, they provide a means to capture those instances of racism/hate that are not flagged/flagged incorrectly by police, events that would otherwise be lost to analysis. Police recorded data on hate crime derived from the use of flags alone are unreliable (Brå 2014; Peutere 2009). Moreover, they also provide access to comprehensive detail of the particular event in question; for example, noting that offensive literature had been used in an incident or that Muslim women had been called 'Islamic Whores' (Peutere 2009, p. 72). As such, data on racist hate crime in Finland and Sweden can offer insights on offences/incidents including their location and type, the time of day, details of the offender including nationality, while details of the victim including nationality, age and gender are also accessible (Brå 2011; Kingspor 2008; Niemi 2011). Insights can also be gained into the faith identity of those being targeted, disaggregated to include Muslims, Christians, Jews, Jehovah's Witnesses etc., and the form of offence they experienced – this even though in Finland there is no hate crime code (Niemi 2011).

The methods of racist/hate crime analysis derived through the use of search terms described above could easily be applied by An Garda Síochána. Indeed, two retired Garda sources that participated in this study stated specifically that data could be generated from the PULSE system through the use of 'search terms' applied to the narrative sections of a crime and non/crime report. As I have demonstrated, the insights that can be gained through the use of search terms go beyond simple rates of racist/hate crime, revealing the identities of vulnerable social groups and broader contextual data. In both Sweden and Finland, search terms are used to complement and confirm levels and forms of racist/hate crime in society (Brå 2014; Niemi 2011). Taken together, the use of data derived from the use of flags/markers and search terms can provide a deep understanding of racist hate crime and non-crime incidents. If deployed by An Garda Síochána, a deeper understanding of racism in Ireland, detailing how it manifests itself and the diverse groups that are targeted – including anti-Muslim racism – could emerge. The technical capability is there but the will of the neoliberal Irish State to recognise 'race' is lacking.

Alternative and complementary data on racism

Police recorded data are not the only sources of information on levels and forms of hate crime.[12] Crime and victimisation and discrimination surveys are an important alternative means to capture data on racist hate crime. According to Brå (2012, p. 37) crime and victimisation surveys (C&V) or 'surveys of self-reported exposure' are a useful source of complementary data on hate crime to that gathered by police. In addition to inadequate police practices vis-à-vis recording hate crime, those who have been targeted may be reluctant to report their experiences to the police for multifarious reasons which I will discuss further below (Kääriäinen and Niemi 2014). The ability to gain an insight into otherwise unreported experiences of crime is of immense value and is arguably the main benefit of conducting C&V surveys (Central Statistics Office 2010; Smith et al. 2012). C&V surveys thereby may offer a 'better reflection of the true extent of household and personal crime' than statistics presented by the police in isolation (Home Office 2011, p. 4; see also Brå 2010).[13]

The Central Statistics Office in Ireland has engaged in Crime and Victimisation surveys on four occasions: 1998, 2003, 2006, and, most recently, in 2010 as a subset of the Quarterly National Household Survey (QNHS) (Central Statistics Office 2007; Central Statistics Office 2010). Not one of the aforementioned surveys has included identity characteristics such as 'race', religion or sexuality as a potential factor in experiences of criminality. This is despite arguments having been made on the need for the inclusion of aggravating factors such as racism in C&V surveys in the National Action Plan Against Racism inter alia (Department for Justice Equality and Law Reform 2005; National Focal Point 2004). As such, there is no other quantitative State source on racist crime outside of the limited data provided through Garda recorded crime figures. Ten years and two C&V surveys since the publication of the National Action Plan Against Racism and 'race', religion and/or other aspects of identity are still not accounted for as bases for criminal victimisation.[14] In terms of best practice and international experience, Ireland fairs poorly by comparison, both in terms of regularity and level of detail provided.[15,16]

Summary reports of hate crime in Sweden, in addition to providing detail on police reported crime include findings from the Swedish Crime Survey (SCS). The findings from the SCS provide insights on self-reported instances of xenophobic and homophobic hate crimes. However, specific experiences of anti-Muslim 'hate' or Islamophobia are not reported and therefore the SCS contribution is somewhat restricted in its own right (Brå 2011a, 2012b, 2013, 2014, 2014a). Similarly, in the UK, C&V surveys conducted in Scotland and Northern Ireland do not elaborate upon the diverse bases upon which one may be a target for hate crime (Campbell and Cadogan 2013; The Scottish Government 2014a). However, the model deployed in England and Wales provides what are arguably the best C&V derived insights of the four referent states discussed in this chapter. Dedicated C&V survey findings on experiences of hate crime are published biannually on the English and Welsh context (Home Office, Office for National Statistics, and Ministry for Justice 2013; Smith et al. 2012).[17] These include data on personal experiences of hate crime on the bases of the following characteristics: 'disability, gender-identity, race; religion/faith; and sexual orientation' (Smith et al. 2012 p. 14). Findings on experiences of hate crime aggravated by religion are disaggregated across the following faiths: Christian, Buddhist, Hindu, Muslim, Other and No religion (Home Office, Office for National Statistics, and Ministry for Justice 2013 (see appendices); Smith et al. 2012). Data on experiences of hate crime such as these are a chimera in the Irish, and indeed other national, contexts. Consequently, the Irish State remains blind to the experiences of racist and other forms of hate crime. However, while 'race' and or religion have been denied a place in surveys of criminal victimisation in Ireland, some efforts have been made in the area of discrimination.

Capturing discrimination: the equality module

The QNHS Equality Module was the first survey of the general population in Ireland to enquire into their experiences of discrimination. Participants were asked if they had experienced discrimination in Ireland during the previous two years. If they answered yes, participants were then asked to define what they perceived to be the basis for this discrimination, citing from the nine grounds covered in Irish equality legislation.[18] The Equality Module has provided some valuable insights into rates of discrimination, context, and how the experience affected people (McGinnity et al. 2012; Russell et al. 2008). This survey was repeated in the fourth quarter of 2010, six years later, repeating the questions that were included in the initial 2004 survey with some additions (Central Statistics Office 2011). Importantly for the purposes of this study, questions were asked as to whether one's 'race' or religion was implicated in their experiences of discrimination (McGinnity et al. 2012; Russell et al. 2008). This has allowed some limited statistical insights into discrimination against Muslim communities to come to the fore. For example, the first module evidenced that Muslim participants experienced discrimination using public transport and the second module demonstrated shops and restaurants as sites of discriminatory behaviour towards Muslims (McGinnity et al. 2012; Russell et al. 2008).

Despite these interesting, albeit superficial insights, the Equality Module is not without its problems. To begin with it is irregular. It has only ever been undertaken twice; and the fact that there are six years between the two tranches raises serious questions in terms of data comparability. Initial statistical releases from the module by the CSO are also limited in the level of analysis they provide. Thus if one is looking to gain a specific insight into anti-Muslim discrimination one has to wait for a third party to take on a project of detailed analysis such as that conducted by Russell et al. (2008) and McGinnity et al. (2012). More importantly, serious questions also remain in relation to the sampling of Muslim and other minority communities (McGinnity et al. 2012). The QNHS model is problematic for surveying experiences of discrimination as it undercounts immigrant communities in Ireland by between 15 to 30 per cent (Barrett and Kelly 2008; Russell 2010; Russell et al. 2008).[19,20]

These factors are particularly problematic when one focuses on Muslim communities in Ireland, given their large immigrant representation.[21] Although the ability to gain at least some level of disaggregated data on anti-Muslim discrimination is welcome, questions must remain as to whether or not the QNHS, and therefore the Equality Module, is representative of Muslim communities in Ireland in light of the acknowledged shortfall in the inclusion of migrant communities.

Thus far I have demonstrated how the Irish State is blind to the experiences of racist and broader forms of hate crime, despite extant examples of alternative models of police recorded hate crime as well as victimisation surveys such as those reviewed in this chapter. Instead of striving to reach these best practice standards, the various instruments deployed by the Irish State continue in their failure to effectively record racist activity in Ireland. As I have demonstrated, the methods employed by the CSO to survey experiences of crime do not acknowledge 'race' or religious identities inter alia as potential factors in participant's experiences of criminality. In the case of discrimination, while religious identity is acknowledged, the aforementioned Equality Module is irregular, questionable in terms of how representative it is, and there is a prolonged delay in the release of detailed analyses. The shortfalls in the different survey mechanisms employed by the CSO discussed here vis-à-vis racism raise serious questions in terms of their utility in policy formation. Taken together with the inadequate recording of racism by An Garda Síochána, it is clear that we are blind to racism in all its guises in Ireland. More importantly, the salience of 'race' in the lives of those who experience racism is denied.

Encouraging reporting

This practice of race denial has real implications beyond the immediate realm of policy in terms of building trust between the state and minority communities. Confidence in the state is vital if people are going to report their experiences of racism, yet findings from different studies demonstrate that trust is lacking. According to Garda Public Attitude Surveys conducted in 2007 and 2008 only 18 per cent of those who experienced a racist incident reported it to Gardaí (Browne 2008, p. 32). These findings were corroborated by further research in 2009 which demonstrated that only one in six Sub-Saharan Africans ever reported experiences of discrimination (European Union Minorities and Discrimination Survey 2009, pp. 51 and 82).

People may choose not to report a racist hate crime/non-crime incident for multifarious reasons including: poor levels of trust in the police; an impression that nothing will be done to address their case; or indeed a perception that racism is to be expected and therefore should be accepted as a normalised part of everyday life (European Union Minorities and Discrimination Survey 2009; Kääriäinen and Niemi 2014; Lynch 2011). This emphasises the importance of effective, consistent policies and procedures that should be followed by members of the Gardaí in Ireland and police internationally when interfacing with members of minority communities and their concerns, especially if trust is to be built and racism challenged, a point that was underscored in the 2004 Garda Human Rights Audit (Walsh 2009). While remaining critical of the anti-racism approaches in Ireland, or lack thereof, it is worth noting at this point that *some* members and departments within the Garda service have made efforts to address racism and engage with minority communities.

According to Fanning *et al.* (2011) the Gardaí have been commended for the measures they have taken in engaging with minority communities. One of the earliest initiatives introduced by the Gardaí relating to minority communities and their experiences was the creation of the Garda Racial Intercultural and Diversity Office (GRIDO). The GRIDO together with the relevant divisional superintendent are tasked to follow up on reports of racially aggravated crime. They are also tasked with contacting and maintaining relationships with members of minority groups (Fanning *et al.* 2011). The GRIDO has been involved in positive initiatives such as the on-going implementation of annual 'Diversity Consultation' and associated with local reach out clinics held regularly in, for example, the Clonskeagh mosque for Jumma prayers (Fanning *et al.* 2011; Lynch 2011).

Related initiatives have included the creation of 'Ethnic Liaison Officers' (ELOs), also referred to as 'Diversity Officers', as well as the implementation of diversity training programmes (Department of Justice Equality and Law Reform 2005, p. 78). Among the various tasks undertaken by ELOs is that of monitoring racist incidents and the provision of information and support to minority communities (An Garda Síochána 2012b). Additional examples of good practice include those also at the local community policing level, whereby individual members of the Gardaí actively engage in designing and implementing mechanisms for addressing the needs of minority groups. Particular initiatives of note include those developed with the NGO NASC in Cork City in the creation of a third party racist reporting mechanism; and also a project designed in conjunction with the Kilkenny Integration Forum aiming to make information available about the role and functions of An Garda Síochána, the support services they provide and how these can be accessed (Fanning *et al.* 2011; Nasc 2011).

The Gardaí have also worked with national groups such as the Immigrant Council of Ireland to address the concerns of those who have experienced racism and their interaction with the service (Charlton, cited in Fanning *et al.* 2011, p. 4). It is worth noting the repeated presence of NGOs in these initiatives. Nonetheless, the effect of good practices such as those engaged in by the GRIDO and local community Gardaí is that they can create an environment of trust wherein people can report experiences of racism. This in turn can serve to increase levels of reporting hate crime (Perry 2009, p. 5).

However, despite these examples of good practice, the experiences of reporting racism detailed by Fanning *et al.* (2011) vividly demonstrate inconsistency and variable levels of support received by people in their interactions with the Gardaí. Such inconsistency results in the professional behaviour of some officers being undermined by the inadequate policing practices of others. Indeed, Lynch (2011) points out that when some members of minority communities have reported an incident to the Gardaí, they themselves have become the subject of investigation and subjected to questions on their immigration status, for example. Experiences such as this undermine police–community relations and lead to a reluctance on the part of vulnerable minority groups to make reports of hate crime to the Gardaí.

Research conducted by Clarke (2013) also demonstrates that examples of good practice by members of An Garda Síochána vis-à-vis racism as outlined above are contingent on the initiative of individuals as opposed to policing policy. In other words, evidence would seem to indicate that anti-racism is not cultural among individual Garda members or the broader organisation. Instead of a managerial focus on racism, there exists an informal approach to anti-racism in practice. Indeed, participants in Clarke's (2013, p. 15) research 'believe there is a lack of will for [Garda] management to prioritise the issue around racial reporting'. In this light, the implementation of the GRIDO group, the creation of the role of ELOs and the hosting of Diversity Consultations become more akin to 'paper policies' that are lacking in any real substance (Fanning *et al.* 2011, p. 21). Indeed, the very creation of the GRIDO and the implementation of Diversity Consultations function to propagate an image of Ireland as a caring state when it comes to addressing racism. Viewed through the lens of neoliberal 'truth', they represent a metaphorical box ticked, thus allowing representatives of the Irish State, such as Ambassador Corr above, to maintain a façade of care while remaining 'blind' to racism. The Irish State has to be seen to toe the neoliberal line in the international context of competitive states.

The Irish State is determined to maintain a facade of 'care' when it comes to challenging racism. If one undertakes a simple web search of the Office for the Promotion of Migrant Integration (OPMI), one can easily find a link to Chapter 6 of the EUFRA (European Union Agency for Fundamental Rights 2013) annual report for 2012. Somewhat confusingly, this report has Ireland listed as having 'good data available – different bias motivations are recorded and data are, in general published' as opposed to the limited data mentioned above, contradicting the report published in November of 2012. How these two EUFRA reports can have differing pronouncements of the efficacy of recording racism and hate crime is arguably an artefact of differing terms of reference in each report and will not be dwelt upon here. What is notable is the manner in which the OPMI are quick to herald the findings from the more positive report, while ignoring the findings from the negative publication. This practice of saving face is arguably being undertaken in the interests of Ireland as a neoliberal state, doing just enough to be seen as meeting international standards. Nonetheless, what is clear on the basis of the evaluation undertaken here is that, in Ireland, data across various hate motivations are neither available nor published regularly. While limited data on racism qua racism are readily available via the Office for the Promotion of Migrant Integration, statistics on anti-Semitism have been removed from the OPMI website (Office for the Promotion of Migrant Integration 2015) for some time. Moreover, there is no facility to systematically record hate crime directed towards members of the Traveller Community, Roma community or, anti-Muslim racism as the contribution from Sgt McInerney demonstrates above.

The selective use of data by the OPMI further demonstrates the manner in which the neoliberal Irish State is more concerned with keeping up appearances than actually investing in mechanisms that can result with meaningful data being collected on racism and broader instances of hate crime in Ireland, a point I will return to in later chapters. Ireland, like other nation states, is today a more diverse and vibrant society than before, with multifarious identities making up the fabric of the nation and the state needs to respond to protect those who are vulnerable from all communities. Yet as I have argued, neoliberal Ireland denies the salience of diverse identities and their policing needs.

Discussion and conclusion

According to Walsh (2009, p. 264) 'victims of crime must not be treated as a single amorphous group whose needs are identical'. One of the outcomes of the MacPherson inquiry into the murder of Stephen Lawrence was the recognition that certain minority groups may require different forms of policing. A 'one policing model fits all' approach does not work. Minority groups may have different requirements from the provision of language services to the protection from hate crime activity that targets their group identity (Ionann Management Consultants 2004). By effectively and publicly addressing hate crime, strong positive relationships can be garnered among members of communities vulnerable to this phenomenon, thereby improving community relations in a broader sense in the process (HM Government 2012). Trust is vital to encouraging the reporting of racist crimes (Lynch 2011). This can be done through community organisations but it can also be increased through the Gardaí acknowledging and recording incidents of racism that may not constitute an actual criminal offence. Simply recording the experience and possibly directing the person towards the appropriate channels may go some way to building trust while also providing invaluable insights on levels and experiences of racism. Recommendations from the International Association of Chiefs of Police state that all racist incidents should be recorded by the police, not only those that can be classed as a criminal offence, thus providing the police with a better, deeper understanding of this phenomena, enabling them to address potentially volatile situations (Lynch 2011).

'Data collection plays a key role in addressing racism. If we cannot measure the problem, we cannot manage it' (Crickley, cited in Lynch 2011, p. 3), or as I prefer – *challenge it*. This is the intention of the Irish State, which true to racial neoliberalism outsources the management of racism to the would-be police of the nation, those who experience it and/or NGOs who can service it. The above evaluation demonstrates that Ireland scores poorly when it comes to recording racism and broader forms of hate crime and remains blind in relation to specifically anti-Muslim racism. The result of this failure to record anti-Muslim racism on a systematic basis limits the policy utility of data on racist crime in Ireland. In addition to An Garda Síochána, the CSO also fails to recognise anti-Muslim racism or indeed racism in a broad sense as being a factor in people's experiences of crime in its irregular C&V surveys. Modules on discrimination conducted by the CSO are also flawed due in part to their irregular nature, low level of initial disaggregation and the question marks that must remain in regards to sampling religious and other minority groups with a large migrant representation.

The lack of disaggregated data on racism limits the ability of those forming policy to do so in a manner that is effective for the state and also supportive of those faced with living in the shadow of this phenomenon. Indeed, by not recognising the diversity of targets that may be visited by hate motivated crime the state, albeit with some individual exceptions, de facto allows for the normalisation of such behaviours. In turn, this further dilutes the trust between the state and minority communities, serving the purpose of neoliberal governmentality as will be argued later. Contrary to neoliberal policy, effective government and organisational policies and the recognition of hate crime targeting communities such as Muslims and others can serve to inform policy. Reporting to the police, and their effectively recording and addressing hate incidents, can strengthen the relationship between all parties concerned, thus challenging the normalisation of racism in Irish society. The next chapter will present the reality of living with anti-Muslim racism in neoliberal Ireland.

Notes

1 An Garda Síochána is the Gaelic language term for the Irish Police service; in pluralised form it is often referred to as the Gardaí. An Garda Síochána are also referred to as the 'Gards' in common parlance, but not to denote guards. I use this common format of 'Gards' when referred to by participants.
2 See Organisation for Security and Cooperation in Europe (2015) Hate Crime Report for 2013, available online at http://hatecrime.osce.org/infocus/2013-hate-crime-reporting-now-available
3 The enactment of the Prohibition of Incitement to Hatred Act (1989) was intended to prohibit the preparation and possession, broadcast/publication or distribution of materials that may incite hatred towards groups identified on the basis of their: 'race', nationality, religion, ethnicity, membership of the Traveller Community or sexual orientation. The efficacy of the Act (1989) has been brought into question given the very limited number of prosecutions that have emanated from this legislation. Questions have also arisen over the content of the Act (1989) and whether or not it is 'workable' (Schweppe and Walsh 2008, p. 56). See Schweppe and Walsh 2008 and the NGO Alliance Against Racism (2011) for further discussion on the Act (1989). Presently, the majority of crimes with a racist motive are dealt with under standard offence types such as public order offences including: offences against the person; criminal damage; and public order offences (Fanning *et al.* 2011, p. 10; Schweppe and Walsh 2008, p. 76).
4 Personal email communication.
5 A limited disaggregation of racist incidents by type of offence is publicly available through the website of the Office for the Promotion of Migrant Integration (2015) but this does not include a disaggregation of victim type.
6 Clarke (2013) somewhat problematically uses the term 'racist incident' to denote both criminal and non-criminal events. Her intention is discernible from the text but to clarify I do not conflate these terms. Here a racist crime is referred to as such; a racist incident refers to non-crime incidents.
7 In addition to denying anti-Muslim racism, the list of 'flags' provided by Sgt McInerney also fails to recognise the experiences of racist crime by members of the Traveller Community, racism towards Roma people, and broader forms of hate crime that would capture data on: for example, anti-LGBT, Transphobic and Disablist offences/incidents.
8 Anti-Semitism is treated differently in the UK to other potential bases for religiously aggravated hostility – all police forces in the UK have formally agreed to collect and publish data on anti-Semitic offences/incidents (Secretary of State for the Communities and Local Government UK 2010, pp. 9–11).
9 The Swedish National Council for Crime Prevention.
10 Bases for Hate Crime Statistics: Xenophobia/racism; Afrophobia; Anti-Roma; Islamophobia; Anti-Semitism; Chirstianophobia; Otherwise anti-religious; Homophobia;

72 *Measuring anti-Muslim racism*

Transphobia-Afrophobic hate crime and anti-Roma hate crime are sub categories (Brå 2012b, p. 19; 2013).

11 Speaking of the Irish context, one retired Garda participant in this study stated that the application of search terms such as this is not that dissimilar to, for example, a word search on PDF or Word files.
12 As the focus of this book lies in understanding the importance of reporting and recording of anti-Muslim etc. hate crimes/incidents and the experience of the individual engaging with the state, I am deliberately not elaborating upon available data on hate crime produced by prosecution services or the courts. For examples of such from the UK context please see Public Prosecution Service Northern Ireland (2014); Home Office, Office for National Statistics, and Ministry for Justice (2013) and Crown Prosecution Service (2014); Crown Office Procurator Fiscal Services (2014).
13 C&V surveys are not a panacea to the problems of generating accurate data on crime. Police records may be preferable in certain respects as they can provide more detailed information on crime when compared to the broader perspectives provided in C&V surveys. Nonetheless, C&V surveys engage directly with participants about their experiences of crime, shedding light on the characteristics of victims, public perceptions or criminality and importantly levels of non-reporting (Central Statistics Office 2010, p. 22).
14 Problematically, participants are asked to select from a list of nationalities instead of 'race'/ethnicity etc. (Central Statistics Office 2010, p. 21).
15 Finland is a possible exception.

> The current National Crime Victim Survey is, as the name implies, a dedicated criminal victimisation survey. The survey ... [is] carried out annually (for now) and the data is collected by other means, i.e. a mix of postal and web survey. So far it has been carried out three times between 2012 and 2014.... The survey has no items tapping religion and no real way to identify victimisation on the basis of religious identity. We have items that can be used to construct immigrant status and ethnic identity, but no religous identity, unfortunately. Also, we cannot identify whether the perceived motive of the offender was racist. (I would like to point out that the new-form Victim Survey is designed to be very light and compact, and so we are forced to leave out many interesting research topics.)
> (Direct communication from a representative of the Institute of Criminology and Legal Policy, University of Helsinki, January 2015)

16 Victim surveys in the Netherlands are conducted in two ways. The *Veiligheidsmonitor* or 'Safety Monitor' survey (Centraal Bureau voor de Statistiek 2012) does not refer to bases of identity such as race or religion for hate crime, although there is an option for special modules to be added by local authorities. The Netherlands does participate in the International Crime and Victimisation Survey but this is outside the scope of this study (van der Veen 2011, p. 44).
17 This was part of what was formerly referred to as the British Crime Survey and is now known as the Crime Survey for England and Wales, see www.gov.uk/government/publications/british-crime-survey-methodology
18 Gender; marital status; family status; age; disability; 'race' (race, skin colour, nationality or ethnic origin); sexual orientation; religious belief; and/or membership of the Traveller Community (Central Statistics Office 2011, pp. 2 and 16; Russell *et al.* 2008, pp. ix and 8–9; McGinnity *et al.* 2012).
19 Reasons for the under-representation of migrants may include the exclusion of those with a poor proficiency in English, the only language the QNHS is delivered in; a hesitancy some may have in completing official surveys, amplified in the case of undocumented migrants; by focusing only on private households the QNHS platform excludes those who live in direct provision centres (O'Connell and McGinnity 2008; Russell 2010).

20 Barrett and Kelly (2008, pp. 195–196 and 204) have argued that the QNHS does not provide a 'qualitatively different picture of immigrants, relative to the Census' and by implication is representative. Russell *et al.* (2008, p. ix) argue the QNHS Equality module survey is 'nationally representative' (Russell 2008, p. 1).
21 According to the 2011 Census, approximately 60 per cent of Muslim people in Ireland have a nationality other than Irish (Central Statistics Office 2012).

5 Conducting hearts and minds
Anti-Muslim racism in a neoliberal state

Introduction

'People spit in my face for being Muslim' – a comment made to this research by a white Irish Muslim man. 'Muhammed is dead, go back to your country' – a slur that was shouted at a Malaysian Muslim woman. These comments in isolation are just two instances of anti-Muslim racism narrated by people who participated in research I conducted with Muslim communities in Ireland. As will be demonstrated throughout this chapter, anti-Muslim racism is a reality for Muslim men, women and children in Ireland. Informed by the hegemonic neoliberal regime of 'truth', symbols of the Islamic faith have come to signify the 'otherised' position of Muslim identity in the Irish context.[1] In addition to these global constructions of the 'other' lies the perception that Muslimness is the antithesis of belonging in Ireland, as in other western states (Hopkins 2006; Triandafyllidou and Gropas 2009; van Nieuwkerk 2004), and therefore must be excluded, alerting those would-be 'police' of the nation to action.

This chapter provides heretofore unknown insights into the levels and experiences of anti-Muslim racism in Ireland. The experiences revealed in this chapter allow for understandings of anti-Muslim racism in Ireland to emerge that, while nuanced by local specificities, resonate with those from the broader international context. Moreover, they also provide vital insights that allow for a deeper theorisation on the factors that might inform perceptions and practices of reporting these experiences in Ireland and abroad. What is made clear below is the manner in which global and local influences direct the public gaze to perceive Muslims as 'other' in the Irish public common sense and the results of these racialised 'truths'.

Anti-Muslim racism in Ireland

In 2008, Strabac and Listhaug, drawing on data from the European Values Survey (EVS) demonstrated the widespread presence of anti-Muslim prejudice in 30 European States, including Ireland. Notably, the EVS sweeps that Strabac and Listhaug (2008) based their analyses upon predated events such as 9/11, subsequent terrorist attacks and the so-called 'war on terror'. Today, these key events form a central aspect of the narrative of lived anti-Muslim hate crime and discrimination. Yet we know little about it. As demonstrated earlier, there is a dearth of data on rates and experiences of anti-Muslim racism in Ireland and abroad. Therefore the findings related here break new ground in our understanding of this phenomenon, particularly in the Irish context. The first phase of this study comprised of a survey of 323[2] Muslim men and women and commenced by asking all those who took part if they had experienced some form of hostility in a specified period. Just over half of all participants who completed the questionnaire indicated that they did experience some form of hostility in that timeframe. Given that this study centres on anti-Muslim racism it was necessary to go a step further and ask a question to validate the centrality of participant's Muslimness in these experiences. The reality is stark. Over one-in-three (36 per cent) of survey participants felt they had been targeted on the basis of their being identified as Muslim.

The rates at anti-Muslim hostility manifested in the Irish context reflected the international experience with verbal abuse predominating, while physical assaults were less frequent (Feldman and Littler 2014). In Ireland participants reported experiencing physical assaults (22 per cent) ranging from being struck, having hijabs forcibly removed, to being pushed, spat at; some reported being threatened or harassed (20 per cent). A white Irish male Muslim recalled his experiences of commonly reported physical forms of abuse: 'I have been pushed and have had people spit in my face, for being Muslim'. Fewer participants (14 per cent) indicated that they had property damaged. Those who detailed how this manifested itself referred to tyres being slashed and having eggs thrown at their home. Unlike other jurisdictions, attacks on Muslim property such as mosques did not feature here (European Monitoring Centre on Racism and Xenophobia 2006). Arguably, this may be the result of the paucity of recognisably 'Islamic' structures in Ireland. As noted, the predominant form of hostility experienced was verbal assault (81 per cent). The verbal abuse meted out to the participants in the Irish context, as will be further elaborated below, frequently makes direct reference to the contemporary form of racialised Muslim identity, indicative of an internationalised prejudicial image of Muslims and Islam.

As with data on anti-Muslim hostility, there is also a dearth of official information on the discrimination experienced by Muslim men and women in Ireland on the basis of their religious identity.[3] As discussed in Chapter 4, the Equality Module, a subset of the Quarterly National Household Survey is the only official source of data on faith based discrimination in Ireland and offers only limited insights on anti-Muslim discrimination (McGinnity *et al.* 2012). Thus the findings presented here offer original insights into experiences of anti-Muslim discrimination in Ireland. As in the case of questions of hostility, participants were asked about their experiences of discrimination during the same period. One third of all participants indicated that they had experienced anti-Muslim discrimination. As with anti-Muslim hostility, the experiences of discrimination elaborated below are heavily gendered with Muslim women

(40 per cent) almost twice as likely as Muslim men (22 per cent) to experience anti-Muslim discrimination.

In the sections that follow I will demonstrate the manner in which neoliberal 'truths' inform experiences of anti-Muslim racism in Ireland. The themes that emerged from the participants' narratives make the effect of global neoliberal discourses clear.[4] There are striking similarities between the experiences of participants here in Ireland with those present in international evidence of anti-Muslim racism (Ameli *et al.* 2012; European Monitoring Centre for Racism and Xenophobia 2006; Open Society Institute 2011; Poynting and Noble 2004; Zempi and Charaborti 2014). In addition to demonstrating the effect of globalised 'truths', these studies also clearly evidence how anti-Muslim racism takes on locally contingent, historically informed characteristics. As will be made evident below, Ireland is no different.

Hegemonic Irishness

Nation states manufacture unity by constructing images of belonging and unbelonging (Essed 2002). Membership of the nation is recognised through 'cultural markers ... assumed or assigned (imagined) indicators of common ordinary belonging' (Goldberg 2002, p. 118), through which the 'racial-cultural identity of "true nationals" ... can be inferred' (Balibar and Wallerstein 1991, p. 60). These constructed images of national inclusion come to represent what it means to belong in 'common sense' definitions of national identity (Gramsci 1971, p. 419).

Notions of belonging in Ireland as in other European States (see for example Triandafyllidou and Gropas 2009 (Greece) and van Nieuwkerk 2004 (Netherlands)) are informed by various histories, politics and religion. To fully understand experiences of anti-Muslim racism in Ireland it is important to first unpack how Irishness has been constructed in the past and today. The Irish have a long history of racialised state practices. British colonialists in early modern Ireland racialised Irish Catholics of Gaelic descent as atavistic, savage and bestial. This characterisation served as a justification for exploitative practices of colonisation (Garner 2009; Rattansi 2007). However, these portrayals also served as a rallying point for counter constructions of Irishness. Over the course of the nineteenth century, a process of auto-racialisation developed forming around the construction of a Catholic Irish nationalist identity (Fanning 2002; Miles and Brown 2003). The narrow imagining of Irishness that emerged from these processes also drew from romanticised 'timeless depiction[s] of Ireland ... [evoking] an ancient and mystical past' (Connolly 2006, p. 23) – a past washed in whiteness. In the decades post-independence (1922), this construction of Irishness assumed a hegemonic position, becoming institutionalised in the Irish State. 'Catholic nationalism became the bearer of a sectarian and exclusionary conception of nation' (Fanning 2002, p. 35), providing an ideological premise for the exclusion and oppression of various social groups on the island. Those most affected included members of the Protestant faith, Ireland's Jewry and the Traveller Community (Fanning 2002).

The minority Protestant population was marked out as 'other' through racialised associations with Britishness which were used to legitimise hostility and social exclusion (Fanning 2012; Lentin 2002; Ní Shúinéar 2002). Ireland's Jewry were classed as a 'people who come to live amongst us, but who never become of us' (United Irishman 1904, cited in Lentin 2002, p. 160). Mac Gréil's (1997) seminal study on prejudice in Ireland noted the manner in which anti-Semitism in Ireland drew on international stereotypes of the Jewish 'other'; a fact that strikingly resonates with constructions of Muslimness today. The Traveller Community also present a clear example of marginalisation and exclusion in the Irish context. The Traveller Community has been constructed as a threatening 'other' associated, through rural mythology, with poor crop returns and a form of Catholic lore that implicated Travellers with the crucifixion of Christ with their fate to be forever nomadic and excluded from the dominant society (Fanning 2012). More contemporary characterisations of Travellers present them as embodying essentialised proclivities towards criminality – a 'suspect community' (Hickman *et al.* 2011; Pavee Point 2010).

A common denominator in the racialisation of these groups was their 'failure' to meet the criteria for belonging, defined as White, Heterosexual, Irish, Sedentary and Catholic (WHISC)[5] (Tracey 2000). This brief adumbration of race history in Ireland underscores that racialising processes are not solely contingent on phenotype (Garner 2009). Furthermore, the exclusion of Protestants and Jews from hegemonic Irishness also emphasises that the marginalisation of religious minorities is not exclusively derived from religious bigotry – membership of another faith can also symbolise outsider status in terms of ethno-national belonging. Dominant constructions of Irishness assume 'Catholic-ness' as atomic in the fabric of Irish-being. Those who do not fit the aforementioned WHISC identity are racialised as 'non-Irish'. In the post-independence era, to belong in Ireland meant to be part of the dominant WHISC identity – a racialised construct invoked in nation making. In the contemporary era the global neoliberal regime 'truth' has reconfigured what it means to belong in Ireland, a nation of individuals.

Neoliberal Irishness

Today, the Irish State is dominated by global neoliberal rationalities of how to govern. Ireland is not alone in this sense. As David Harvey argues, today

> [a]lmost all states, from those newly minted after the collapse of the Soviet Union to old-style social democracies and welfare states such as New Zealand and Sweden, have embraced ... some version of neoliberal theory and adjusted at least some policies and practices accordingly.
>
> (2005, p. 3)

In the Irish context, state policies and practices that centre on idealised notions of 'Ireland Inc.' and the valorisation of the individual entrepreneur permeate political and popular discourses (Bord Bia 2013; Department of Jobs, Enterprise and Innovation 2013; Murphy 2012; Phelan 2007). Neoliberalism as hegemonic ideology is inherent in the rationalities of the dominant political parties in Ireland (Allen 2009; Phelan 2007). Indeed, neoliberalism is so embedded that changing from a government led by one of the main parties to another simply results in the continued maintenance of the neoliberal consensus (Allen 2009; Phelan 2007). According to Allen (2009, p. 35), 'neoliberal ideology ... was [still is] largely diffused throughout the population by the political establishment'. In addition to the political, media discourses play a 'key role in the ... production and reproduction of an Irish neoliberal hegemony' (Phelan 2007, p. 30), inculcating neoliberal ideals throughout the popular consciousness. The education system is also a key site for the inculcation of neoliberal ideals. According to Keohane and Kuhling (2014, p. 127) educational practice from second level onwards promotes entrepreneurship and the 'cultivation of the individual', further embedding neoliberalism as the dominant 'truth' in Ireland. Instead of citizens depending on community and shared public services, the populace comes to be defined as a collective of 'customers who could choose' encouraged by a state that promotes care for the self (Allen 2009, pp. 65 and 152).

'Neoliberalism as an economic theology' (Keohane and Kuhling 2014, p. 90) has assumed a hegemonic position in political and popular consciousness. In neoliberal Ireland, individualism is worshipped while

> [T]he Republic is de-symbolised as a historical, national, public, collective identity and re-symbolised as 'Ireland Inc.', a re-privatised corporate enterprise of individual entrepreneurs; and the values of Community are re-coded in terms of economic actors exercising individual rational choices.
> (Keohane and Kuhling 2014, p. 161)

Hegemonic Irishness has become infused with neoliberal ideals that reframe the nation as an oxymoronic collective of individuals; national belonging operates as a holding device for the effective conduct of conduct. On this basis I argue that the concept of WHISC can be reformulated as neo-WHISC – neoliberal White Heterosexual Irish Sedentary and Catholic to encompass the primacy of neoliberal individualism in Ireland.*

Neoliberal processes of individuation require the breaking of ties with other collective identities in order to construct a 'rational' individualised society wherein self-reliance is prioritised over notions of social solidarity. Group solidarity is frowned upon as a form of 'moral hazard'. One should cast off one's identification with collective (contrarian to ideas of nation) identities representative of the 'non-citizen ... trapped within group based identities' (Razack 2008, p. 166; see also Giroux 2008). Communal identities are anathema to neoliberal thought as they provide a potential repository for group-care, grating with the sacralised place of the individual. The only exception is that of making nation which acts as a discursive conduit which through neoliberal governance can manage the collective of individuals – conducting their conduct through a 'truth' that admonishes contrary solidarities. Hence the power of national collective discourses is not removed but infused with neoliberal discourses that valorise the individual. Thus neoliberal individualism challenges 'other' group identification to make 'them' like 'us'. Neoliberalism fragments 'othered' identities only to re-massify them under a governable neoliberal collective.

Not part of the neoliberal tribe

The following sections detail the implications that this revised ideal type of Irishness holds for Muslim communities in Ireland. As will be demonstrated, at the level of the state, affiliation with a 'non-national' out-group is policed through discourses and practices that pathologise Muslim collective identities as different to the norm of Irishness. In addition, global discourses of Muslimness as 'other' add another layer to the locally derived constructions of contrarian identifications – that of impending 'threat'. Together, global and local 'truths' serve to legitimise the acts of individuals who use the neoliberal norm of nation as their reference point to constantly police Muslim identities through the social panoptic gaze. The goal of such panoptic micro management of populations is to bring those who are perceived as resistant into the neoliberal reality, into the fragmented collective of self-caring, 'properly' Irish individuals.

According to Zempi and Chakraborti (2014, p. 14), 'in the British context, national identity and examples of Muslim "difference" are cast as mutually exclusive'. Moreover, the wearing of signifiers of Muslimness is deemed evidence of a failure to integrate on behalf of the bearer (Zempi and Chakraborti 2014). This is problematic not only for migrant communities who simply must become like us to belong, but also to those who are already integrated, those born and bred Muslim and Irish in contemporary neoliberal Ireland. Irishness and Muslimness are deemed so 'abnormal', so incompatible, that they are often met with incredulity. Arabic-Irish, Dublin born Sara explains, 'If I go I'm Irish they're like "no, you're not."'... It happens so many times I kind of gave up on that ... [doing so] saves the saliva of conversation'. White Irish revert[6] to Islam, Aalia, recalling her dealings with state authorities, also relates how, 'as an Irish girl ... I think basically ... sometimes you lose your identity ... just because I put a scarf on my head.... I'm still Irish actually you're taking my identity away from me'.

These examples demonstrate the manner in which Muslimness remains outside of the 'norm' of Irishness. Treating Muslimness as pathologised vis-à-vis Irishness has a profound effect on the person as Aalia demonstrates, she feels her identity as an Irish Muslim woman is being taken from her; it is defining who is excluded from the nation while concomitantly reasserting the identity of those who 'really' belong. Importantly, the above brief quotes demonstrate the more benign manner in which membership of nation is policed. Frequently, as I will now demonstrate, being an Irish Muslim, especially for reverts to Islam, means being equated with treachery and being met with verbal and physical responses by would-be 'police' of the nation.

'... you're betraying Ireland'

If one reverts to Islam one is deemed to be a traitor, further underscoring the synonymous place of Christianity, particularly Catholicism, with constructions of Irishness and also the proscription of 'other' group identities. As one white Irish female Muslim survey participant stated: '[I've been] told by a lot of people on the street I'm Irish ... [I] don't need to follow Islam and betray Ireland'. This chimes with studies in France and the Netherlands which also document how Muslim reverts, particularly Muslim women, are perceived as 'traitors' to their nation or 'race' (Open Society Institute 2011, van Nieuwkerk 2004; Zempi and Chakraborti 2014). The following quotes are all provided by white Irish reverts to Islam. Here, they elaborate how they are perceived by some in Irish society as 'other' and the experiences of verbal and physical abuse that can ensue on the basis of a perceived betrayal.

> When they find out you're Irish they feel that like traitor ... but what because you've put a scarf on your head? Or because you changed your religion? ... then [you] are no more an Irish person, you have then lost your identity of who you are, you are ... classed as non-Irish.
>
> (Aalia)

Faced with this perception of being a traitor, participants were keen to emphasise their own Irish identity and how they do belong here in Ireland, something which they saw as being taken away from them. The comments of a white Irish male Muslim revert who participated in the survey are indicative of such sentiments: 'my family have been traced back to the 1700s in Ireland on both sides'.

During a group discussion, Jada, a white Irish female revert to Islam, shared her experience as she went about her duty as a nurse where a male patient 'said take that thing rag off your head you're too good looking for that ... you're betraying Ireland'.

It is worth quoting Zaheen's narrative at length to capture her experience of anti-Muslim hostility. Zaheen participated in an interview and is also a white Irish female revert to Islam and her experience reveals a number of interesting points. First, Zaheen's experience demonstrates the perceived juxtaposition of Muslimness and Irishness; second, the invocation of global racialised anti-Muslim tropes are clearly present; and third, Zaheen is singled out here because she is Muslim and deemed representative of her community, as is common to experiences of hate crime (Hall 2013; Iganski 2008).

> My son was for his six weeks check-up in the doctor, when I was coming out ... there was this man at the cross roads and I was waiting for the lights to change so that I could cross over and there was three other women behind me, and then this guy and he started muttering things like under his breath and they started getting louder and louder and he was like 'you F'n terrorist', 'you are all a pack of murderers ah you're a foreigner in this country'; and just really, really, violent things.... I was, I was scared but I

was afraid what he would do to the buggy like because my baby was there ... and he was so loud and these three women said nothing behind me, and I just told him look I'm not a terrorist and I'm not a foreigner I'm Irish and he just kept going and going just getting more and more [aggressive] then we crossed the road and he turned around to me and he spat in my face and I was just really shocked because, that was the fi[rst], I've had like comments before just about terrorism and bin Laden's wife and all these things like whatever, but that was the first kind of like physical abuse.

Zaheen's assailant continues the theme of Muslimness/Irishness incompatibility through his assertion of 'foreigner in this country'. Moreover, Zaheen's assailant not only targets her as a 'foreigner' but in the process he is also implicated in the recreation and reaffirmation of ideas of what it means to be Irish, demonstrating his role as an agent of governmentality in asserting the norms of Irishness. The invocation of symbolic terms such as 'terrorist' also reveals the connection of the global neoliberal discursive constructs to the micro social spheres of racialisation. Zaheen's experience represents an encapsulation of the discursive relationship between global neoliberal 'truths' and their effects on the national common sense of what it means to belong to the neo-WHISC collective.

Markers of Muslimness such as the hijab are deemed alien to Irishness as Aalia notes: 'They label the hijab as Pakistani'. Van Nieuwkerk's (2004, p. 235) research in the Netherlands demonstrated how for Muslim reverts 'being Dutch and veiling is ... totally incomprehensible and reprehensible. It is a choice to become like a foreigner'. Van Nieuwkerk's (2004, p. 236) participants were subjected to similar practices of interrogation by members of the public on the basis that by becoming Muslim they had 'renounced their [Dutch] origins'. These insights into the Dutch context bear a striking similarity to comments made by female reverts in this study who recalled how they were subjected to their own interrogations.

Zaheen recalls from her confrontation with an angry male stranger in the market: 'Why did you convert? If you're an Irish person why did you choose to change your religion?'

Jada tells of how she was asked: 'You were born Christian, why did you have to change?'

Given the prime position of Catholicness in definitions of Irish identity, those who choose to revert to Islam, in the eyes of their inquisitors, are choosing to 'become like foreigners'. The incredulity in the comments addressed towards Zaheen and Jada clearly indicates a suspicion on the part of those asking the questions as to their true motives. As Muslimness is not associated with definitions of Irishness, Zaheen and Jada, by reverting, become 'cultural others' (van Nieuwkerk 2004, p. 245). By reverting, suspicions arise which centre on questions as to why they would leave the civilised self for the atavistic 'other'. Thus, reverts can become 'suspects' on the basis of their motivations for reverting in addition to perceived racialised proclivities towards terrorism.

Suspect communities

Research undertaken in the British context has clearly demonstrated the manner in which Irish communities came to be perceived as a 'suspect community' in the eye of the UK state (Hillyard 1994, p. 52). Here, Irish identity, Irishness, came to be associated with terrorism (Hickman *et al.* 2011; Nickels *et al.* 2012). According to Nickels *et al.* (2012, p. 136), Irish and Muslim communities in the UK have both been subjected to 'negative stereotyping, intelligence profiling, stop and search, wrongful arrest, anti-Irish and anti-Muslim sentiment'. This history of Irishness as 'suspect' is an interesting lens through which to view the current practices of the Irish State towards Muslim communities in Ireland.

The co-location of Muslim and terrorist is a key trope in international neoliberal racialising 'truths' about Muslimness. These hegemonic discourses construct Muslimness as synonymous with an alleged threat to 'our' presumed homogenous Western values. Muslims, we are told, are continually plotting against 'us', devising new ways of removing 'our freedoms'. The purpose of such discourses is twofold. First, the construction of Muslims as putative threat serves to legitimise imperialistic, expansionist campaigns that aim to bring freedom (neoliberalism) to the oppressed. Almost ironically, such discourses of liberty are contemporaneously invoked to legitimise increases in the state technologies that police populations in the West with the attendant curtailment of civil liberties through for example increased state surveillance (Cincotta 2011; Goldberg 2002, 2009; Hanniman 2008; Kumar 2012; Runnymede Trust 1997). The racialised figure of the Muslim is constructed as such a threat that securitised incursions into our freedoms avoid public opprobrium. Informed by global neoliberal discourses, Muslim people have become a suspect community both in the eyes of the Irish State and in the gaze of the Irish general public. It is Dean's (2010a, p. 10) neoliberal regime of 'double truths' made manifest.

The following interview contributions of Ehan and Aatif detail the manner in which Muslim identity is 'suspect' in the eyes of the Irish State, chiming with the mind-set and practices of other 'Western' states wherein Muslims are the subject of practices of surveillance and suspicion. These Muslim men, Ehan who is a brown South-Asian and Aatif white and Irish, are united by their common Muslim identity. The following examples detail their experiences of religious profiling by the Irish State, singled out purely due to their Muslim identity. Aatif, an Irish revert to Islam, explicitly presents the core of the concept of 'suspect community' wherein a person is assumed to be a 'threat' or suspect on the basis of an association with a group identity, in this case Muslim.

> I remember the first day I came [back to Ireland] in 2003 ... within three weeks there was a Garda car unmarked ... outside the [prayer house] for weeks watching us, we knew this and I accepted it, at times maybe it was a bit annoying ... from my memory now this is back in 2003/4 after 2004 they stopped [surveillance], obviously they were satisfied we weren't harbouring any terrorists, I don't know??!! I mean what else can I think??... They must

have checked me out, they must have tried to find out a lot about me ....
I'm sure they just were satisfied that this person is not a danger to society ...
he is not a Muslim terrorist.

Sometime afterwards Aatif was involved in an Islamic event in Dublin. A colleague at the event arranged a meeting with a member of the Garda 'multicultural' office. Aatif recalls the meeting:

I remember when I went in [to the Gardaí] ... when I first sat down at the table and started introducing myself the response was don't worry Aatif we know everything about you. I said everything? He said everything all your movements so I went ok, ok.

Aatif perceived this as a 'warning shot across the bow' alerting him to the fact that they 'know everything about you ... we're watching you'. It is interesting that when probed on being singled out on the basis of being Muslim, Aatif responds with the term 'potential terrorist'. This suspectification of Muslims by the Irish State is further underscored by Ehan's recollection of one particular occasion when he and some Muslim friends were 'singled out ... [because] we just happened to look different, we all happened to have beards'. They just happened to be and look Muslim.

It was one of the anniversaries of the Iraq war or something like that ... there was a big crowd going from Dublin ... we went down with everybody else [from] the Anti-War movement.... Obviously am [when] it was time to pray so we prayed, you know its normal thing to do ... [at the end] we went to the car park to sit down and turn on the car ... we're just reversing to come out of the car park and head back ... with the rest of the crowd and then Gards came. Two Gards in plain clothes and then two others in uniforms were standing like in the near distance ... they came to us and I could see most of our colleagues ... going; it was just our car left in the car park near the Shannon airport. ... I was sitting in the back, so two guys [Gardaí] came ... inside the car ... we just took it easy ... they're [asking] what's your name? Do you have an ID on you? You know, whose car is this?? Where did you get it?? Where do you live?? When did you come to Ireland what do you think of Saudi Arabia?? What do you think of Hezbollah?? They asked me this question what do you think of Saudi Arabia, they asked the other guy what do you think of Hezbollah ... there was a mixed Q&A thing ... we asked them why did you single us out? And he said we just have to do our job.

Ehan and Aatif are both are presumed guilty through association, regardless of evidence or the committal of a criminal offence. These governmental practices further demonstrate the boundaries of who is allowed be part of the neoliberal Irish nation.

According to Aatif, the effect that such governmental practices can have on Muslim people is that they 'manage' their Muslimness: 'many of my colleagues when they go to airports they just hide their identity, they try to go as westernised as they can' (Aatif). A study published by the Migrants' Rights Centre Ireland (2011) on ethnic profiling noted how one Muslim woman changed her appearance so as not to be recognised as Muslim in an effort to reduce being profiled. Moves to manage one's identity such as this are unsurprising given the international security discourses which frame markers of Muslimness as synonymous with suspect. This is especially common when it comes to air-travel, wherein experiences of institutional racism are 'something that is expected' (Ehan).

'Random checks'

'Random checks' are a common experience for Muslim men and women entering or leaving the Irish State. This is a phenomenon that is by no means peculiar to Ireland (see Engage 2012; Poynting and Perry 2007). Various participants indicated that they had similar experiences in different countries. Constant in all of these security checks is the presence of Muslim identifiers. During a group discussion, Sara (Arabic-Irish), Nasirah (South-Asian Irish) and Samira (South-Asian Muslim female) almost in unison referred to their experiences of 'random checks'. Female Muslim survey participants also noted how they are 'much more scrutinised by airport staff than most other people' (Northern European hijabi Muslim female survey participant). A Malay Muslim female survey participant notes how she has 'to step aside for a full body check-up even though the alarm was not beeping when we pass through'. These Muslim women hail from diverse ethno-national backgrounds. As with Ehan and Aatif, what unites them is their Muslimness. The effect of international securitisation policies and discourses is to contribute to the collocation of words such as Muslim/Islam with terrorism in the popular lexicon (Hickman *et al.* 2011, p. 4). By focusing on Muslim communities as the domain of 'extremism' and an alleged threat from within, state policies that aim to counter terrorism become harmful and set Muslims apart as a suspect group, a 'fifth column' against whom hostility becomes socially acceptable (Fekete 2009; Hickman *et al.* 2011; Pantazis and Pemberton 2009).

Ehan, South-Asian and 'Muslim looking', clearly demonstrates how he was set apart from the 'us' in the following example:

> We were going to Turkey, me and my friend just on a holiday ... we were waiting in the ... lounge to board the plane.... I went to the toilet ... and as you come out ... you come out of a corridor and there was a Gard guy in a suit and tie, nice and smiling he stopped me there and then a guy came from behind ... it just happened ... he said can I have your passport please ... he showed me his badge ... he took my passport and then I realised that my friend also was taken aside, his passport taken ... he [police] was nice about it he was just ... where are you going? How long are you going? Where do

you work? Etc.... They brought the passport back in about ten minutes but we ... had to stand ... out there in front of the public between these two big guys.

The last few lines reveal the impact that being set apart from other passengers can have not only on self-esteem but also in perpetuating the cycle of racialised constructions of Muslimness. Ehan feels that religiously profiling in security practice 'gives people or the public ammunition to say oh look you know our police officers are doing some ... or that [he] could be a threat that's why they're stopping him ... it makes you look very awkward'. According to Poynting and Perry (2007, p. 164, their emphasis) it reinforces 'the public perception that Muslims *are* questionable' in terms of loyalty to nation and as a terrorist threat.

In a manner reminiscent to the preceding examples, Asif (South-Asian Muslim male) also recalls how he and his wife Zaheen experienced the suspecting gaze of the state. What is notable here is the additional incredulity that the border official seemingly demonstrates towards Zaheen's, now Muslim, identity. Asif explains their experience arriving at

Dun Laoghaire [port in their] Irish car ... everybody was going through ... when they see ... my car ... he [Garda] just took us and he was looking in my passport, and then she [Zaheen] was wearing hijab that time and she had her passport without hijab, and it was very young ... her picture ... and he was looking at her and her passport for so long ... [and started asking questions] where are you from, what's your name? ... he was looking at the picture he could see next name is there you know and still asking her her name, her date of birth her address and everything. Where did you go? For how long? What you was doing there? and all this question like this. [I] said oh forget it you know because I knew these sort of things happen so kind of used to it you know, you expect things like this sort of things happen.

This expectancy of being exposed to extra scrutiny by the apparatuses of state security is also demonstrated by Aatif's reflection on the securitised construction of the 'other' compared to the 'safe' Irish:

[I]f you have a Garda coming down the road and he sees an Irish guy ... he chats to them normally: how're you going? Then the same Gard goes down the road and he sees an Asian and a Muslim: where are you coming from? Where are you going? Do you have your GNIB[7] card? That's only one reason they see a Muslim ... whether they see it as a threat or they just don't like it or they don't want it.

These open practices of securitisation whether in the seaport, airport or on the High Street further inform the collocation of Muslimness with threat in the public perception. Furthermore, they also act to reassert the boundaries of the state, a form of symbolic exercise of putting under the microscope those who 'do not belong'', concomitantly underlining their identity as problematic to the national 'us' while reaffirming the globalised figure of Muslim as 'other', providing what Poynting and Perry (2007, p. 161) refer to as 'permission to hate'. I will present further evidence of institutionalised racist practices in the following chapter. In the next section I will elaborate the effect of global discourses of the Muslim suspect on the Irish public gaze.

Suspicious communities

The impact of anti-Muslim discourses and securitisation policies has not only been discriminatory state hostility but also the stigmatisation of Muslim communities as a threat in the public perception, bringing the global discourses and distal effects of the so called 'war on terror' into the proximal, lived experiences of Muslim men and women. In addition to the state, the role that media actors play in communicating hegemonic neoliberal discourses cannot be underestimated. Research conducted in Ireland has demonstrated the manner in which media outlets regurgitate neoliberal ideological messages into the public common sense, often targeting minority groups in the process (Power *et al.* 2012; Phelan 2007). These messages not only reinforce localised discourses but also serve as key outlets wherein global neoliberal 'truths' deployed to justify the 'war on terror' can permeate into the public 'common sense'. Again, it is somewhat ironic given the history of Irish communities in the UK and their subjection to practices of suspectification (Hickman *et al.* 2011), that Muslim people in Ireland now form a 'suspect community'.

In 2007, the National Consultative Committee on Racism and Interculturalism (NCCRI) noted an 'increase in alarmist, selective' media reporting in relation to Muslim communities in Ireland. Among the headlines referred to by the NCCRI were: 'Fascist fundamentalism is rife among young Irish Muslims' and 'The green jihadis'. The NCCRI report also noted that any efforts to counter these sensational reports were frequently 'buried in the letters page' (National Consultative Committee on Racism and Interculturalism 2007, pp. 4–5). In the aftermath of the killing of Osama bin Laden, the *Irish Sun* newspaper printed a front page headline of 'AL-QAEDA'S IRISH TERROR CELL' accompanied by the sub-headlines 'EVIL IN OUR MIDST' and 'Jihad fanatics hiding out amongst us'. Coverage of the story inside the same paper continued the theme of 'TERROR IN OUR MIDST' and featured a map of Ireland with the eyes of Osama bin Laden imposed over the island (McElgunn 2011). Contentious, intentionally sensationalist TV productions have also attempted to depict Muslims as an enemy within, purporting to uncover the 'true' threat that Muslims allegedly pose to Irish society (Raidio Teilifís Éireann 2013).

Portrayals such as these add to practices of profiling conducted by the Irish State to solidify the co-location of Muslimness with threat in the Irish 'common sense'. These ideas gain public traction so much so that they are invoked in experiences of anti-Muslim racism. Repeatedly throughout this study, survey participants recalled how they have been subjected to taunts of 'Muslims are terrorists', 'Suicide bombers!' and 'Taliban, go back to your cave'. The association inherent in these comments is that Muslim men and women may really be a terror threat, that 'Islam is not good because Islam teach people the hate and make them think to kill and be terrorists' (Arabic male survey participant). Zaheen relates the impact of such essentialising media discourses: 'the media's so got the role of showing ... [that] we're all from the same flock ... [but] we're not, ... [not] all Irish people weren't supporting terrorism [during the Troubles]' (Zaheen).

The impact of pathologising Muslim identity goes beyond slurs and taunts and can end up in extreme cases of hostility being meted out to Muslim men and women. Just days after bin Laden was killed, two female Muslim students were approached by a group of teenage girls on the upper deck of bus in Dublin. Mona recalls how they were asked, 'Are you upset 'cos bin Laden died? Was he your Da?' The public suspectification to which Muslim participants were subjected was particularly heightened in certain locales. Realised terrorist attacks in New York, Madrid, London and Scotland utilising various modes of transport, in addition to increased security measures in airports, for example, have positioned public transport as a central location where Muslimness is deemed suspect. Almost one third of participants (32 per cent) reported experiencing discrimination in the sphere of public transport, ranking it second among all of the choices offered in the survey. Experiences of discrimination at the hands of staff and fellow patrons on various modes of transport were reported. These experiences chimed with the instances of anti-Muslim hostility elaborated above. Consistent across these experiences is the internalised norm of Muslim 'otherness', continuing the theme of Muslims as a suspect group.

> I was on the bus in Jan '11 and a man kept telling the bus driver there was a suicide bomber on the bus.
>
> (Irish Muslim female, survey)

> In June 2011 – at the Luas station – an older man said to me and shouted, 'She has a bomb in her bag, she has a bomb in her bag', because I was wearing (burqa).
>
> (Arabic Muslim female, survey)

> What have you got under your dress ... is it a bomb?
>
> (Zaheen)

> So [I] was going to 'X' street from the 'Y' street.... I saw a few guys there already drunk ... and I just stopped.... I said I'll let them go ... because sometimes they just come into the car and they will shout ... so I was thinking ... I will let them go so I stopped but it didn't help me; actually when they see me stop they come more to me and they said oh, do you have bomb in your car? And all this you know you're bin Laden and all this.
>
> (Asif)

The evidence I have presented thus far demonstrates the palpable, visceral manner in which anti-Muslim racism manifests itself in Ireland. Writing in relation to the niqab, but also of relevance here, Zempi and Chakraborti (2014, p. 2) note how visible markers of Muslimness are associated with, among others, 'Islamist terrorism' as is clearly evidenced here. Moreover, neoliberal 'truths' repeated through stereotypical associations of Muslimness with terror and threat legitimise acts of state and public violence against Muslim men and women. Resonating with international experiences and true to processes of racialisation, these discourses build on 'fiction or fragmented "fact"' (Carr and Haynes 2013) to construct Muslimness as the enemy *de jour*.

Religious identifiability and 'selective (in)visibility'

Muslim communities in Ireland are incredibly diverse. In this study alone there are over 50 different countries of origin and multifarious ethnicities. This diversity means that a Muslim person may be exposed to exclusionary practices on the basis of any one of their identity characteristics including but not restricted to gender and skin colour. Bearing this diversity in mind it is necessary 'to account for multiple grounds of identity' and how they might intersect in the participants' experiences of anti-Muslim racism (Crenshaw 1991, p. 1245). Survey participants were asked to indicate which aspects of their identity they felt played a role in their experiences or racism. Skin colour (47 per cent), cultural identity (45 per cent) and real or perceived immigrant status (37 per cent) as markers of 'otherness' all featured strongly as intersectional factors in the participants' experiences, demonstrating the multiple bases of exclusion that Muslim men and women can encounter in Ireland. Chiming with the UK context (Allen *et al.* 2014), qualitative commentary also highlighted how 'traditional' racisms intersect with anti-Muslim sentiment – '[been] called: nigger, bin Laden, go back to where you came from' (Male, Arabic-Irish survey participant).

However, of all the personal identity characteristics to be cited by participants, the overriding trait indicated as being a factor in experiences of anti-Muslim racism was religious identity. In experiences of hostility the vast majority or participants (81 per cent) stated that their religious identity played a role in their being targeted for abuse. A similar number (87 per cent) felt their religious identity factored in their experience of discrimination. As is made clear throughout these research findings, anti-Muslim racism operates on discursively informed markers of Muslimness that set Muslim identity apart as 'other'. These markers convey an alleged threat, a suspicious identity to be subject to social sanction. Studies from across Europe underscore the importance of markers of Muslimness in experiences of anti-Muslim racism (Allen and Nielsen 2002; Allen *et al.* 2014; Open Society 2011; Zempi and Chakraborti 2014). The importance of Muslim identifiability here is made perfectly clear in comments shared by participants. One female Muslim focus group participant recalls how she was treated by a staff member in a restaurant – when she 'was in the line waiting to get a seat when it was my turn, the man ignored us and got the next customer' (Arabic-American Muslim female). Fahima, a female Irish revert to Islam details the experience that a female Muslim friend from Britain had when out with her young son.⁸ What is crucial here is the manner in which the sales staff internalise glocalised discourses of Muslimness as 'abnormal' and contrary to homogenous neo-WHISC constructions of Irishness. Fahima explains:

> [A] lady [at] one of the kiosk sweet sections in the centre of the shopping centres [with] her young son he was two years old wanted a packet of crisps ... this lady wears the niqab ... she stood there [at the counter] ... the lady [staff member] was engrossed in a conversation with a friend across the counter ... she [Muslim woman] said 'Excuse me!' she was ignored, she said four times and she was ignored, completely dismissed ... another lady came up to purchase something and was served immediately. she [Muslim woman] said ... 'Excuse me why didn't you serve me?' ... [Staff member] said 'You can see me talking to somebody' ... [the Muslim woman] turned ... just erupted ... told her how ignorant she was ... [the staff member] stood back in amazement ... the other lady [staff friend] left in embarrassment ... the woman ... didn't apologise though just stood there shocked. ... [the little boy] started crying he sensed the distress ... she said 'I wouldn't have imagined that was out there.' She said it was most shocking for her.

Even when you do get served it does not necessarily mean that you will be treated with respect. Survey participants detailed how they experienced poor service, and were often 'treated aggressively' (Arabic female Muslim) by waiting staff in restaurants while those customers who were deemed acceptable were served appropriately.

> It was so obvious that we were the only customers who got treated aggressively than the others because she was taking the order from other customers with a smile and she was laughing, and telling jokes, but as soon as she finished from them, she turns to our table with a scary look full of hatred. She was pulling the menus and throws the orders on our table.

Others recalled experiencing discrimination when trying to access accommodation.

> Once when looking for a house to rent, we had reached an agreement by phone (before they had met with us). After viewing the house, the landlord came up with some excuse (apparently because of the fact that we are Muslims).
>
> (Northern European Muslim female, use of brackets is hers)

Given the racialised constructions that pervade international and local discourses, sometimes making oneself 'invisibly' Muslim can mean one can avoid experiencing discrimination – 'I regularly changed my name when speaking to landlords on the phone simply because they are quick to judge on Muslim names' (South-Asian Muslim male). This last quote highlights the agency individuals can employ in the form of micro-resistances such as obfuscating their identity (see also Open Society 2011a). Being the bearer of putative signifiers of Western identity, such as a name or an accent, may reduce one's chances of being identified as Muslim. Yet, once your Muslimness is recognised the exposure to discrimination is arguably the same. Even if the identification as Muslim is misplaced.

> My [friend] ... was stabbed ... there was two guys, he was outside his door ... they shouted you fuckin' Osama bin Laden ... [a] knife ripped through his hand.
> (Kulvir, a South-Asian Sikh male whose friend was assaulted on the mistaken assumption that he was Muslim)

Statistical analysis of the areas that participants in this study identified as locales of discrimination further bears this out. Muslim men and women both experience high levels of discrimination in areas where their identity as Muslim becomes apparent. The sphere that participants reported as having the highest rate of discrimination was 'looking for work' (36 per cent), while almost a third (31 per cent) experienced discrimination 'at work'. Muslim men experience more discrimination than Muslim women at work (49 per cent to 18 per cent) and also in terms of looking for work (43 per cent to 33 per cent). This, even though Muslim women reported an overall higher level of discrimination than Muslim men (40 per cent compared to 22 per cent). What these findings demonstrate is that both Muslim men and women experience discrimination when they are identified as Muslim. When we think of markers of Muslimness we first think of the hijab, niqab or the long beard. However, revealing one's name in a job application also reveals one's Muslimness. The following male participant found his job interview focused inappropriately on his faith even though he was devoid of embodied, overt, markers of Muslimness, with the possible exception of his name.

> During job interviews, questions are more focused on religion, although that I do not practice it. It is more like hiring an Irish [person] for management position and ask him/her about being Catholic. For every single interview I attended, it is exclusively about Islam and Muslims, the fact of being secular doesn't mean anything, then and during the interviews. I know it very well that I was asked to come for questioning and having a job, after an interview focused on what type is my religion rather than my educational background or previous multinational experience, [the interview] was ending as it always used to end. I became intimidated of attending further interviews because of the religious or ethnic prejudice [that] has already formed in the mentality of the interviewer and I became guilty until proven innocent.
> (Arabic male survey participant)

Male participants also demonstrated how they were faced with barriers when it came to fulfilling their religious duties, despite having made alternative arrangements: 'was told on Eid day that we cannot go for prayers although I changed the schedule for my patients so that the patients' care is not affected' (South-Asian Muslim male survey participant, not identifiably Muslim); and sometimes under duress: 'management complaining about staff using their break period to observe their prayer and threatening to relieve the individual of their job' (Black African Muslim male survey participant).

A female perspective on employment discrimination is provided by Jeehan, a Black African Muslim woman who wears the hijab. She recalls her experiences of looking for work during an interview:

> I went to a clothes shop and a restaurant/coffee shop. The girl in the coffee shop actually she smiled, 'I don't think you'll get work here', meaning because of the way I was dressed. I left CV for the manager who was out.... I left CV in sports clothes shop. The guy working there, not the manager, said, 'I don't think you will get a job because of the way you are dressed ... he didn't even hide it ... when I left him I thought maybe he said that because he compared with my clothes to the uniform of the shop. At this point I was wearing a full long hijab, I was new here.

Experiences of discrimination in accessing accommodation, employment education, etc. revealed in this research are remarkably similar to those evidenced in studies undertaken across Europe (Open Society 2010). Here, analyses of the different areas where participants reported experiencing discrimination reveal an interesting pattern when broken down across the sexes. In areas where Muslim men become more identifiably Muslim – for example where they have provided their names in job applications or in accessing education – they experience similar or higher rates of anti-Muslim discrimination than Muslim women. However, in areas where being identified as Muslim requires the presence of more overt markers of Muslimness, Muslim women reported higher rates of discrimination in locations such as public transport (44 per cent) or restaurants (16 per cent), compared to the respective rates (14 per cent and 6 per cent) for Muslim men.

That female Muslims demonstrate higher rates of discrimination looking for work (33 per cent) than those Muslim women who are in the work place (18 per cent) may be indicative of efforts at identity management undertaken by some of this group. There is an awareness of instances of discrimination in the employment sphere among Muslim communities and this may encourage a process of identity management so that one becomes more like the neo-WHISC 'us' or is discouraged from seeking employment altogether.

> I know more than one Muslim lady who want to work in shops like Marks and Spencers and Tesco; the management told those ladies openly that the problem is the Hijab.
> (Arabic Muslim female survey participant)

These findings raise the gendered theme of anti-Muslim racism so prevalent within neoliberal discourses of the Muslim as 'other'. I now want to turn specifically to the experiences of female Muslims in Ireland and the gendered inflections of anti-Muslim racism flowing through neoliberal discourses and the manner in which they locate Muslim women.

'Liberating' the oppressed

As has already been demonstrated, the racialised identities of Muslim women, as with Muslim men, are perceived as threatening, treacherous, and not belonging; they are representative of group solidarities that jar with neoliberal visions of Ireland as a collective of individuals. However, differences arise in terms of gender and how recognisably one is as Muslim. The vast majority of Muslim women (86 per cent) that took part in this survey stated that they were 'identifiably Muslim' compared to less than half of the Muslim men (46 per cent). Moreover, the overwhelming majority of Muslim women (96 per cent) who experienced hostility in this study reported that they were religiously identifiable compared with just under half of the Muslim men. A similar pattern emerged in relation to discrimination, where again the vast majority of Muslim women (98 per cent) who experienced discriminatory practices stated they were religiously identifiable compared to a much smaller number of Muslim men (45 per cent).

The implications of this greater identifiability for Muslim women are stark. While the identities of Muslim women and men are both replete with racialised symbolism, in terms of experiencing hostility and discrimination, disparities present themselves in the association between sex and anti-Muslim hostility and discrimination.[9] Survey findings are clear on this point, with Muslim women (44 per cent) reporting higher levels of anti-Muslim hostility than Muslim men (28 per cent);[10] and, as already noted, female Muslims (40 per cent) reported overall higher levels of discrimination than their male co-religionists (22 per cent). Nuanced differences also emerged in the survey and interview data that demonstrate that while taunts such as 'terrorist', 'suicide bomber', 'foreigner' and 'Paki' may be deployed in a similar manner across genders, others are peculiar to men or women. There are clear differences in the perceived commodification of Muslim women – for example, in that while Muslim men are called 'bin Laden', Muslim women are referred to as 'bin Laden's wife'. The following quote details experiences of both verbal and physical abuse experienced by a female Arabic Muslim survey participant:

> Been called 'filthy Arab', hijab pulled, drenched with beer Tuesday August 2010.... Empty can [was] thrown at me from moving car while yelling 'F-ing terrorist' Midweek afternoon September 2011.
>
> (Arabic Muslim female)

These findings demonstrate that, in the Irish context, one's sex has real implications in terms of being targeted for anti-Muslim hostility. The targeting of

Muslim women is directly related to their identifiability as Muslims. Signifiers of Muslimness, infested with pejorative anti-Muslim meaning, indicate a 'common-sense' difference not only between Muslims and non-Muslims but also a difference between Muslims, denoting Muslim women as 'imperilled' and Muslim men as 'dangerous' (Razack 2004; 2008). The 'hyper-visible' markers of female Islamic identity are racialised targets associated with assumptions of patriarchal oppression, inferiority, foreignness, refusals to integrate and impending threat (Hoodfar 1993; Khiabany and Williamson 2008; Open Society Institute 2011; Razack 2004; Zempi and Chakraborti 2014). These characterisations resonate with the following themes that elucidate the manner in which gendered racialised images of Muslim women have become common in the Irish public sense.

Oppressed: 'imperilled Muslim women'

Dwyer (1999, p. 7) argues that Muslim women are perceived in the West as 'passive victims of oppressive cultures ... the embodiment of a repressive and "fundamentalist" religion'. The figure of the female Muslim is putatively positioned as outside the 'norm' of Irishness. Practices of veiling among women are not unusual in Irish history. However, the hijab has become invested with racialised meanings associated with oppression and patriarchy. According to Razack (2008, pp. 4–5), there exists in the West a perception that Muslim women need to be saved from 'hyper-patriarchal' Muslim men, an image frequently invoked to legitimate military expeditions to free Muslim women. The repercussions of these discourses are clear as Ghadir, a white Irish revert to Islam demonstrates: 'they think that like everyone that wears a scarf is oppressed.... Oh look at the poor woman she's depressed because she's wearing a headscarf'. Despite the temporal, cultural and political complexity of veiling practices (Dwyer 1999; Open Society Institute 2011); the racialised symbolism of Muslim women being oppressed is a powerful theme in this study, evident in both manifest and latent hostility. 'You get the same questions, you know, the women are put down ... is your husband domineering? And, you know, this stuff' (Jada, Irish Muslim female).

'I have my own brain!'

This perception of being oppressed is met with frustration. Female participants demonstrated 'oppression fatigue' as succinctly put by Samira: 'It's really tiring' and Sara: 'You no longer care. You are like: yeah I'm oppressed!!' Not only do the women express their tedium at racial typecasting as oppressed, submissive 'victims', they are also keen demonstrate that they are their own agents, that they are intelligent, engaging people, despite the stereotype of Muslim women as intellectual 'dopes' that cannot save themselves. In the case of Irish reverts to Islam, a common perception they are greeted with is one whereby they are deemed lacking in both agency and intellect and must have been coerced and simultaneously duped into taking the *Shahadah*.[11] This marks a further point of frustration for female Muslim reverts who are keen to underscore that it was their decision to follow Islam, not their husbands:

> I chose to be this religion. It's not because I'm married to a Muslim because everyone meets me [asks] 'Oh you must be married to a Muslim then and that's why you're a Muslim'. Hello!! I have my own brain! I can think for myself!
>
> (Ghadir, white female Irish Muslim and revert to Islam)

The power of racialised Muslimness in the Irish and international common sense is such that women are perceived as coerced into their faith, the implication being that they must be informally educated about the 'superiority' of Western ways and the perils of their faith, rescued by non-Muslims who 'really know' the 'true nature' of Islam (Hoodfar 1988; Razack 2004). Zaheen recollects an encounter she had with a middle aged Irish man in a local market buying an ice-cream for her infant son. Zaheen's experience exemplifies the multifaceted aspects of the racialised identity of the Muslim woman in Ireland. Her assailant challenged her intellect and what he perceived as unconscionable breaking from the Irish tribe to become Muslim, underscoring the perceived incompatibility between Irishness and Muslimness.

> [H]e was like you know your religion is full of hatred and am you're so you're really bad to women.... I told him no, no Islam is not bad to women, in fact like if I'd be a bit stupid if I changed my religion knowing that it would be bad for women like when I'm a woman. Why would I do that??!! Like I'm a little bit educated enough to think, oh I'm going to go into this religion I'm going to get beaten or locked in a room like this like phobia thing. And I said ok, no, no, Islam is not like that in fact like it uplifts the women, I'm very happy with my religion and with my choice. And he was very, very, aggressive to me and I said ok, you know what I don't need this. I just sat down and he followed me to this chair and he kept at me and at me.... 'In you Qur'an it says you kill other people that are not Muslim, in your Qur'an ... beat your [women]', and I thought ok I'm sorry but you're not reading the Qur'an, it must be something else but this is definitely not Qur'an. 'Oh! no, no, I know more than you I worked in Saudi Arabia for many years, I know more about your religion than you.' I thought, ok, ok, ok, I said ok you know more than me, ok, but I know for a fact this is not true. And he kept on and on and on.

Liberation tactics

The characterisation of female Muslims as subjugated and oppressed is not only insulting and a source of frustration for the participants but central to legitimising the policing of who belongs in the nation. The discourse of oppressed

Muslim women also serves to legitimise the deployment of 'liberation tactics' by those would-be 'liberators' of the oppressed. The impact these 'tactics' have on the Muslim female participants in this study includes shock, depression, feelings of fear and vulnerability. Jada, explains how she was told to 'take that thing rag off your head' by a patient in the hospital she works in. The impact this had on Jada was

> You just feel low, you just feel like, you know, he's really almost taking all my clothes he's exposed me and he did it in front of everybody ... it's not just him either I've had it a few times and am this is just one case I can think of.

At times these tactics manifest as assaults which sometimes involve threatening behaviour and vulgar sexualised practices. A Muslim woman in Cork City related how she was 'Followed home, pulled aside, asked if I was "open for business" then vomited on building doorstep' (Arabic female Muslim survey participant). The fear and shock this Muslim woman experienced is understandably palpable and the resonance with Orientalist obsessions with the Muslim female form does come to mind. Fahima details a 'very shocking ... atrocious' experience that her young teenage daughters (aged 15 and 16) were subjected to on the LUAS in Dublin.

> [M]y two daughters, coming home, they took the LUAS one day and there was some people ... a couple, a young man and a young girl and they were remarking on ... they used the term the alleged chastity of the girls and they performed oral sex on the LUAS that day and that was absolutely, I remember my daughter being absolutely distraught she actually jumped off the LUAS at the spot.

The young couple who engaged in what could be perceived as a vicarious sexual assault, targeted the young Muslim women on the perception of their being oppressed, repressed individuals. It is impossible to say what was in the minds of this couple. Nonetheless the effect of the performance of this lewd sexual act was to shock and intimidate the young Muslim women who were targeted. Arguably, the couple were demonstrating how liberal and free 'we' are in the West and, by implication, how oppressed and repressed the Muslim women are, presumably based on their modest, racialised attire. It is ironic that, in all of the examples above, Muslim women, assumed to be oppressed and repressed, the alleged property of Muslim men, are being 'liberated' through acts of coercion and (re)appropriation as property of the West. Instead of being liberated, Muslim women become oppressed at the hands of their assailants (Poynting and Noble 2004).

These acts of 'liberation' are not always of a sexual nature, yet the hijab and the niqab retain a central role in the experiences of anti-Muslim hostility as directed towards Muslim women (see also Zempi and Chakraborti 2014).

Participants recalled, with notable similarities, the manner in which their hijab or niqab had been forcibly removed by complete strangers. Indeed, it is almost expected. As one survey participant puts it: 'since I am a female Muslim I got to experience that my scarf got pulled down off my head in school' (Arabic Muslim).

> Once my Mam and my two sisters and my youngest sister were walking toward the sea in peace; my Mam and my little sister came from Saudi Arabia in the summer Holliday to Dublin and [were] visiting my sisters who study there.... They all went to the sea without any man with them, two big Irish men came to them, one of them tried to take off my sister headscarf. It was really bad experience for my family.
>
> (Arabic male survey participant)

Aatif recalls an experience his wife was subjected to wherein she was left in no doubt that her Muslim dress was deemed as 'other' and a 'legitimate' target for sanction in Irish society:

> [W]hen she was going to her car with the shopping ... the woman started shouting things at her things like 'We don't want you type of people here' ... then they came close to her and again.... 'Why you people have to come to this country we don't need you in this country.' My wife was trying to be polite to them by saying look 'I'm sorry ... what have I done to you' or things like that and because actually they were talking to my wife and obviously they couldn't see, they just could see the veil [niqab] so one of them felt the need to just pull this veil down.

Racialised imaginings of Muslim women operate on and through symbols associated with Islam and Muslimness (Allen and Nielsen 2002; Zempi and Chakraborti 2014). Stereotypical associations and co-locations of Muslim women as oppressed 'others' serve to justify exclusionary practices directed towards these women. These practices are lived by Muslim women as both latent and manifest forms of hostility, with profound effects ranging from frustration and tedium to feelings of shock and vulnerability for those on the receiving end of such 'tactics of liberation'.

Discussion and conclusion: 'day in and day out'

The findings discussed in this chapter on lived anti-Muslim racism illustrate not only the fact that this form of racism is alive and well in Ireland, but also the complex and multifaceted manner in which it persists. Historic state-maintained notions of Irishness collide with the global racialised image of the Muslim 'other' in discourses of nation that idealise, fetishise, an ideal type neo-WHISC identity. These notions of nation merge with global, neoliberal, political discourses, policies, media representations, and a public 'common sense' which separates Muslim men and women from a presumed homogenous 'Western us' to legitimise anti-Muslim hostility and discrimination. The experiences detailed in this study may not be those of every Muslim in Ireland. However, for those participating in this research, racism is perceived as 'normal'. It is worthwhile, indeed necessary, to underscore this point by foregrounding the participants' own voices. For example, Zaheen:

> [Y]ou take it as a norm, you know people don't like Islam you're going to get that racism but we just think like, ok, it's going to happen we just have to take it and be strong from it like because there's nowhere we can report it or if we do report there's nothing done about it.

It is striking and indeed disheartening to hear repeated, in so many narratives, not only that racism is something so commonly experienced, but also implicit resignation to the normalcy of this reality on the part of some participants. If the Irish State, or indeed any state is serious about policing racism, effective action must be taken to change this normalisation as described by participants. Not only is there a need for the state to become reflective of a diverse society, it must demonstrate this by engaging with racism in a meaningful manner, not just rhetoric; otherwise Muslims, and indeed other 'others', will continue to be left to negotiate racism in their lives.

Notes

* It is a topic for further research if the passing of the very recent Marriage Referendum will have implications for the heterosexual aspect of this proposed concept. Unfortunately, homophobic hate crime remains a concern in Ireland (see http://glen.ie/news-post.aspx?contentid=27831).
1 As I have argued in Chapter 3, Islam and Muslims have a history of being 'othered' in the West to meet differing ends (Esposito 2011, p. xxii; Iqbal 2010, p. 575; Said 2003 [1985], p. 59). These historical constructions should be perceived as a repository from which contemporary anti-Muslim racism draws. In and of themselves these symbolic forms may inform racialised perceptions of Muslims as 'other', in isolation from hegemonic discourses. However, I contend that in the contemporary period these historically contingent 'truths' and racialised symbolic forms are deployed in neoliberal discourses to justify governmental campaigns, filling the social 'common sense' with constructions of Muslim 'otherness'. I accept that not every instance of anti-Muslim racism is the product of the neoliberal regime of 'truth'. Nonetheless, I argue that the experiences of participants in this study underscore the effects of global neoliberal discourses on the public perception in constructing Muslim as 'other' informing and legitimising experiences of anti-Muslim racism.
2 49 per cent of participants were male, 51 per cent were female and participants were drawn from 14 towns and cities in Ireland; questionnaire was predominantly comprised of closed questions but did provide for some open answers; multiple locations were identified in the bigger cities. See the Appendix 1 for more on methodology.
3 The questionnaire was divided into distinct sections: the first focused on experiences of hostility; the second, experiences of discrimination; the third investigated experiences of reporting; and the final section comprised of detail such as age and ethnicity.

4 In addition to drawing on responses to the open questions in the questionnaire, I also undertook focus group discussions and one-to-one interviews with Muslim men and women; the themes discussed here derive from a thematic analysis of the words shared with me by participants.
5 WHISC is conceptualised in this study as an ideal type premised on normative assumptions of belonging to the historically dominant social group. It does not denote levels of religiosity or necessity of affiliation to Catholicism, but the presumption, for example, that because one is Irish she is therefore Catholic. Furthermore, I am not blind to the agency of those, like myself, who would resist such categorisation. This equally applies to the concept of neo-WHISC being proffered here. We do not all subscribe to neoliberal 'truths' but they do dominate global and local discourses on how to conduct conduct.
6 I used the term revert as opposed to convert.
7 The commonly referred to Garda National Immigration Bureau Card is an Immigration Certificate of Registration document for all non-EEA nationals.
8 Although children did not participate in this study, it is important to note the presence of children when parents or other siblings are racially abused. Not only did this cause them upset but it was also worrying to see children being socialised into 'otherness'.
9 The relationship of 'Sex' and experiences of anti-Muslim hostility proved significant in terms of statistical testing with a Chi-squared statistic of 7.7194 and a $P<0.005$ of independence.
10 In terms of relative rate, Muslim women are 50 per cent more likely to experience anti-Muslim hostility and discrimination than Muslim men.
11 Hewer (2006, p. 223) defines the *Shahada* as: 'The principal statement of [the Islamic] faith: "I bear witness that there is no god save God, Muhammed is the Messenger of God"'

6 Neoliberal governmentalities of 'care'

Rhetoric and anti-Muslim racism in Ireland

Introduction

The realities of anti-Muslim racism in Ireland, as the previous chapter demonstrates, are stark. The experiences lived by Muslim communities in Ireland behove a state response, but the reality is somewhat different. Before engaging in the experiences participants shared of reporting anti-Muslim racism to the state it is important to first gain an understanding of the duplicitous neoliberal state in action. As will be argued below, the Irish State is an exemplar of neoliberalism in practice; engaging in the rhetoric of anti-racism but in reality devoid of substance. As will be noted below, there are individuals within the state who do endeavour to challenge racism in all its forms. But while it is important to acknowledge their efforts, the fact remains that these microchallenges toward racism are not cultural within the arms of the state tasked with challenging racism. Maintaining the focus on the police in Ireland, I contend that the Irish State is engaged in processes of 'truth' creation when it comes to antiracism, manifesting itself through high profile rhetorical displays matched with inconsistent policing and policies which are part of a broader consistent neoliberal race-blind practice to conduct those vulnerable to racism away from the state.

The neoliberal (non)racial republic

In the previous chapter I argued how hegemonic neoliberal discourses pervade the 'truth' of how society should be in contemporary Ireland. Markers of 'otherness' indicate membership of contrarian collectives which may still hold vestiges of communal care that grate with the neoliberal goal of atomised societies. Neoliberalism is not about collective care derived from group responsibility; care is the responsibility of individuals and privatised actors. Global neoliberal discourses encourage governments to roll back on their commitments toward social care programmes deemed unconducive to maintaining the dominance and expansion of the neoliberal regime of 'truth'.

In this context, having and implementing a policy on addressing racism would not only contradict neoliberal doctrine by recognising collective identities, but it would also create an expectancy of state care. However, the neoliberal state,

Ireland included, must also engage in practices that present a mirage of care by signing up to, for example ,the UN Convention on the Elimination of Racial Discrimination (CERD). Not being seen to do so would send mixed messages as to how advanced and (neo)liberal Irish State really is. In turn, this could negatively impact on attracting corporate investment, tourism revenue and also much desired resource-*ful* immigrants. This results in contradictory policy positions wherein the Irish State must be seen to address issues such as racism and other human rights obligations, while concomitantly remaining loyal to the hegemonic neoliberal 'truth' that valorises self-care, self-reliance and the outsourcing of myriad forms of previously state provided support to privately funded philanthropic organisations.

It is important to preface the analysis that follows by acknowledging again, in line with Foucauldian thought, that the Irish State, as with others, is not perceived here as a monolithic actor – it is far more layered and complex. Different arms of government tasked with different goals are frequently positioned against one another, each with their own organisational priorities and resources. At times one department can engage in practices that essentially contradict the other. Historically, it is possible to trace these contradictory practices in action. In 1998 the National Consultative Committee on Racism and Interculturalism was formed, funded primarily by the state. Between 2001 and 2004 the 'Know Racism' campaign on racism and diversity was launched by the Irish State (Office for the Promotion of Migrant Integration 2013). In 2001–2003 An Garda Síochána commenced recording racism as a potentially motivating factor in a criminal act, while also creating what was then known as the Garda Racial and Intercultural Office and the position of Ethnic Liaison Officer. In 2005, the then Department for Justice, Equality and Law Reform launched a National Action Plan Against Racism which was to run until 2008. All of these measures radiate an impression that neoliberal Ireland was a state intent on challenging racism, not blind to it. However, these represent just one side of Janus-faced Irish policies.

Even as the aforementioned anti-racism policies and practices were being enacted, the Irish State was also engaging in the formation and imposition of overtly racist policies and procedures. The early part of last decade witnessed a particularly regressive period on the part of the Irish State towards the Traveller Community. In 2002, the Irish Government bowed to pressure from lobby groups in the hospitality sector, changing equality legislation in a manner particularly problematic for those who do not fit the neo-WHISC ideal type, in this case the Traveller Community, by moving the facility to make claims of discrimination vis-à-vis accessing goods and services in the hospitality sector from the Equality Tribunal to the local District Court (Equality Authority 2006).[1] Also in 2002, the Irish Government enacted legislation which, according to Crowley and Kitchin (2007, p. 128) specifically 'targets a minority, Irish Travellers' making it nigh on impossible for Travellers to maintain their nomadic culture without infringing upon the law.[2] In 2004, four years after ratifying the CERD, the Government baldly refused to acknowledge the status of ethnic group sought after by the Traveller Community, despite increasing acceptance that Traveller ethnicity should be officially recognised (McVeigh 2007). Apart from Travellers, in 2004, the Irish Government held a referendum on citizenship which targeted the children of migrants born in Ireland. By aligning citizenship under blood line conditions, the Irish State excluded those from citizenship who, up to this point, were granted citizens status as a birth right; a project of racial, national-social engineering to maintain the dominance of the neo-WHISC group defined by blood (Ní Chatháin 2011).

The apparent inconsistency between state rhetoric and substantial policy implementation demonstrates a consistency of sorts: the Irish State predominantly addresses racism at the level of rhetoric, rarely in substance, thus meeting its neoliberal commitments. As I will demonstrate further below, whatever the wont of individuals working for the state to challenge racist practice, their desire is not matched by a similar overriding energy at governmental level that perceives challenging racism as a state priority. This pattern has not been contingent upon any one political party. A formerly dominant party, Fianna Fáil, presided in coalition government with different partners[3] from the drafting of the aforementioned National Action Plan Against Racism until the implementation of the so-called austerity cuts. These cuts have been continued under the current Fine Gael and Labour Party coalition government (Department of Justice and Equality 2013; MacDonald 2011). While certain individuals can act as points of resistance within the state apparatus, they are overwhelmed by the hegemonic neoliberal rationalities that dominate policy and practice.

Throughout the analysis that follows here I will present the manner in which the Irish State engages in rhetorical anti-racism, the latent purpose of which is to conduct those vulnerable to anti-Muslim racism away from the care of the state. In what follows, I will first adumbrate some positive instances of state 'care' recalled by participants. These positive examples represent the points of resistance wherein individuals within the state endeavour to challenge racism. This is followed by a mapping of the boundaries that delimit the efforts of these actors, marking out the hollow character of governmental discourses in terms of challenging racism. First, Janus smiles.

The smiling face of Janus: the Irish state and anti-racism

As I have argued above, neoliberal states, Ireland among them concomitantly engage in practices conducive to maintaining racism while also endeavouring to present an image of a 'caring' state. These are the contrarian faces of Janus in neoliberal anti-racism. The smile of Janus presents a façade of 'care' for those who are vulnerable to racism. The opposing face demonstrates the benighted reality wherein racism is something that is not treated seriously but only rhetorically. Behind the smile are those actors within the Irish State that, tasked with building community relations, engage, some passionately, with racism and diversity as seriously as they are permitted to, bearing in mind the constrained resources emblematic of selective neoliberal intervention.

In the Irish context, community policing is perceived as a vital conduit for the generation of trust and confidence between the police and myriad communities (An Garda Síochána 2009). Positive perceptions of state 'care' vis-à-vis racism have particularly been encouraged through examples of outreach on the part of members of An Garda Síochána, particularly by Community Gardaí and members of the Garda Racial Intercultural and Diversity Office (GRIDO). In real terms, community relations with minority groups are extremely important and can have positive implications for the reporting of racism. Such relationships can create a platform wherein members of diverse groups feel that they can raise issues in a non-threatening environment with members of state bodies they may otherwise be wary of. A frequent barrier to reporting experiences of racism is a fear of the police, in particular, and that by reporting one may expose oneself to secondary victimisation or even self-incrimination in the case of undocumented migrants (Lynch 2011, Perry 2009).

Community representatives from diverse aspects of Islam participating in this study related their positive experiences of Garda outreach, including the benefits of having a regular Garda presence at the mosque. According to community representative Azim: 'the community Garda ... they come once a week and every Friday after prayer they'll sit down here, they'll hear the complaints' thus creating a platform wherein trust can be engendered. Azim noted during our interview how he relied on his local Community Garda as a first point of contact for any issues that may arise. By simply being there to take questions or address issues, trust can be built with members of minority communities that may otherwise mistrust agents of the state. Outreach such as this on the part of the state can go a long way towards encouraging people to report experiences of racism (Kielinger and Paterson 2007).

Discussions with various community representatives evinced an appreciation of the need for Muslim men and women to report their experiences of racism to An Garda Síochána. They also noted the importance of generating data on anti-Muslim racism and the role such data can play informing policy. In one interview, local Muslim community leader Saad demonstrated first-hand the role that outreach by local Community Gardaí played in encouraging him to report his experience of racism. Saad encountered anti-Muslim hostility during a quick visit to a local supermarket where he was subjected to verbal abuse by a man and a woman. During the course of the abuse Saad informed them he was going to use the video function on his phone to record the tirade of abuse he was being subjected to:

> I thought ok what should I do, should I tell the Gards or not? ... it was not my intention to ... but ... week before or two weeks before I had visits from the Gards and they gave me some leaflets about [reporting] racism and all this thing so I thought, ok, I was brave about this thing so I better go and tell the Gards ... so I rang one of the community relations Gards ... I think by chance he was on duty so I went straight to him and I explained the scenario and I played the recording ... he was shocked, he said wow you know if I

had told this thing to people here they would think this doesn't exist so he gave me a CD ... I went to my laptop ... recorded and handed it over to him, after a while maybe about few weeks ... I met up with him again and he told me that they managed to track that guy ... they located his car registration from [the supermarket] security camera and he was asking me.... 'Do you want us to prosecute him?'

When asked about the importance of the earlier Garda visit in terms of encouraging him to report racism, Saad's response is telling, revealing the importance of community policing but also, the normalised place of racism among negatively racialised communities:

[I]f they didn't come I don't think I would have reported it ... maybe I would have just had the same feeling of everyone, like there is no point in reporting to the Gards I'll just keep it to myself.

Muslim community representatives were also clear regarding the esteem in which they held members of the GRIDO and Community Gardaí, and the benefits of regular interaction with members of the service. Fahima sums it up:

Oh yes, I would always applaud anybody to be in touch with them, they're fantastic ... they'll come ... here ... I've known the reaction ... a GARDA came and spoke to [a] women's group ... and left those women ... they couldn't believe not only for the Gardaí but that such PARTICULAR GARDAÍ existed ... how well it worked with the Muslim community and how well he was able to dispel a lot of the misconceptions about Muslims in general without being Muslim.

Members of various Irish-based NGOs also shared positive perceptions of members of Community Gardaí and the GRIDO during interview discussions. Representatives from various NGOs referred to the dedication and passion of individual Community Gardaí and staff in the GRIDO office. Brian Killoran, CEO and former Information and Referral Service Manager with the Immigrant Council of Ireland (ICI), a leading national immigrant advocacy and support organisation, noted that the ICI has a 'great working relationship' with the GRIDO and related that they have a 'fantastic understanding of all the issues and a fantastic understanding of under reporting [of racism] and why people are under reporting and encouraging people to report'. Jennifer de Wan, Campaigns and Communications Officer with the highly respected immigrant support and human rights advocacy group Nasc,[4] in Cork, paid tribute to the local Community Garda who she felt was 'such a strong person so passionate' when it came to addressing racism.

Jennifer continues, 'I suppose we are quite kinda reliant on our relationship with Community Gards for managing the issues' we encounter in the course of our work assisting immigrants. The importance of strong relationships and outreach to those who are vulnerable to racism and those interfacing regularly with minority communities cannot be understated; it is vital in building 'trust and encouraging people to report' racism (Brian ICI). However, while Fahima may 'applaud' people for contacting the Gardaí it is important to bear some additional considerations in mind. Representatives of community groups are privileged in terms of their accessibility to members of the GRIDO and Community Gardaí. It is highly unlikely that the average member of the public will have the same level of access and familiarity as those who regularly interface with appointed Community Gardaí or members of the GRIDO. Indeed, the experience of the average Muslim person is, as will be demonstrated below, very much at odds with those of the aforementioned community representatives.

It is also important to bear the problems of relying on the personalities and passion of individual Gardaí. A 'retired very senior officer, who has had experience in the development of policing responses to dealing with racism, both at policy and operational level'[5] referred during an interview to some of the good practices he was engaged in. In particular he noted how, on the basis of a 'need identified locally', and in conjunction with local minority communities, he established a public forum to address issues particular to them. The purpose of this forum was to build trust and provide a means of communication between the local Gardaí and minority groups. This forum was so successful that members of minority communities came from outside of his district for advice and to engage with An Garda Síochána. While this again demonstrates some of the good work carried out by individual Gardaí, this 'retired very senior officer' noted in our interview discussion that when he moved location, the initiative 'crashed'. The damage that this may have had to community relations was clear in the mind of the retired senior officer on the basis that 'you build expectations out in the community', expectations that may not be met if one is reliant solely on individual Gardaí.

Positive experiences with Community Gardaí and the GRIDO must be understood within the context of conflicting policies and practices further discussed below. Fundamental in the smile of Janus is the presentation of Ireland as a caring state. In this case, Community Gardaí and members of the GRIDO serve that purpose in that they create and help maintain a facade of 'care' while in reality the state denies the salience of racism. While taken seriously by at least some of those involved in community policing, anti-racism in Ireland is not afforded the level of institutional importance and leadership it clearly requires. This is borne out below by community representatives and NGO participants whose experiences evince an inconsistency between practice and policy, between reality and rhetoric.

Janus turns: the Irish state and rhetorical anti-racism

As the above comments demonstrate, a number of community representatives spoke highly of the GRIDO office. However, one does not have to look hard to reveal the superficiality of Irish State approaches to anti-racism and the lack of importance assigned to racism. There was a shared feeling among Muslim representatives in this research that the GRIDO itself was under-appreciated and not receiving the level of recognition it deserved within An Garda Síochána. 'I don't think they are appreciated enough, I don't believe they are recognised for ... the great work they do ... I don't believe they're perceived ... with any huge respect' (Fahima). Instead of being viewed as an important section within An Garda Síochána, the GRIDO office is perceived, according to Azim, as 'a weak office, a lot of talk and there is not much action ... we have some result from that office but we felt there's not much happening in there'. Azim continues the office is 'just few people ... trying to get involved in intercultural things but they don't have much authority'.

The perceptions of Muslim community representatives are echoed by NGO participants. Matt Cannon, Integration Policy Officer with Limerick-based migrants' rights NGO Doras Luimní,[6] perceives the GRIDO as 'isolated to some degree' and unsure of 'what influence they have across departments' within An Garda Síochána. Jennifer from Nasc concurs:

> [E]veryone I talk to there [in GRIDO] is very passionate about what they do and very passionate about ensuring that the Gards are seen as prioritising diversity and integration, but again they are a very small office in a very big force ... the fact that they're there ... it's something.

Given the good work undertaken by Community Gardaí and members of the GRIDO noted in this study, it is worrying, but not unsurprising, that they are not being given support by the broader Garda organisation. Even in the midst of the mythical 'Celtic Tiger', when 'belt-tightening' was less of a concern, the resources allocated to offices such as the GRIDO were in no way sufficient for the effective policing of racism and recognition of an increasingly diverse Ireland. The resources allocated today are relatively lower given the increased role of the office. The remit of the GRIDO has widened to incorporate all nine strands of Ireland's equality legislation in the absence of an attendant increase in resources (An Garda Síochána 2009).

> [I]n the good old days when there was resources, there wasn't a recruitment ban, and there wasn't stations closing, there wasn't serious problems with the financing, even then it was still quite a small office within the whole Garda force ... There would be an argument definitely that they've [the GRIDO] never had enough resources and continue to not have enough resources ... especially now when they have taken on such a broader remit, their remit has multiplied eight fold to take on all the other areas of discrimination and diversity ... but there hasn't been a corresponding increase of resources.
>
> (Brian, ICI)

To this could be added the under resourcing of the position of 'Ethnic Liaison Officer' (ELO – now known as Diversity Officers) created in 2002. In 2009 the number of ELOs stood at 550; today, it is estimated that there are 322 ELOs serving in An Garda Síochána (An Garda Síochána 2009a; Office for the Promotion of Migrant Integration 2013). Not only have the numbers of ELOs reduced but, already noted, their role has actually expanded to incorporate 'caring' for and assisting LGBT communities (Garda 2013a). A retired Community Garda interviewed for this research stressed the impact of broader resource restrictions on the ability of an ELO to do their work:

> [I]f you appoint an ethnic liaison officer then you decide tomorrow morning you actually need three community policemen to do this [other task] ... the ethnic liaison officer is [now] gone [the communities he has been working with] might not see him for a week, they might not see him for twelve days, they might not see him for a month depending on the resource issue.

All NGO representatives that participated in this study referred to the issue of reduced resources and how this impacts on community policing. The implication, as regards the priority placed on anti-racism, was not lost on the participants.

> [C]utting community policing ... shows that kind of underlying structural or cultural ... lack of prioritising of those aspects of policing ... we would be concerned that it shows a lack of engagement ... that the retrenchment is to just focus on policing crime at its most fundamental level and that it would be a concern to us in general because it shows that things like racism, things like ethnic profiling, are not seen as priorities; or integration or community building relationships, things like that are not seen as priorities by a police force, which is a pretty significant issue.
>
> (Jennifer, Nasc)

I argue on the basis of the findings presented here, resonating with research conducted by Fanning *et al.* (2011), that there never was a serious investment in the GRIDO office and that resourcing has always been just enough to maintain an appearance of a 'caring' Irish State with real 'care' outsourced to NGOs. Similarly, as the retired Community Garda put it, the the fulfilment of position of ELO was a 'box ticked'. This was also exemplified in the manner in which the ELO was chosen which was not based on any particular competency but merely a case of

> [Y]ou're the ethnic liaison officer ... simple as that ... you could be a racist you could have crosses burning in your garden going around with a white cape over your head and the eyes cut out of it ... there was no criteria, no interviews.

'Ticking the boxes' enables the perpetuation of an image of an inclusive, welcoming Ireland on the international stage, while being disingenuous when it comes to building trust and challenging racism. The manner in which the community police and those tasked with engaging with diversity are hampered by insufficient resources not only erodes trust in those particular offices but also signals that what is espoused at management level is, to quote Fanning *et al.* (2011) but a 'paper policy'. This superficiality or rhetorical approach to racism is further evidenced in the experiences shared by various community and NGO representatives regarding their interactions with the state in what up to 2013 were high profile 'diversity' events.

'[T]he annual farce'

Each year since 2007, An Garda Síochána has hosted an annual Garda National Consultation Day. This high level event included representation from senior Garda management, including the Commissioner, as well as representatives from NGOs and academics. The aim of the day was to showcase good Garda practice while also allowing minority groups an opportunity to participate in workshops on the topic of diversity and their needs as a community (email communication from the GRIDO). The National Consultation Day provided a welcome opportunity for community groups to interface with Garda management. Sab (a Muslim representative) explained the immediate benefits of attending the consultation: 'I went over there – we did have a serious complaint ... I raised that issue with ... senior staff ... and they were very responsive'. While this event has been well attended in the past and welcomed by communities, participants demonstrated a belief that the initiative is superficial with the perception that points emanating from the consultation would not translate into effective meaningful policy outcomes:

> I think what they are saying is very positive, excellent, it's remarkable ... but my worry is only this, is it superficial? Ok, the people who are leading it the people who are organising it are all done by those people who are mostly community police officers ... I am worried ok if you have all these people here who are supporting this, the commissioner spoke this year and he was upfront about it that racism has no place in the police force and then you had the ... deputy commissioner, then it went down to superintendent etc. now these guys spoke fine; my worry is how far is that filtering down.... I applaud the conference I will attend it every time ... but I'm wondering how far is it coming down this is my biggest concern.
>
> (Aatif)

Aatif clearly underscores the need for the rhetoric proffered in the forum to be realised in policing practice. Likewise, Brian from the ICI feels that while the Consultations were 'worthwhile', there was 'not an awful lot of follow up', with concrete outcomes failing to manifest themselves on the ground.

Ken McCue, Cultural Planner at the Global Development Education Office of NGO Sport Against Racism Ireland (SARI), is blunt in his criticism of the Diversity Consultation, referring to it as 'the annual farce'. If rhetoric is not supported by real policy outcomes, events such as the consultation day – and, arguably, broader anti-racism initiatives – may actually push communities away from co-operating with the state. This serves the purpose of neoliberal governmentality and indeed racial neoliberalism, as elaborated above, and the aim to conduct those vulnerable to racism away from the state and into the realm of self-care, or, towards the outsourced arm of government that is the NGO sector. One particular community participant, simply stopped attending the Diversity Consultation:

> [W]e used to go a lot to these Garda national consultative meetings and their forums but ... we don't go anymore because it's just talk, talk, talk ... just nice catchy words ... nice plans but nothing happening on the ground. They have liaison officers but I don't know what's the use.... I don't know how many years they have been just talking about policies and nothing happening on the ground, no significant change on the ground.

Institutional initiatives that proclaim they encourage better police/public relations and challenge racism are in reality left at the venue of the Consultation and are counter-*productive*, in that groups vulnerable to all forms of hate crime are pushed to seek assistance elsewhere (hence the productivity as will be demonstrated in the next chapter). Superficial approaches to racism at the level of management send a clear signal that anti-racism is not cultural in An Garda Síochána. This, in turn, has the effect of creating a two-tier police force where some, a minority of officers tasked with 'saving face', are attuned to addressing racism – namely the GRIDO and Community Gardaí – while others are not required to see it as part of their role as police officers.

While constrained by limited power and resources, Community Gardaí and members of the GRIDO interact with minority communities in a manner that is sensitive to their concerns and which, in turn, can generate trust among Muslim and other minority communities. Saad's positive experience with local Gardaí clearly demonstrates this point. However, a 'second' tier of policing exists, as demonstrated also by Fanning *et al.* (2011), that is more akin to what Greene (2000) refers to as a traditional policing model. Here, mainstream Gardaí fill the ideal type of 'crime-fighter' more concerned with addressing individual incidents than building relationships or trust (Zhao *et al.* 1995, p. 24). Brian and Aatif differentiate between experiences of interacting with Community/GRIDO Gardaí with that of 'crime-fighter' members of the service:

> [I]n a lot of individual instances you'd meet individual Gards who are very good, but people have come to us ... since we started taking reports [feeling] that the local Gard for whatever reason ... is not responding to them at all about the incident, or not communicating to them how an incident can be handled, or how an incident can be treated, and in some instances ... we've had to go a very long route to get the local Gardaí to act on an incident ... we'd go maybe to the GRIDO to get them to talk to the local Gard to say look into the situation ... in some cases we've gone right to the head of community relations.
>
> (Brian, ICI)

[C]ommunity Gardas are brilliant, they understand everything they are brilliant ... their response and their attitude is completely different, they're very careful what they have to say they don't want to hurt your feelings so they are very sensitive to they're not offending you as a Muslim ... they are well trained, I mean these are the type of Gards you need ... whatever training they were getting should be filtered down to every Gard.

(Aatif)

This inconsistency in Garda service essentially means that, in most instances, members of minority communities are dependent on the idiosyncrasy of the attending police officer as to whether or not they will be treated professionally and with respect should they make a report of racism (Clarke 2013; Fanning et al. 2011). For members of minorities, this results in uncertainty and ambivalence regarding contacting the Gardaí. Furthermore, it is consistent with standard definitions of institutional racism as the needs of certain groups within society are neither being recognised nor acted upon (Mac Éinrí 2007; see also Ionnan Management Consultants 2004). Efforts to encourage trust and develop community–police relationships are being eroded due to inconsistent police practice, where, upon reporting racism to regular on duty Garda, in the opinion of Ken from SARI, they would 'laugh at you' and tell you 'that's a heat of the moment ... kind of answer'.

While Fanning et al. (2011) argue the presence of an organisational inconsistency vis-à-vis anti-racism in Ireland, I contend the opposite – that, on the basis of the evidence presented in this and other studies (Clarke 2013; Fanning et al. 2011; King O'Riain 2007), these experiences should be interpreted as a consistency in the contradictory manner in which the neoliberal Irish State addresses racism. The neoliberal Irish State has left anti-racism to the individual 'victims' of racism themselves and to the vagaries of the market, doing enough to satisfy external appearances while providing a service that is unable to meet the needs of a diverse society. Contradictory policy measures combined with a policy of 'not caring', as evidenced in the roll-back of the state in the evisceration of the equality infrastructure in the name of austerity, demonstrates the real level of 'care' and attention that the neoliberal Irish State is willing to afford to racism. Consistent inconsistencies in regards to anti-racism serve to ensure that people are conducted away from the state towards a reliance on the self or an NGO.

Organisational blindness

The inconsistency between organisational rhetoric and substantive practice is further evidenced in the lack of recognition afforded to anti-Muslim racism in Ireland. In Chapter 4, I demonstrated how anti-Muslim racism is not recognised by An Garda Síochána. This blindness to racism is not peculiar to the Gardaí and the impact this has on reporting anti-Muslim racism is very real. One Muslim woman in particular related the manner in which her experience of anti-Muslim racism failed to lead to a successful outcome through the other established equality mechanisms as it was not recognised as racism. The failure to recognise anti-Muslim racism discourages people from making any future reports to the state.

> [B]ecause I had gone to the Equality Tribunal once before and lost because they said it was not racism because I'm white Irish, although it occurred because my Muslim dress makes me appear foreign.
> (White Irish female Muslim survey participant)

This blindness is not restricted to the type of racism. Research conducted by (Nocon *et al.* 2011) demonstrates that crimes that target people on the basis of their identity have a more profound emotional impact than standard offences. To put it simply, 'hate crimes hurt more' (Iganski 2001). Furthermore, racist/hate crime is also perceived as a 'message crime' that permeates the broader community of which the victim is part (Iganski 2001, p. 630, see also Perry 2001). Nasimah (a female Arabic Muslim) narrates this distinction between standard criminality and those offences that target a person on the basis of who they are:

> [I]t's not about like your own security like, [it is] not a thief will come and ... steal your stuff, but it's my something ... like it's not a bad person who wants something – your car or bag or whatever – it's ... just someone he just he want to insult you and I think that's worse ... because if someone he want my bag, he want my car, he just need money ... he will do the same for man or for boy, for Muslim for non-Muslim, for any nation, but when a person he just want to insult you that mean you are an open target all the time.

The difference between standard non-aggravated offences and those that are, for example, motivated by or demonstrate anti-Muslim racism, requires state actors to be cognisant of the various bases upon which racism can manifest. However, despite the rhetoric, the lack of substance and recognition of racism as a phenomenon in Garda practice is clear. Different communities have different policing requirements, racism cannot then be just perceived as a standard offence (Ionann Management Consultants 2004; Walsh 2009), nor can all racisms be grouped as the same phenomenon. Anti-Muslim racism, as this research demonstrates, has a profoundly gendered dimension. This alone demands that Gardaí are cognisant of the specific circumstances and requirements of Muslim women when they report racist hate crime/non-crime incidents. However, a recently 'retired very senior [Garda] officer' that took part in this study notes how racism qua racism is policed by An Garda Síochána: 'its racism or it's not ... that was the approach'. Indeed, the following quotes from an interview I undertook with a retired Garda Inspector demonstrate a lack of understanding of the multifarious bases upon which one may be targeted for racist crime and the importance of recognising these differences.

Racism no more than any other crime or offence committed would be dealt with the same attitude there'd be no question about it, but the biggest problem was that people didn't report it ... it doesn't matter what creed you are or what, you know racism is racism ... my point being, from a policing point of view ... whatever it is [that] becomes a problem you deal with it ... legislation will come out like the umbrella effect it will cover everything and [the offence] it will fit in.

(Retired Garda Inspector)

Members of An Garda Síochána need to engage with reports of racism in a manner that is alert to the different communities that may be targeted and the more profound impact racist incidents can have on victims. It would seem that the rhetoric of Diversity Consultations has failed (or, from a neoliberal perspective, succeeded) thus far to translate into policy. Instead, there remains an ignorance of how to engage with racism, let alone record a racist crime and non/crime incident on PULSE. Despite the simplicity of doing so, as outlined by Sgt McInerney, a retired Community Garda that took part in this study was unaware of the presence of a 'racism' motivation flag on the PULSE system – even though it was in place for at least five years before he retired.

[P]ersonally ... [training on recording racism on PULSE] was never given to me. All that was given to me basically was how to record [a standard] incident on the PULSE system.... I suppose the reality of the situation would be, for me, if you have a particular category or type [of crime] ... if you are writing information in the incident box [you must ensure] that that information correlates with the type of category of crime that you have ... [for example] if somebody was to record a public order incident ... it could have ... [had] a racist element in it to a degree, but that would never have been recorded as a racist incident it would have been recorded as a public order incident.

(Retired Community Garda)

These findings underscore previous research undertaken by Clarke (2013) who demonstrated differences in terms of practice and levels of uncertainty on the part of Gardaí in relation to how one should record a racist incident. The lack of awareness of how to record a racist crime/non-crime incident on PULSE has real implications in terms of recognising racism as an issue in Ireland. Catherine Lynch, formerlly from ENAR Ireland, is clear as to why she feels the Irish State is reticent in recording racism effectively:

I think it's something very specific around racism; we also cannot ignore the generalities.... Ireland is not good on data collection ... once you have the data you have to do something with it, ... racism is just not seen as being that serious or being that different, ... Well-meaning and willing [Garda] individuals do honestly feel it's not going to make any difference [if they record it as racism] ... [they feel they are] just building expectations by recording it ... But there is, and this is where it's not just around state structures, there is a prevailing sense that Ireland is not that racist ... that is a myth, it is a myth, it's a myth we live by and no one wants to break that myth ... Why is there this reluctance [to recognise and legislate for racism]? 1. People don't think racism exists first of all; 2. People think that the system is ok; 3. Where you have real resistance, I think it's around if the data is collected then we're going to have to do something about it, or does this make us look [bad].

Change is difficult. Catherine's contribution captures key aspects of the neoliberal zeitgeist that pervades the Irish State, including the denial of racism and a rationale for not recording racism effectively. If the state does not collect figures on racism in any form, then racism does not exist because there is 'no objective evidence', to quote Ambassador to the UN, Gerard Corr (Your Rights Right Now 2013).

Discussion and conclusion

The Gardaí have been commended for the measures they have taken in engaging with minority communities (Fanning *et al.* 2011). Steps have been made in building relationships with diverse and vulnerable minority groups, in particular through the GRIDO and community police. In cities such as Cork, Kilkenny and elsewhere, Community Gardaí have played an important role in the creation and implementation of third party reporting mechanisms designed to encourage the voices of those that have experienced racism to be heard (Fanning *et al.* 2011; Nasc 2011). The findings in this study provide evidence of the importance of these initiatives and the role they play in supporting the victims of racism. However, the examples of good practice at the level of individual Gardaí, detailed above, must be set in a context wherein there exists a clear disconnect between what is espoused at Diversity Consultations and substantive Garda practice. While speaking of diversity, An Garda Síochána fails to recognise anti-Muslim racism as a particular form of racist activity.

From the neoliberal perspective, recognising diverse communities is anathema to the ideal of a collection of individuals thus denial or race blindness, as opposed to the recognition of anti-Muslim racism, is preferred. The role of the neoliberal state is to promote the creation of self-responsible individuals, not dependents. The Irish State whole-heartedly embraces global hegemonic neoliberal discourses of governance. As I have demonstrated, this results in the state maintaining an illusion of care, all the while following the neoliberal doctrine of reducing anti-racism supports, outsourcing them to the responsibility of those who experience racism themselves, who may or may not turn to privately funded NGOs. The state engages in a rhetorical anti-racism which is rich on sound-bites and optics but lacking in terms of substance. The purpose of this policy of rhetorical anti-racism is that it serves as a form of neoliberal governmentality to conduct those who are vulnerable to racism away from the state who, as part of the neoliberal project, is invested in remaking the social on the basis of ideals of individualism, choice, care of the self and competition. The next chapter will engage with participants' experiences of and perceptions towards reporting anti-Muslim hostility and discrimination in Ireland and the recording practices of the police. Through the voices of participants the difference between rhetoric and reality will be set in stark relief.

Notes

1 According to Niall Crowley (Equality Authority 2006) the implementation of the Intoxicating Liqour Act (2003) made it

> particularly difficult to challenge the discrimination they [Travellers] experience in public houses.... These cases can be heard by District Court. This presents barriers to Travellers ... in terms of the risk of costs being awarded and in the need to be legally represented.

2 Housing [Miscellaneous] Provisions Act 2002.
3 The Progressive Democrats and the Green Party (Fianna Fáil 2013).
4 Nasc is the Gaelic language word for 'link'.
5 This quote reflects the way in which this participant wanted to be referred to.
6 Doras Luimní literally translates from Gaelic into 'Limerick City Door', meaning point of access for immigrants for support and information.

7 Janus turned

(Counter)productive policing

Introduction

A central argument proffered in this book is that anti-Muslim racism needs to be recognised as a distinct racism by, in this case, the Irish State if it is to be challenged. This recognition, for example in the form of statistical data, is but a starting point which could be used to create evidenced anti-racism policies, thus challenging the norm of anti-Muslim racism in the contemporary context. However, as the previous chapter demonstrates, anti-racism policies in the neoliberal state are replete with a rhetoric of care that is, in reality, hollow and without substance. This rhetorical anti-racism will be further evidenced below, this time in the voices of those who have experienced anti-Muslim racism in Ireland. This chapter will focus on the topic of the recording and reporting by those who have experienced anti-Muslim hostility and discrimination in the racism-blind neoliberal Irish State. Drawing again on an analysis of quantitative data combined with a rich thematic analysis of participants' qualitative contributions, I will demonstrate how the Irish State is perceived – focusing particularly on the police – by those who have experienced of anti-Muslim racism, and the effect this perception has on their reporting practices. I will argue that the Irish State is disengaged when it comes to caring for those vulnerable to racism. Indeed, instead of addressing racism as a core function of state responsibility, the Irish State, intoxicated with neoliberal rationalities, privatises anti-Muslim racism, outsourcing responsibility to the self (those who experience racism). The effect this has on those who have been the targets of anti-Muslim racism is clear.

(Not) reporting racism in Ireland

Official statistical rates of racism in Ireland demonstrate a decline in racist incidents over the past seven years (Office for the Promotion of Migrant Integration 2015). According to Fanning *et al.* (2011), this may be indicative of a reduction in rates of reporting[1] as opposed to any actual decrease in racist crime.[2] However, the underreporting of racist incidents is in fact well-documented in Ireland. As noted in Chapter 4, various studies have demonstrated that rates of reporting experiences of racism range from a poor one in five to a dismal one in ten, meaning the vast majority of racist incidents go undocumented (Browne 2008; European Network Against Racism Ireland 2015; European Union Agency for Fundamental Rights 2009; McGinnity *et al.* 2012). Common factors in the under-reporting of racism include: poor levels of trust in the police; a belief that nothing will be done should one report; the view that racism is so regular as to be impossible to report each incident; a lack of awareness as to where to report; fear of secondary victimisation; poor past experiences of reporting; self-reliance (Smith *et al.* 2012; European Union Agency for Fundamental Rights 2009; Lynch 2011; Poynting and Noble 2004; Spalek 2002).

Of those who had experienced anti-Muslim hostility as part of this study, one in three (36 per cent) said they reported it. This rate of reporting is arguably higher than expected, and this may be an artefact of the sample in this study, which includes a large number of students and professionals. Research has demonstrated that higher levels of education and an awareness of one's rights and where to report racism increases the likelihood of one making an official report (McGinnity *et al.* 2008). In all cases, the vast majority of reports were made to An Garda Síochána. Those who stated that they had experienced anti-Muslim discrimination reported at a rate of one in five (22 per cent). Interestingly, An Garda Síochána was also the site where most reports of discrimination were made in addition to statutory equality bodies. The numbers are too small to make any generalisations regarding service levels. The sections that follow below will elucidate the various factors that guided participants' decisions when it came to reporting (or not) experiences of anti-Muslim racism.

Eroding trust: all part of the neoliberal service

In Chapter 5 I demonstrated how anti-Muslim racism, informed by neoliberal rationalities, acts as a means of creating and maintaining the nation as a collective of individuals. The following sections demonstrate the manner in which the state through An Garda Síochána also encourages this concept of nation. International and national research studies demonstrate that querying of immigration status, ethnic profiling or other negative experiences at home or abroad can impact upon perceptions of the police, leading to suspicion and distrust (Fanning *et al.* 2011; Perry 2009; Poynting and Noble 2004). Negative interactions with the police have a profound impact on the person(s) involved and their confidence and trust in the service (Kääriäinen and Niemi 2014; Skogan 2006). This is especially true for those who have been the subject of 'police initiated contacts' (Skogan 2006, p. 104).

Profiling practices undertaken by police towards certain communities on the basis of their real or perceived identity are also very problematic in terms of maintaining trust and police cooperation (Kääriäinen and Niemi 2014). Policing in the name of 'preventing terror' is particularly relevant to the relationship between the police and Muslim communities and the trust they will have in the service (Spalek 2010). A report published by Cork-based NGO Nasc (2013), demonstrates the manner in which Roma women have been racially profiled by members of An Garda Síochána based on their cultural appearance. Research undertaken by the Migrants' Rights Centre Ireland (2011) demonstrates the lack of faith that Muslim women have in the Gardaí on the basis of being 'racially' or as I prefer, religio-profiled[3] to reflect the role that their religious identifiability plays in their experience. Chapter 5 of this study detailed the experiences of Aatif and Ehan and the manner in which they were subjected to religio-profiling by members of An Garda Síochána constructed as part of the 'suspect community' *de jour*; they were singled out purely due to their Muslim identity, wherein a person is assumed to be a 'threat' or suspect on the basis of an association with terrorism and their group identity (Hickman *et al.* 2011; Spalek 2010). These practices build on other negative experiences of policing at home and abroad that can result in minorities holding a suspicion of the police which can militate against chances of reporting any crime, let alone racism. As Sab demonstrates:

> [S]ome people would report things to the Gards ... others would not because people are a little bit hesitant to go to the Gards ... could be because they might have had difficult experience ... in the home country and they might have had difficult experience in Ireland with the Gards here so it could be one way or the other ... some of them would go and others would not.
>
> (Sab, Muslim community representative)

This lack of trust in the Gardaí is not restricted to migrants. Aatif, an Irish revert to Islam has experienced a diverse range of interactions with An Garda Síochána, reporting instances of criminal damage to property and assault. Experiences of religio-profiling noted in Chapter 5, and demonstrated in the following more 'mundane' interaction, serve to encourage distrust and alienate Muslim communities from the Gardaí. Aatif recalls his experiences of reporting a traffic accident to the Gardaí:

> [M]y wife's car was hit.... When the Gards turned up here's a woman standing in long niqab, hijab standing on the side of the road with her husband with his with long beard and topi [skull cap], the Gards came straight to us and said: 'So did you hit this car?' They assumed we were the ones that hit the car ... we weren't assumed to be the victims.... The Gard assumes it must be the fault of the foreigner rather than the fault of the native of Ireland.... The first question he put to me was, 'How long are living here?'.... He asked, 'Do you have residence, do you have your GNIB card?'.... I went Garda, 'You're here to investigate a car being hit, not whether we have residence or permit'.... That's when he asked me where are you from, where do you live. I said, 'I'm from Ireland I'm born in Ireland, I'm Irish' and things changed immediately.

Important here is the effect of the process as opposed to the outcome (e.g. retrieving stolen goods) of engaging with Gardaí and the manner in which it has impacted Aatif's perceptions of interacting with the Garda service (Kääriäinen and Niemi 2014; Skogan 2006). The manner in which Aatif has been treated above and in other incidents by some Gardaí has induced a hesitancy in him when it comes to interacting with members of the service. Clearly, for Aatif, not fitting the ideal type of neo-WHISC has resulted in a different type of policing experience (oversight rather than protection) which in turn engenders a well-founded lack of trust in the police service:

> I often go on the High Street preaching.... Any Gard that approaches our table, I always now I'm hesitant with them because I don't know why they are coming and that's bad for me ... when I lose the confidence of trusting a Gard ... will he treat me properly, will he treat us properly; that's quite bad, that's quite bad.
>
> (Aatif)

The following narratives of racism are perhaps some of the most disturbing given that they were committed by members of an agency tasked with protecting the vulnerable – An Garda Síochána. The finding of racism in An Garda Síochána is not new. The Garda Human Rights Audit (Ionann Management Consultants 2004) found the service to be institutionally racist. A claim which is argued here remains equally valid today based on the findings presented in this book and made clear in the quotes below. I was particularly struck in one of the interviews I undertook with a former Garda, who left the service just over a decade ago. He recalled his experience of observing racism in the service, in this case towards the Traveller Community, another group outside of the neo-WHISC ideal type.

> I was in 'X Town Station' at the time and I was on my nine month probationary, my nine month placement there and it was one of my first times out in the patrol car with my new colleagues so I was trying to suss them out, what they're like, what's their attitudes like to ordinary people.... I remember on one occasion we drove up to a halting site where Travellers lived ... at about maybe three or four in the morning and the Garda who was driving the car a guy who with maybe 8 or 10 years – experience he turned on the full lights in the car and blew the horn several times to wake up the family, the Traveller family in question and he was laughing as he was doing it and I said, 'What are you doing that for?' And he said, 'Just letting them know that we're here' ... I was actually shocked ... I was really, really shocked.

At a different incident, Irish female revert Fahima recalls one experience that was related to her by a member of her community:

> [O]ne of the community members ... was going into his local police station because of an on-going issue with his family and the Gardaí.... When he

was entering in to make a complaint about two Gardaí that came to his house the [same] two Gardaí exited the police station and wouldn't allow him enter; [they] blocked him and told him ... allegedly ... told him what to do with himself.... His English wasn't great so he came to me ... distressed completely distressed, he said obviously I can't go, I'm afraid now so we made a report to the Ombudsman and they took it very, fair play they took it as serious.

The quote from Alia (female Irish revert to Islam) below refers to the case of a Cork couple and the impact their arrest and detention has had on perceptions and levels of trust in An Garda Síochána. In 2010, seven people were arrested in Waterford and Cork on suspicion of being linked with a plot to murder Swedish cartoonist Lars Vilks who had sketched images of the Prophet Mohammed. Evidence existed that an American revert to Islam, Colleen LaRose, aka 'Jihad Jane', was communicating online with a male Irish citizen of Algerian origin, Ali Charaf Damache. As part of an international policing operation, intelligence was communicated by the FBI to An Garda Síochána who in turn placed LaRose under surveillance; seven arrests were made subsequently (Brady 2010; Irish Times 2013; McDonald 2010; Sheehan 2011). In addition, 25 other people were interviewed on the basis that the seven were known to them in a way reminiscent of the policing of Irish communities during the troubles in the UK (Hillyard 1994; Sapsted 2010). Of the seven arrested, LaRose was extradited to the US. The American female revert to Islam who had married Damache also returned voluntarily to face charges related to terrorism and of attempted murder to which both pleaded guilty. Damache was charged with sending a menacing text message, while another male was charged with an immigration offence. A married couple from Cork and another man were freed without charge. Internet communication formed the main body of evidence underlying the charges that connected LaRose with Damache; however, according to Brady (2010) the Cork couple involved 'did not communicate directly with Ms LaRose but were aware she held strong views'. The effect of this operation, and the manner in which the Cork coupled were detained, was clear for Aalia:

[L]ook at ... the Waterford 7 ... they were [in] hell for weeks, he lost his job, he lost everything because they did what we do Islamically: If a sister is in need and she needs [shelter] ... if you got a call tonight and there's a sister on the street you'd be like, ok, I have a spare room for her immediately.... . They did that and because they did that ... their [the couple] life was destroyed by the Gards ... their kids were four days in the house with no [support] ... the 18 year old was afraid to go out because click, click, click, media were there, so how can you say we trust the Gards? They [Cork couple] got the Irish Immigrant Council [to assist] ... they were fighting for an apology, they wanted a public apology because they were told that they were harbouring.... Taliban.... Their life was destroyed, and like where can you have faith in the Gards.

The above examples clearly evidence why a person would be afraid to report a crime to An Garda Síochána on the basis of previous interactions with the force and the erosion of trust they engender. As Aalia's experience above and those below demonstrate, these experiences need not be direct; even hearing of these events can generate distrust and have the effect of discouraging a person from making an approach to a member of An Garda Síochána. There is an interesting resonance here between the 'message' implicit and explicit in acts of hate crime which endeavour to communicate 'otherness' and subordination, and the manner in which this message spreads throughout the targeted communities (Chakraborti and Garland 2009; Iganski 2008; Perry 2001). The difference here is that the message being shared among communities is not to report experiences of racism to the police.

Various participants made reference to stories they had heard of peoples' experiences of reporting to An Garda Síochána. As a migrant, Jeehan (Black African female Muslim) has been informed by fellow immigrants of the 'dos and don'ts' if one is to secure citizenship: 'If you tell [report to] the Gardaí it will be written in your report and will damage your chances of citizenship.... People advise me not to report because of this'. A'idah, an Arabic Muslim woman, recalls a discussion she had with another female Muslim about making reports to the police. Here again A'idah demonstrates the effect that negative community discourses and knowledges of past experiences can have on the likelihood of one making a report to the Gardaí in this instance:

> I ask one of my close friends in the community.... 'Did you report that to the police?' 'No ... I didn't report because they won't listen'.... One time she said that she knows a story about a friend in the community, Arab Muslim woman she reported but the Garda never listened to her, never come back or never called her back, or never check on her again later to see if her problems are resolved or not; and why? Because Garda knows they are Muslim woman so they know already that the Garda doesn't care about them because they are a Muslim.

An awareness of institutionally racist practices is clearly evident in the above quotes and experiences of Muslim men and women in Ireland. The participants demonstrate that they are being subjected to a type of policing that differs from that accorded to those who fit the desired neo-WHISC profile. It is interesting to note that the Cork couple implicated in the 'Jihad Jane' affair sought recourse not through the state but through an NGO, further demonstrating the neoliberal practice of outsourcing care. This theme will be taken up again below. For now it is important to emphasise that state practices as described above encourage distrust and create an (intentional) uncertainty among communities, conducting them away from the state as a source of support to the self or privatised sources of support.

Normalised acceptance

Participants repeatedly referred, directly and indirectly, to ignoring their experiences of racism instead of taking any action such as making a report. This finding resonates with studies such as those undertaken by Poynting and Noble (2004) in Australia and the European Union Minorities and Discrimination Survey (2009). The rationales employed by participants who chose to ignore their experience of racism instead of reporting it varied. For example, some 'did not find it important to report' while others chose 'not to prolong the incident'. Likewise, Fahima perceives that 'there's a certain reluctance to report because ... people will see if I don't report maybe it will go away'. Some participants did not see the need to report their experience of racism at all 'because I think that is not common and it's just from some people' implying that a certain level of racism is 'acceptable'.

Iganski (2008, p. 5) describes this normalised view as one where those who are targeted for racism perceive it to be a 'part of the routine incivilities of everyday life'. Participants in the Leicester Hate Crime Project (Chakraborti *et al.* 2014, p. 44) also evidenced what is referred to as 'normalised hate' wherein experiencing 'hate' was something to be expected. In terms of responding to these incidents, in this study, ignoring the incident was the most frequently reported reason for not going to the authorities upon experiencing anti-Muslim racism. For Nasirah there is nothing exceptional about experiences of racism which are:

> [P]retty normal when you are walking around the town sometimes people will pass by you and they'll just say something.... You ... learn to ignore it ... if you pay attention to it you're bringing trouble on so it's like bullying you just ignore it, don't look at them or don't look them in the eye they kind of move off.
>
> (Nasirah, South-Asian female)

When racism is deemed 'normal', part of the everyday, it has a far lower chance of being reported (European Union Agency for Fundamental Rights, 2009). Participants in this study noted that racism is so common that they engage in a process of 'grading' their experiences in terms of severity before deciding whether or not they should report. Herek *et al.* (2002, p. 335) argue that those who are targeted in a hate incident enter into a 'cost–benefit analysis' as to whether they should report the incident or not. Or in Foucauldian terms, the person attacked or abused becomes the neoliberal ideal: homo-œconomicus, rationally assessing their options (Foucault 2010). Here, participants grade their experiences of racism for severity: the more threatening or hostile the incident is, the more likely that it will be reported. If it is not so serious they will care for themselves as prescribed by neoliberal ideals. The state is seen as a last resort when it comes to reporting, not a resource that could be drawn upon if one required support as Jeehan demonstrates.

[W]here I have been called insults or bad words I would not call the police. I don't think there is anything they could. ... If something causes injury I will definitely report it, something easy [less severe] I will not report. I don't want to keep on going back to 4–5 times per month.

Fear

Participants also expressed a fear of reporting their instances of hostility to the Gardaí. This is unsurprising given the experiences already referred to above which may be compounded by policing practices engaged in within certain states abroad which at times can be lethal (Perry 2009). Jada, an Irish female revert to Islam, felt that some Muslim migrants 'wouldn't find the Gards approachable' because of corrupt policing abroad. However, in some cases this fear of reporting was grounded in past experiences with An Garda Síochána here in Ireland, as demonstrated in the examples outlined above and reflected again in the comments of a male Muslim participant in this study who stated that 'actually, I face discrimination several times from Garda' and as a result would not report his experience.

Worryingly, even when those who have experienced hostility are encouraged to report by other Muslims, the fear of repeat attacks from the original assailant and the feeling that agents of the state, An Garda Síochána, will not support them may result with reluctance towards making a report. Zaheen, an Irish revert, narrates the process of decision-making torn between advice, fear and the perception that her report will not lead to a successful outcome. A fear of reprisal and a lack of faith that any official action will be taken eventually wins out and she decides not report.

[L]ike he [my husband] kept telling me go, go, go and I was like what they're [Gardaí] not going to do anything why am I going to go there like I was just really, really scared and I thought ok, if I report it then if they catch him then he is going to come after me again and then like I was thinking ok no like they're not going to do anything it's just a waste of time.

(Zaheen)

This underscores the necessity for a 'safe environment' wherein people can report their experiences of racism with the knowledge that their security is paramount and the chances for repeat hostility are minimised (European Union Agency for Fundamental Rights 2009, p. 54). The rationale of not reporting to avoid an escalation in instances of racist abuse is not restricted to experiences of hostility but extends to contexts such as accessing goods and services as well as the workplace.

Samira, a female Muslim of South-Asian origin, explains why she, as a customer, would be wary of reporting discriminatory treatment to a restaurant manager:

[I]f the manager is just like their employee they're not going to do anything ... they'll just be even more rude to you ... I've never reported anything like that because you're never sure.

Similarly, a female Black African Muslim survey participant believes that if she reported discrimination at work it would affect future prospects: 'I believe if I complained it may affect my ability of getting another job'. Decisions of whether or not to make a report of discrimination include a consideration of the potential for a negative escalation should one report. Fears such as this mean that people are forced to live with discrimination (Poynting and Noble 2004, p. 15), forced to manage their experiences themselves, living the neoliberal dream. A central issue here is the current lack of any real outreach on the part of the various equality bodies. The 'rationalisation' of the state's equality infrastructure was a huge step towards privatising the care of those vulnerable to racism; again the limits of neoliberal intervention in the care of the social are clearly marked.

Practices of escalation avoidance are also compounded by the fear that if one reports to the state one may self-incriminate. A common factor that unites participants who expressed this fear is their immigrant identity (current or historic), common to many Muslims in Ireland. According to Jennifer, from Nasc, 'it does not help that the GNIB[4] services are attached to the Gards ... it doesn't create a positive experience for anyone'. According to Lynch (2011) upon reporting experiences of racism to the Gardaí, members of minority groups have in the past been asked about their status as an immigrant although this detail was extraneous to the event being reported, leading to a reluctance on the part of some to report instances of racist crime with undocumented migrants as an especially vulnerable group. This results in a situation where there is insecurity that if one should report a racist incident, and by logical extension any form of criminal activity, to the state one will instead become the subject of investigation to negative effect. As Aatif, a community representative, states:

> I used to try and encourage them to report.... The answer has always been no there's no point because they won't believe us or they'll treat us like second class, or rather than focusing on the incident they ask us for our GNIB card, they ask us for our status, and they're saying we're reporting a racial incident and we're being investigated on something else.

Also notable in the comments of Aatif and Saad is the implicit hierarchy in terms of who can and who cannot report experiences of racism to An Garda Síochána. Those described by Aatif who have a valid GNIB card are in somewhat of an advantageous position to undocumented migrants who have made Ireland their home.

> [S]ome people ... for example might not have you know correct documentation and they're fearful that if they go and report this thing to the Gards they're instead reporting themselves.... This also increases the fear.
> (Saad, a community representative)

This hierarchy is broadened further by Jeehan, a female migrant who is awaiting Irish citizenship. Only once she acquires citizenship will Jeehan feel empowered, secure enough to report her experiences of racism to the Gardaí without incriminating herself:

> I am always so hesitant to report my complaints to police stations but the fear of not reporting to Garda station will be much less if I get citizenship. I strongly believe that being citizen of this country will enable me to find my rights.

Research undertaken by the Migrant's Rights Centre Ireland (2011, p. 46) demonstrates that coming to the 'adverse attention' of the Gardaí for those in the process of naturalisation can negatively impact chances of obtaining citizenship. Thus to have rights, even notionally, one must first obtain Irish citizenship. Even if one does acquire citizenship, the fact that one does not fit the neo-WHISC ideal type of Irishness may nonetheless preclude them from fully actualising these rights.

It is my contention that the persistence of the kinds of fears revealed by participants in this study demonstrates neoliberal state governmentality in Ireland, directing those vulnerable to racism away from the state towards privatised 'carers'. As discussed above by NGO representatives, members of An Garda Síochána are aware of the issues in terms of barriers to reporting. The failure to address these barriers cannot be based on a defence of 'not knowing'. The intentional racism denial, combined with cuts to support for state equality bodies that are tasked with addressing reports of racism, evidences the roll-back of the state to outsource 'care' for anti-racism to the private sector. Clearly, the choreographed optics of high level consultations do not translate into effective anti-racism in practice, but remain as optics. Instead, the privatisation of anti-racism is evidenced in the manner that people are being conducted away from the state through the maintenance of feelings of fear and, as will now be further demonstrated, feelings of futility among those vulnerable to racism.

Futility

International research demonstrates that perceptions that 'nothing will happen' are common among those who experience hostility and discrimination, leading to feelings of futility that are significant barriers to reporting (Chakraborti *et al.* 2014; European Union Agency for Fundamental Rights 2009). Informed by past experiences and shared community discourses, participants here elaborated the perception that their reports would not be taken seriously, and, even if they were to report, there was a lack of faith that any ameliorative action would be taken. A male Muslim survey participant from the Balkans clearly felt that it was pointless to report instances of racism to the Gardaí:

> What is the good reporting it, what Garda will do about? I believe they can do nothing; I even have meet [*sic*] racist Garda, so I do not believe they can help.

Aalia, a female Irish revert to Islam, elaborated numerous instances of racism that she and her wider family had experienced to the point of physical violence. However, bringing her experiences to attention of the Community Gardaí in the past provoked such feelings of frustration and futility that she would not direct others to report their experiences of racism to the Gardaí. Aalia recalls:

> I called them immediately. ... The Community Garda rang four days [later] and within the time they were supposed to come down to me. I spoke to a community Gard and she said to me, 'For God's sake do you not get on with anyone down there?'.... That's what I was told ... so that was in 2009 and the last time I let my children out to play.

Aalia clearly demonstrates the results of neoliberal governmental practices in the advice she would give to other Muslim women, the process of conducting of those vulnerable to racism away from the state to privatised care in action:

> [T]hey have things ... up in [the] Garda station if you're a victim of racism call 1800 ... I'm going for what? There is no point. If any girls came to me and said this is happening to us I'd say go to an NGO!.... I certainly wouldn't say go ring that number ... because I did give them a chance and the racism came ... personally affected me and my children and my husband and it wasn't one issue, it was a ten years of it ... and it still goes on.... The Community Gard ... had a big meeting and [with] their sergeant and they said they'd do a, b, and c for us and nothing was done, nothing was done.... We had another incident on our road and I rang them again I was hysterical they were all chanting outside my door ... '2 4 6 8 get the Pakis off the estate', this kind of thing was going on and I broke I was so upset going in with my kids and I was waiting four days for the Gards to come ... four days!

When asked if she would encourage someone to report their experience of anti-Muslim hostility, Aalia reiterates that she: 'would probably feel like a hypocrite if I advised her [friend to report). I just don't think there's any ... I didn't see anything constructive help to me and my family at all'. Being taken seriously and having a perception that action will be taken can encourage victims of racism to report their experience (Poynting and Noble 2004). Effective action on the part of the police when faced with hate activity can reassure those being targeted and challenge the norm of hate activity. Through professional policing, trust can be built with groups that otherwise perceive the police as lacking sensitivity towards their situation, as demonstrated in Saad's experience outlined above and the efforts of the 'retired very senior officer' in his local community forum. These experiences, however, are not the norm.

The argument that binds the findings presented in this study is the omnipresence of a hegemonic neoliberal rationale that undergirds Irish State constructions of neo-Irishness and also the manner in which vulnerable minorities are to be managed vis-à-vis racism. Despite the good work of certain individuals and offices within An Garda Síochána that demonstrate the presence of multiple rationalities among the technologies of government, the overriding neoliberal logic has the desired effect. The resultant lack of faith, combined with the inability of NGOs to take direct action against perpetrators, leads participants to feeling, through frustration, that to get 'justice' they may need to take action themselves, they need to be self-reliant to take 'care' of the self. They need to be neoliberal.

In Chapter 5, I argued the Irish State is implicated in maintaining the dominance of a homogenous, historically informed construction of Irishness. In addition to the WHISC ideal, in the full light of the hegemonic discourse *de jour*, Irishness is now infused with neoliberalism constructing a neo-WHISC ideal type. As discussed, not all Irish people, in reality, fit this type; there are multifarious points of resistance. However, it is the discursively informed ideal type that is the goal 'we all should strive to attain'. A central aspect of the dominant neoliberal discourse is the primacy of the individual and 'care' of the self. Inherent in this principle is the belief that if you are subjected to racism then it is your responsibility to take appropriate action. Given state inaction, one is left with the choice of going to an NGO for care, just treat it as the norm, or take matters into your own hands.

Managing space, managing hate

The narratives of those who experienced anti-Muslim racism indicate that, in the vacuum left by the state in terms of addressing racism, Muslim men and women have developed 'coping strategies' to deal with these phenomena (Chakraborti *et al.* 2014, p. 51). One strategy employed by interviewees, already noted, is to refuse to respond, to ignore the perpetrator. This strategy can be construed as another means of preventing further escalation of the situation and is a common response to racism on the part of many (Ziemer 2011; Ahluwalia and Pellettiere, 2010; Herbert *et al.*, 2008). Responses of this variety are often infused with acceptance, i.e. an acceptance that the microaggressions of everyday racism will always be with us as elaborated by Sikh interview participant Kulvir: 'you have to tolerate certain amount of racism if you have to live in Ireland'. Repeated experiences of the 'everyday' sort of racism, while not always 'serious' in and of themselves, can have the effect making those on the receiving end feel as though they do not belong (Poynting and Noble 2004).

Left to care for their own experiences and exposure to racism, participants cope with the fear and anticipation of hostility by taking measures to ensure their own security, and also by altering and indeed limiting their use of public and commercial space in order to reduce vulnerability to attack. Zempi and Chakraborti (2014, p. 60) refer to the importance of managing space, recognising the existence of 'no go zones' wherein Muslim women may experience higher levels of abuse than in areas deemed safer that accommodate difference (see also Chakraborti *et al.* 2014). Self-management of space, both personal and social, also emerged as important considerations in this study. While these participants may be taking care of themselves, experiences of racism, either lived by themselves or shared by others through community discourses, impact upon the daily movements and lifestyles of Ireland's Muslim population, as explained in an interview with Arabic Muslim female Nasimah (it is interesting again to note the presence of community discourses and the message of hate crime in action (Iganski 2008)):

> [L]ike the first thing I do [is] lock my doors [of my car] even like in the town during the day and then like in the traffic light or something like that, I always close my window and I always shutting my door because, well, like I know it's never happened to me, it just like being ready.
> JC: Is that based on your own experience or have other people said things to you about it?
> NASIMAH: Yes, yeah other people. Like I remember there was this story about a girl she was doing her shopping in x shopping mall and it was like at seven o'clock like in the summer it wasn't ... in the winter and she's a doctor.... She was putting her grocery [in the car] two guys came they pull off her scarf and they start [stamping on the hijab] and they were screaming at her face, don't wear it again.

Poynting and Noble (2004) note that the public sphere, within which anti-Muslim racism is experienced, includes not just streets and parks but also hospitals and schools and workplaces. This strategy holds the possibility of limiting not just movement through public space but engagement in the broader public sphere, excluding people from equal participation in society, unless of course, they cast off their contrarian identity and become neo-WHISC.

> [T]here are small things which small decisions you can make ... you know while going outside ... you can avoid some streets, you can avoid some ... encounters with teenagers, you might prefer ... driving your own car rather than travelling by ... public transport.
>
> (Kulvir)

Similarly, Mona, a young Arabic-Irish Muslim, recalled how on the basis of repeated intimidation, she 'stopped taking the LUAS' in order to avoid hostility. Lack of confidence in the police and feelings of self-reliance in the face of criminality result in a 'strategy that has absence as its basis'; that is, faced with the absence of state support, communities may take action themselves (Sharp and Atherton 2007, p. 755). This is not uncommon. The absence of sufficient redress on the part of the state has resulted in some participants taking it upon themselves, directly or indirectly, to address experiences of racism. At times this has manifested in direct and risky confrontation with perpetrators of racist hostility.

> I was coming to the door [of the mosque] here and I felt something go past my head, 'Foom!!' ... it was a bottle.... I looked across and there was an Irish guy standing there and ... I said to him, 'Why did you do it?' I approached him, I actually approached him. I mean I was furious I said, 'What ... what are you doing why are you throwing the bottle?' And he said, 'You, because ... you're a Muslim.' I said, 'But why even if we're Muslims why, what have we done to you?
>
> (Aatif)

Sara fantasises about such dangerous and risky methods of managing racism:

> To be honest ... if I knew who assaulted me specifically I'd just get people to beat them up. The police don't do anything ... just kinda like ok we'll do something and three weeks later did you do anything? Oh no we still have to do this and that ... it gets really annoying.

Feelings of fear and futility demonstrate the manner in which members of Muslim communities are effectively denied care from the state. Although clearly vulnerable to racism, Muslim men and women are conducted towards managing their own care, which, as the findings demonstrate, can put people at great risk. The only other alternative is to go to a civil society actor – a privatised site – for care.

Managing care

Ireland has a history of outsourcing the 'care' of minority communities which can be traced to state policies and practices wherein programmes for government were premised on consensus between the state and a variety of corporate and civil society actors (Gray 2013). This policy of outsourcing the 'care' for migrants continued into the most recent policy document, *Migration Nation* (Office of the Minister for Integration 2008). The civil society actors that participated in this research provide important assistance to those who are conducted to them by practices of minimal 'care' which manifest themselves in ineffective state practices that fail (by design) to challenge racism. In recent years the state has cut funding for the National Consultative Committee on Racism and Interculturalism, thus shutting it down, and 'rationalised' the Irish Human Rights Commission, the Equality Authority and Equality Tribunal. The state may talk of anti-racism but in reality it is involved in a process of downsizing the bodies that can challenge racism, outsourcing the 'care' they could provide to NGOs.

Faced with an uncaring neoliberal state, Muslim men and women who experience racism are left with little choice but to resort to caring for themselves, embodying the neoliberal ideal of self-reliance over communal care, or referring their case to NGOs. As noted in Chapter 4, the European Network Against Racism Ireland (ENAR Ireland), an umbrella group for various Irish based NGOs, coordinates a third party racism reporting mechanism iReport.ie (European Network Against Racism (Ireland) 2015). The iReport system provides those who experience racist hostility and discrimination with an outlet through which they can have their voice heard or at least share their experiences. The aims of the iReport system, from the perspective of the NGOs, are telling of the current lack of substance in the approach of the Irish State towards anti-racism. In particular, they reveal the absence of data on levels, experiences and forms of racism in Ireland.

By reporting the [racist] incident you will help ENAR Ireland:

1   Understand how often racist incidents occur in Ireland.
2   Understand in greater detail who is experiencing racism in Ireland.
3   Understand more about the different kinds of racism in Ireland.
4   In some cases, if you are willing, take action against the people responsible.
5   Devise effective local strategies for combating racism.
6   Inform our arguments for stronger anti-racist policies at national level.
(European Network Against Racism (Ireland) 2013a)

Similarly, the Immigrant Council of Ireland (ICI) also operates a facility wherein one can make a report of racist hostility and discrimination. As with the ENAR Ireland reporting mechanism, the aims of the ICI model again evince the lacunae in substantive policies vis-à-vis anti-racism by the Irish State and the paucity of available data.

> The aim of the service is to provide supports and information to people who have experienced or witnessed a racist incident and to monitor the extent of racism in Ireland. The types of supports we can provide range from referrals to counselling if that is required, information about avenues for redress, support in making a formal complaint to an appropriate agency and information as to where to seek legal representation. The data we gather about racist incidents will be used to inform advocacy for legislative or policy change.
> (Immigrant Council of Ireland 2015)

Thus, in addition to receiving reports these bodies can also offer advice on how one could pursue their case, provide emotional support and also make people aware of any available legal options they may have:

> … from the NGO perspective obviously [we] identify and see what we can do as an NGO to assist the person who's making the report … to encourage the party to make the report.
> (Matt, representative of Doras Luimní)

> [W]e would have a hotline to the Gards and I would ring Dave McInerney … straight away and he would then, he would get, where ever it happens in the country he would get the local ELO to check it out.
> (Ken, representative of SARI)

NGOs provide an important service to those who are fearful of approaching the state for the purposes of reporting racism. Moreover, NGOs endeavour to fill the void of 'care' that the state should be fulfilling. Catherine, formerly of ENAR Ireland, explains:

> NGOs provide a support around racism that the government has got a responsibility to provide, but in terms of reporting racist incidents.... we know some people are never going to go to the state and there actually is a clear role for the NGOs ... that role is there no more than the responsibility is there, but absolutely for sure, if we look at the practice.... The reporting incident system went from the NCCRI with the closure of the NCCRI and we took it up ... you can see very clearly that things the government wasn't doing we did, and things that they had dropped, we took up.

Nonetheless, while acknowledging the positive role played by NGOs, it is important to critically assess how these civil society actors de facto allow, unintentionally, the Irish State to abrogate itself from the responsibility of 'caring' for racism. The wont of the neoliberal state is to outsource the responsibility of care for those who experience, for example racism, to privately funded, 'marketised civil society' (Gray 2013, p. 78) actors. State care withdrawn, NGOs populate the spaces vacated by government. But in doing so, NGOs effectively become an arm of governance, a means to govern at a distance without having to take responsibility to care for those vulnerable to racism. They are already being 'cared' for by NGOs, so there is no need for the state to intervene. This issue will become even more pertinent between now and 2016, with a serious reduction in the amount of philanthropic support for NGOs forecast (Crosbie 2013).

The lack of supports at the level of the state presented an interesting finding in that, faced with lacking institutional support, members of An Garda Síochána have themselves referred those vulnerable to racism toward NGOs for 'care'. Clearly, even members of the state apparatus recognise the problems inherent in the neoliberal Irish State when it comes to challenging racism and caring for the vulnerable. Catherine again:

> We actually had Gards come to us, I'll give you one example where a guy went to the Gards, really it was his family who was affected; his window was broken on a regular basis. So this particular Gard drives up and down on that street every day deliberately to show people that it's being monitored to give out that message. He said it's not effective; the windows were broken six times by the time they [Gards] came to me and ... said he was concerned for the person, implicitly around his mental health.... Would we have any supports to offer?
>
> [W]e made a criminal report and trying to follow it up and trying to push them to investigate it; push them to send the file to the DPP ... it was [certain Gardaí] saying you've got to keep pushing, keep pushing, keep

> pushing because that's the only thing that's going to change.... Basically they were saying that it was up to NGOs to be pushing that agenda.
>
> (Jennifer, Nasc)

An interesting, and indeed unexpected, finding is the manner in which agents of good practice within An Garda Síochána also utilise NGOs as potential conduits to push for broader institutional change vis-à-vis racism. As one NGO participant put it, to 'ask the questions that [serving Gardaí themselves] would want to ask but he can't' – this demonstrates again the contrasting priorities within the apparatuses of the state. In particular, the issue of criminal legislation in the area of racism has increasingly become an issue:

> [I]n the early stages we wouldn't have such a response around hate crime legislation from the Gards ... but I will say certainly in the last couple of years both at a local level and at a higher level there has been support for us to actually go and lobby on legislation, that bit around if it's a crime then there is something that we can do about it and if it's a crime it's a bit of a deterrent.
>
> (Catherine, formerly of the European Network Against Racism, Ireland)

To sum up, faced with experiences of racism and inadequate state support, Muslim men and women are conducted to the private sector for 'care'. It is important to note the positive function that NGOs can fulfil as an outlet where racism can be reported to and assistance provided. Moreover, the areas that NGOs look to provide assistance in demonstrably reveal a lack of understanding and an absence of substantive policies on the part of the Irish State vis-à-vis challenging racism. However, the supports that NGOs provide are precarious and subject to the vicissitudes of philanthropic funders. Moreover, these civil society actors play an important role in the neoliberal governance of minority communities, allowing the government to channel the responsibility of 'care' away from the state. The invaluable provision of advice and comfort for those who experience racism permits the state to relieve itself of the 'burden' of caring for those with identities that are contrary to the neo-WHISC ideal. This has to be challenged. NGOs will always be required as an alternative to fulfil a range of necessary supports when it comes to challenging racism but they are not a replacement for the state. They cannot legislate nor can they penalise racist activity. While they can inform policy they cannot *form* policy. The state has to take the lead in this area.

Discussion and conclusion

The findings I have presented here and in the preceding two chapters demonstrate the concretising of neoliberal governance in the care of vulnerable minorities in Ireland. Anti-Muslim racism is normalised in Irish society and this is met with a lack of 'care' on the part of the Irish State in terms of recognising and challenging this phenomenon. Consistent inconsistency has been the 'truth' of Irish anti-racism heretofore. This chapter, and the one before, clearly demonstrate organisational (in)consistencies in the policies and in the practices of An Garda Síochána in addressing racism and assuring minorities of their security. As discussed above, 'race' and broader forms of hate crime have a greater emotional impact than other non-aggravated offences or incidents (Iganski 2008; McDevitt *et al.* 2001; Zempi and Chakraborti 2014). As Nasimah's comments above demonstrate, in instances of racism/hate crime the person being targeted is selected on the basis of who they are, not what they might possess. However, there is a reluctance on the part of those who have experienced anti-Muslim hate crime to report it.

Trust is vitally important if people are to report their experiences of anti-Muslim racism to the police. Participants here and in preceding chapters have recalled negative experiences of interacting with the Gardaí, whether as a result of religio-profiling or through poor responses to previous reports. Negative interactions such as these leave an indelible mark on those who have experienced them and serve to discourage people from making reports, serving to foster distrust between the Gardaí and those who they are supposed to serve. Filled with uncertainty and a lack of trust, participants, to draw on Chakraborti *et al.* (2014), are forced to accept 'normalised hate' in their lives. This lack of trust is further informed by the fear of what might happen if one was to make a report, whether at the hands of the perpetrator through retaliation, or through secondary victimisation at the hands of the Gardaí. Others are more despondent; reporting for them will be an exercise in futility as no action will be taken that could ameliorate their situation. Distrust, the normalisation of hate, fear and futility result in members of Muslim communities taking steps to manage their exposure to hate, self-policing their use of space and limiting their exposure to risk – managing their exposure to hate as good neoliberal citizens. Moreover, faced with the evident neoliberal racism blindness on the part of the Irish State, those who experience anti-Muslim hate are directed, if they should so desire for care, to the NGO sector for support.

NGOs populate the spaces for care that are evacuated by the neoliberal state and these NGOs and their staff strive to support those who are targeted for hate in its multifarious guises. NGOs fulfil an important role and provide those who do not want to go to the state with a space where they can find support. However, it is argued here that the supports that are required to challenge hate need to come from the state if they are to be fully and securely resourced today and into the future. Moreover, anti-racism has to become part of the culture of the Gardaí (as a critical actor in the fight against racism) and indeed other state agencies if race hate is to be challenged. At the moment, however, the primacy of neoliberal thought dominates rationalities of government. However, in keeping with Foucault, where there is power there is resistance. The following, final chapter will discuss opportunities for change in the recording and reporting of anti-Muslim racism in neoliberal Ireland.

Notes

1 Reporting here refers to the reporting of instances of hostility and discrimination as defined above.
2 It is worth remembering that racist incidents not defined as a crime are only catalogued in the narrative section of a report made to the Gardaí. Statistical data are not available for non-crime racist incidents.
3 Religio-profiled is suggested here as a term to denote the manner in which members of religious communities, in this instance Muslims, can be selected and subjected to closer scrutiny by, for example, state security practices on the basis of identifiers of their faith – hijab, long beard or name, for example.
4   All *non-nationals who are not citizens* of a member State of the European Union, the European Economic Area or Switzerland, must register with An Garda Síochána and at all times have a valid registration certificate in the form of a GNIB [Garda National Immigration Bureau] Card. From the 19 November 2012 a fee for this card is €300 and must be paid by credit card, laser card or bank giro. This fee cannot be paid by cash.

(Ann Garda Síochána 2013c, my emphasis)

8 Opportunities for positive change in the recording and reporting of anti-Muslim racism in neoliberal Ireland

Introduction

This concluding chapter draws together the strands of the various arguments that I have been making throughout this study: the hegemony of neoliberal governmentality and the 'race' blind state; the role of racialising process and the prevalence of the pernicious phenomenon that is anti-Muslim racism; and the international landscape in terms of best practice when it comes to recognising racism and the opportunities this may afford informed policy creation. Arguably most importantly, I have presented the realities of anti-Muslim racism as lived by Muslim communities in Ireland. Faced with such experiences it is vital that the Irish State starts to seriously engage in meaningful anti-racism policies. Yet, as I have argued, neoliberal rationalities have seeped into the pores of belonging and notions of ideal Irishness at the level of the individual and of state practice. However, true to Foucault, I argue here that resistance is possible – on neoliberal terms. Thus, in addition to bringing this book to a close, I will present opportunities for positive change in the recording and reporting of anti-Muslim racism that I have identified on the basis of my findings. Before I present these recommendations, it is necessary to again present the theoretical and empirical premise upon which this argument is based.

Neoliberal governmentality: 'truths' and rationalities

In the neoliberal regime of 'truth', as rational individuals, one and all, we are endowed with the freedom to choose, to be responsible, charged with caring for ourselves, managing risks and developing our human capital. We are '*Homo-œconomicus*', entrepreneurs of the self (Foucault 2010a, p. 226). This primacy of individual care and responsibility takes on an additional edge when positioned in tandem with the neoliberal deployment of 'race'. Foucault (2003) perceived 'racism ... as the basic mechanism of power as it is exercised in modern states'; racism introduces 'a break into the domain of life that is under power's control: the break between what must live and what must die'. One of the central concepts at the heart of neoliberal governmentality is that of 'race' or, more appropriately, racism. 'Race', racism and racialising discourses are deployed as 'truth' to legitimate the manner in which the neoliberal state acts to expand both at home and abroad. Furthermore, according to Goldberg (2009, p. 334) 'the more robustly neoliberal the state ... the more likely race would be rendered largely immune from state intervention'.

The neoliberal state denies the importance of 'race' in the lives of those who are vulnerable to racism resulting in little, if any, real investment in measures that could challenge this phenomenon. In the place of policies that could explicitly address racist practice are platitudes of encouraging/welcoming diversity (Davis 2007). In the era of self-care, the salience of 'race' is obfuscated by the neoliberal 'truth', wherein one's failure to succeed in society is held not just to be the fault of the person themselves but of being their 'race', of failing to assimilate. The denial of the importance of 'race' allows racism to operate unmolested in society (Goldberg 2009).

If one experiences racism, they should not look to the state for care but to the self or a privatised provider of 'care'. The neoliberal state takes responsibility for racism only where it benefits a rational *telos*; calculating the costs and benefits of the 'care' of those who experience racism. I will return to this point below. For now, it is important to note the role 'race' serves to meet the neoliberal aim of fragmenting society with the aim of remaking the social as a collective of individuals. Racialised 'truths' present 'races' as naturally distinct groups; the concept of 'race' fragments the population that is the target of power, it is 'a way of separating out groups' (Foucault 2003, p. 255). These constructions draw from history and the present to 'conduct conduct' through social interaction. Racialisation and the construction of different 'races' is at the heart of the neoliberal state. Those who belong to negatively racialised communities, contrarian solidarities, are to be cast out from the neoliberal collective of rational individuals and are presented as a threat to the neoliberal way of individualised responsibility (Roberts and Mahtani 2010). Collective solidarity is anathema to the neoliberal ideal of individualism – they must revoke their communal identity or face the consequences. Neoliberal 'truths' promote expansion at home through the creation of more individuals through the process of fragmentation only to massify again under the guise of a manageable 'nation' of individuals. The process of expansion at home is matched by expansionist aspirations abroad.

In the contemporary era, predominantly Muslim majority states are firmly in the cross-hairs of neoliberal expansionism. This requires the creation of the Muslim as 'other' par excellence to justify expansionist aims abroad. Muslimness is constructed and presented as being synonymous with homogeneity, barbarity, atavism, misogyny and an innate inability to self-govern amongst other things (Kumar 2012). All of these racialised tropes are invoked in discourses that serve to justify military intervention with the aim of (neo)liberalising the 'other'. These constructions of the Muslim as 'other' proliferate in the media, the public, political and 'you and I' discourses, becoming in the process a 'truth'. This 'truth' of the Muslim as 'other' that legitimates the expansion of neoliberalism abroad, through proliferating discourses, presents Muslimness as contrary to neoliberal ideals of individualism at home. Muslim identity, despite myriad diversity, is presented as a monolithic collective that is contrarian to neoliberal ideals.

Neoliberal Ireland and anti-Muslim racism

Drawing on Giroux, I contend that neoliberal Ireland is an oxymoronic collective of individuals, a gathering of 'one-man [sic] archipelagos' (2008, p. 592). Membership in the neo-WHISC collective of individuals is contingent upon those traditional imagined markers of Irishness – whiteness and Catholicism, for example – but also requires the added 'quality' of being inculcated with neoliberal 'truths'. This contemporary manifestation of imagined Irishness helps to maintain the collective of individuals through the holding device of 'nation', clearly delimiting those who belong and those who do not.

Anti-Muslim racism operates in Ireland as it does abroad, targeting Muslim men, women and children who do not fit within historical notions of nation. Moreover, discursive constructions of the Muslim as the 'other' that utilise symbols of the Islamic religion, alert and empower those who would police the nation to fulfil their outsourced role. Central to the 'truth' that these would-be police have accepted as common sense is the perception that Muslimness is not only representative of some amorphous terrorist threat, but is also alien to Irishness – as it goes, one simply cannot be Muslim and Irish. Catalysed into action, those who fill the space where the state will not be seen to go, engage in overt racism to let Muslim men and women and children know they do not belong. Anti-Muslim racism operates to police the boundaries of the neoliberal Irish State, conducting the 'other' through subjugation by the 'rightfully' deserving population. Racial regulation is outsourced in the name of constructing the neoliberal nation. All the while the neoliberal Irish State engages in practices of 'race' denial, subjugating the knowledges of anti-Muslim racism in Ireland.

This study clearly reveals these heretofore subjugated knowledges of anti-Muslim racism in Ireland. Over one third of those who participated in this study stated that they had experienced anti-Muslim hostility in Ireland. The vast majority of participants in this study have experienced anti-Muslim verbal abuse. Taunts of 'Taliban', 'bin Laden', 'get that thing off your head' and 'terrorist' are a common experience. Muslim women reported experiences that held sexualised overtones manifesting as 'you're too pretty to wear that', 'are you open for business' or more shockingly in the performance of fellatio as a form of visual assault. Over one in five of all those who took part in this study reported experiencing explicitly anti-Muslim assaults. Hijabs have been torn from heads, niqabs have been pulled from faces, people have been punched and pushed, bottles and fruit have been thrown, people have been spat at and one girl was beaten so badly with a can of soda that it exploded on impact with her head. These are some of the subjugated knowledges of anti-Muslim racism in Ireland, manifesting as hostility, that target Muslim people on the basis of their religious identity which is presumed alien to neoliberal Irishness.

One in three participants in this study reported experiencing anti-Muslim discrimination. Religious identity was a decisive factor in their experience. Whether on public transport, at the job interview or simply distributing CVs, the participants' Muslimness is focused upon regardless of religiosity and the diversity of personal realities. Experiences of hostility and discrimination operate as a microgovernance of identity encouraging those who are members of the contrarian collective to become more like the neo-WHISC 'us', or face the consequences in the social. This is anti-Muslim racism in Ireland, true to racial neoliberalism, successfully outsourced.

Muslims in Ireland, as across the West, are a suspect community. Experiences revealed in this research demonstrate the manner in which Muslims in Ireland are selectively identified and profiled on the basis of their religious identity. This is despite the long and recent history of Irish men's and women's subjection to securitised processes of profiling on the assumption that Irishness represented a threat (Hickman et al. 2011; Hillyard 1994). Yet again, the presence of macro-hegemonic discourses and their effect on government are clear. Neoliberal discourses present Muslimness as synonymous with threats to 'our' security and 'our' presumed homogenous values. Apparatuses of the Irish State police Muslim identities through macro-informed discourses of Muslim as threat, which also seep into public perceptions to inform the micro-level policing of Muslimness in Ireland, a policing that differentiates along gendered lines.

The Muslim body, particularly of the Muslim woman, is held as symbolic of how not to be neoliberal but a member or the contrarian collective de jour. This study found that Muslim women are approximately twice as likely to experience hostility and discrimination on the basis of their Muslimness when compared to men. The issue of identifiability as Muslim is central here. As has been argued throughout this study, markers of Muslimness are infused with neoliberally informed negative connotations and act as symbolic referents that catalyse anti-Muslim sentiment. Indeed, differences in the experiences of discrimination across various domains demonstrate that where one's Muslimness is uncovered, for example in the job application or interview, differences between the genders become less salient. The gender dynamic is contingent on the identifiability of Muslimness. It is no coincidence that Muslim women reported being religiously identifiable at a rate of almost twice that of Muslim men and also experience higher rates of anti-Muslim sentiment in areas where Muslimness is read on the basis of symbolic markers such as the hijab.

These same markers of Muslimness also distinguish Irish Muslims from the 'real' Irish. Irish reverts are separated through practices of anti-Muslim racism which set them apart from those who 'really' belong in Ireland. Ongoing processes of creating 'nation' in state and public discourses, now with the additional character trait of neoliberalism, present Irishness and Muslimness as 'ab*norm*al' bedfellows, so incompatible that their collocation is often met with incredulity.

Constructions of Muslims as 'other', true to the Foucauldian perspective on racism, fragment society in order to control who should be cared for and let live and who should be let die. But the neoliberal project of racialisation also massifies Muslims as a homogenous threat so that it can then fragment these communities to become part of the manageable Irish nation through practices that police 'race'. This is a process of (re)asserting neoliberal 'truth' over those who, due to an increased flow of bodies, are new here or those who continue to demonstrate an alternative collective identity that jars with the neoliberal promotion of self-care, self-responsibility and freedom. As Razack (2008, p. 166) argues, the anti-thesis of the neoliberal idealised subject citizen is the 'non-citizen ... trapped within group based identities'.

Ireland and post-racial neoliberal governmentality

The neoliberal Irish State has a history of being consistent in its inconsistency toward racialised minority groups. One need look no further than the treatment of the Traveller Community to witness this inconsistency in practice. While the Irish State was busy preparing for the now defunct National Action Plan Against Racism, it was passing a referendum that realigned citizenship status along blood lines, engineering the Irish 'race'. We now know, of course, that the Irish State was never serious about challenging racism. Agencies that did so were the first casualties of the so-called austerity measures of 2008. The National Consultative Committee on Racism and Interculturalism (NCCRI) was erased effectively overnight and with the NCCRI went the only evidence that was systematically collected, albeit by a quasi-NGO.

Despite the efforts of the Office for the Promotion of Migrant Integration (2015) to obfuscate the reality and create a different 'truth', as has been demonstrated above, the manner in which 'race' and broader hate crime are recorded in Ireland is poor in the extreme, and experiences of racisms thus denied. Currently we do not have any official data in Ireland on anti-Muslim racism. Indeed the findings presented in this research are the most inclusive and comprehensive account of anti-Muslim racism produced in Ireland to date. At the time of writing only 41 racist crimes were recorded by An Garda Síochána for the first half of 2014 for the entire state (Office for the Promotion of Migrant Integration 2015). This figure vastly underestimates the prevalence of racism in Ireland but is not surprising given the inconsistencies present in the manner in which An Garda Síochána engages with minority communities, the lack of an anti-racism culture within the service, the severe under-resourcing of bodies tasked with addressing racism in the service, and the lack of legislation in the area of hate crime qua hate crime with the exclusion of incitement offences (Clarke 2013).

Not reporting anti-Muslim racism

Previous research conducted in Ireland has demonstrated the low levels of reporting of racist crime to An Garda Síochána (Browne 2008; European Union Agency for Fundamental Rights 2009; European Network Against Racism Ireland 2015, 2015a). The majority of participants in this study also refused to report their experiences of anti-Muslim racism to An Garda Síochána or any official body. The reasons people gave for not reporting fit with classic accounts in the literature and can be surmised under the themes of distrust, fear, futility and a normalisation of hate. This raises huge concerns in terms of the vulnerability of those (particularly undocumented) men and women in Ireland who can have no recourse to state support if they are subjected to human rights violations.

The manner in which the Irish State has policed Muslim communities has damaged levels of trust between these communities and the authorities, resulting in Muslim men and women not perceiving the state as something to be trusted. In addition to not trusting, some participants chose not to report their experiences on the basis that this is the norm, something to be tolerated in neoliberal Ireland, part and parcel of the everyday micro-aggressions one experiences if one is the 'other' in Ireland, while for others still reporting racism was perceived as a futile exercise and their experiences remain suppressed. Some participants expressed feelings of futility informed by past experiences with the state in reporting of racism that, should they report, 'nothing will happen', demonstrating the lack of substance in Irish anti-racism. Sharp and Atherton (2007) argue that if minorities feel they are not being taken seriously when they report a crime, they will lose confidence in the police and be reluctant to do so in the future. Participants related how they received a differential level of policing to the 'normal' Irish. By this I do not mean they received a standard of policing that met the needs of their community, but conversely they were treated as 'other' by members of An Garda Síochána. Nonetheless, some people do persist and turn to the state as a potential source for support as detailed by Sgt McInerney and Saad above. How a person is treated is vital if future reporting is to be encouraged.

Experiences such as those detailed by participants do nothing to engender trust between the state and minority communities in Ireland. Feelings of fear and futility if one should report a racist incident unquestionably demonstrate that anti-racism is not cultural in the Garda service. Instead, those who experience racism do not report to the state but internalise their 'otherness' and carry on with their heads down. Racism is normalised and the social-psychological impact this must be having on members of minority communities is barely conscionable. Racism is not a crime like other crimes. However, people who experience racism have *learned* to accept it as the norm in Ireland. I argue that this acceptance is the product of fear and futility, where it is perceived that there is no effective recourse to the Irish authorities for those vulnerable to racism. Instead, the vulnerable are left to manage their own care and cope with (the fear and anticipation of) hostility by altering and indeed limiting their use of personal and public space in order to reduce vulnerability to attack. The lack of substance in policing racism meets the requirement of neoliberal governmentality which restricts state intervention in the social unless it has utility in furthering the neoliberal agenda. Those who experience it are turned away from reporting to the neoliberal state for care and conducted to the self or the private market for 'care' should they experience anti-Muslim racism. They become *homo-œconomicus*, measuring their options as to whether they should keep their experience to themselves or report to an NGO. All the while the Irish neoliberal state engages in maintaining a facade of care which is easily unpicked as the following sections will continue to do.

'A lot of talk ... not much action'

The findings presented in this research evidence that commitment to address racism, including anti-Muslim racism, fails to make it beyond rhetoric. There are some instances of good practice. As stated in Chapter 2, I do not perceive the state as being a monolithic actor; there may be multiple rationalities at play within the apparatuses of the state. Evidence above demonstrates that there are micro-resistances within the apparatuses of the neoliberal state on the part of individuals who, albeit tasked with maintaining a facade of 'care', actually do endeavour to challenge racism in all its forms. Participants in this study, be they from NGOs or Muslim communities, were quick to praise Community Gardaí and members of the Garda Racial, Intercultural and Diversity Office. Both were perceived as being populated by passionate, dedicated, responsive and understanding staff. Indeed, there was a reliance on members of these offices by representatives of minority communities and NGOs. However, challenging racism cannot solely be within the remit of a select few Gardaí but has to be an integral part of policing in twenty-first century Ireland. This research demonstrates that this is not the case. Anti-racism is not cultural in the service; at best, racism is treated as any other crime, at worst it is dismissed and its victims criminalised.

A 'ticking the boxes' approach enables the perpetuation of an image of an inclusive welcoming Ireland on the international stage and this is vitally important if 'Ireland Inc.' is to be marketed. As is discussed further below, our safe and friendly society is a key selling point in our efforts to attract resource*ful* migrants. Another example of this box ticking can be found in the annual Diversity Consultation characterised by one participant as 'the annual farce'. The discourse engaged in at the Consultation remains at the level of managerial rhetoric, does not transfer into practice, and fails to 'filter' down into the culture of the broader Garda service. Inconsistent policing and the lack of understanding by members of Gardaí of how to record a racist incident are emblematic of the low level of priority afforded to racism by the state. The failure to follow the rhetoric of the Consultation day with substantive policy outcomes and broader initiatives has the effect of further pushing those in need of the assistance of the state towards self-care or care from privatised sources in the form of NGOs.

The neoliberal Irish State does not want to record racism, including anti-Muslim racism, as it fears it will have to intervene further in providing for the 'care' of those who experience anti-Muslim racism, contrary to the ideals of the neoliberal regime of 'truth'. As has been argued throughout this book, neoliberalism promotes the erosion and minimisation of state intervention for social wellbeing. Where the state does intervene, it does so on the premise that the intervention serves the ends of the neoliberal state. Neoliberalism does not simply talk the talk of laisser-faire socio-economics, the neoliberal state actively intervenes to ensure that market principles dominate in the social. The effect this has on social aspects of the state is that they are curbed, perceived only through their economic rationale. Their utility lies only in how they can support neoliberal goals.

What is required, among which recording anti-Muslim racism is one step, is meaningful intervention by An Garda Síochána to address racism beyond the level of optics. An Garda Síochána must recognise anti-Muslim racism and broader forms of hate crime and, in doing so, move from empty rhetoric to substantive measures. Furthermore, real change must come from management, be maintained by management and disseminated throughout the service as a priority. Making these changes will be no easy task for the Commissioner enlightened and brave enough to try. The Irish government is intoxicated on macro neoliberal discourses and is wont to roll back on programmes that are deemed non-conducive to maintaining the dominance and expansion of neoliberal hegemony. The neoliberal state promotes the creation of individuals, not dependents. The findings I have presented in this study are stark in this regard. However, true to the work of Foucault (1998), where there is power, there is resistance. It is on this premise that the following suggestions for change will be based.

Resisting anti-Muslim racism in the neoliberal era

Power and resistance are co-constituents in an almost permanent relationship. Power is met by resistance, power works on resistance, the absence of resistance means the absence of power, or at least that it is not as visible (Foucault 1998). While power is dispersed throughout society, so too is the possibility of resistance. When power arises, freedom does not just fade away; when power manifests itself it does so in the presence of freedom (Foucault 1998; 2000). Struggles emerge as a response to the effect of power relations associated with the control of 'knowledge, competence, and qualification', invoking investigation and inquiry into how 'knowledge' operates and permeates through society (Foucault 2000, pp. 330–331 and 347). Foucault referred to such movements of resistance as particular constructions of 'truth', and the manner in which our conduct is conducted as a 'counter-conduct[s] ... against the process implemented for conducting others' (2003a, p. 70). Researches such as this, working with those whose voices are silenced, can act as insurrections of subjugated knowledges, in this case of anti-Muslim racism, and provide a platform from which the aforementioned counter-conducts can be vitalised (Foucault 1980a). Foucault (2003a, p. 70) argued that 'the history of race struggle is a counter-history' against the dominant racialised group. It is time for a counter-history to the mythicised construction of a historically homogenous Irishness. It is also time for a counter-history that challenges the neoliberally informed racialised constructions of Muslims as 'other'.

Constructions of what it means to be neo-WHISC and Muslim permeate the political, academic, media and 'you and I' discourses. Yet I contend that they can be challenged through the collection of data that speaks to the truth of anti-Muslim racism in Ireland, revealing the levels of this phenomenon on a regular basis and providing a platform upon which the lived experiences of anti-Muslim racism can be exposed. I assert, however, that this will require an almost Faustian engagement with neoliberalism on *neoliberal* terms. As I have argued throughout, neoliberalism is hegemonic in the contemporary era (Harvey 2005); thus to resist neoliberalism requires us, drawing on Thompson (2007), 'partly ... embrac[ing] it so as to manoeuvre for more "progressive" positions within it'. In other words, to engage in a counter conduct (Foucault 1998) and turn the audit culture of governmental neoliberalism back on itself. In doing so it may be possible to focus the gaze of the state and international partners back on itself in terms of how Ireland does, or does not, challenge racism – in the name of competitiveness.

Ireland, as with other states in the neoliberal era, is in competition to attract skilled labour and thus must send a message that Ireland is a desirable destination to at least some migrants (Gray 2011). As the former Minister for Integration once espoused, 'We [nation states] are all competing for talent and labour power and must seek to make ourselves attractive in certain areas' (Office of the Minister for Integration 2008, p. 34). As a case in point, the Irish State is keen to attract resource-*ful* immigrants including many university students and medical professionals from Muslim majority societies.

The Irish government's International Education Strategy 2010–2015 (High-level Group on International Education 2010) seeks to raise the numbers of international students in Ireland by 50 per cent by the end of 2015. According to the strategy document, international education is 'an important internationally traded service and an important sector in Ireland's trade relationships' (High-level Group on International Education 2010, p. 31). The strategy document emphasises the benefits of attracting international students to Ireland. In the longer term this includes creating longer term advocates for 'Ireland Inc.', networks of influential actors who can engage in advocacy for 'brand Ireland' (High-level Group on International Education 2010). In the more immediate period, the document notes the targeted financial impact anticipated from the increased international education sector to be in the region of €1.2 billion (High-level Group on International Education 2010, p. 31). The importance of such revenue is not lost on Muslim communities. According to one Muslim representative

> [T]he number of Muslim students studying in Ireland ... these Muslim students ... are paying to the Irish economy €50m a year, and that is only study fees, let alone the money they spend on the living in this country. So it is in favour of everybody that people should be comfortable.
>
> (Sab)

One of Ireland Inc.'s unique selling points in attracting international students is the friendly and safe environment that the state purportedly has offer. This safe environment is held as giving Ireland the edge in the competitive international space for 'student farming' (Enterprise Ireland 2014; High-level Group on International Education 2010). However, as this book has made clear, the reality is different. Muslim communities in Ireland, including students, do experience anti-Muslim racism in the form of hostility and discrimination. Indeed, threats to Muslim communities have not gone unnoticed by governments of Muslim majority states. In response to the hate mail campaign discussed in Chapter 3, the office of the Saudi Arabian Cultural Attaché to Ireland, on 2 December 2013, sent an email communication to Saudi students in Ireland. The following translation details the concerns of the Saudi government as communicated to its citizens:

> Important notice:
> The Saudi Embassy in Dublin has announced that there are some threats aimed Muslim residents in Dublin.
> We advise all Saudi students and their relatives to take good care and stay away from suspicious groups and do not go to any inappropriate places.
> (Translation provided by Saudi and Libyan Postgraduate students)

Concerns related to incidents of racism, such as the above, have been shown in the Australian context to negatively impact rates of students willing to study there (Education in Ireland 2014a).[1] Racism, then, is a risk factor to attracting inward investment in the form of international students, giving other states a competitive advantage over Ireland; hence the emphasis on presenting Ireland as a safe environment for international students. This image of a safe and pleasant Ireland is jeopardised by hate mail campaigns and instances of racism meted out to Muslim communities. On purely (I repeat) Faustian neoliberal terms, this increases the imperative for the Irish State to make sure that anti-Muslim racism, and indeed other forms of racist activity, do not jeopardise economically preferred forms of migration such as student farming. To construct policies that could effectively challenge racism, the state needs data on the phenomenon to understand how, when and where it manifests itself, thus creating informed policy decisions.

One could argue that greater transparency on levels of anti-Muslim racism will result in negative publicity for the Irish State. However, substantive efforts designed to combat anti-Muslim racism could 'competitively' advantage the Irish State by demonstrating its commitment to be exceptionally proactive on this phenomenon, unlike other international 'competitor' states. Not engaging with anti-Muslim racism at the level of the state will not make the problem go away. Instead, resource-*ful* migrants will continue to experience anti-Muslim racism and disseminate a negative perception of Ireland that will circulate among their communities at home, resulting in Muslim students going elsewhere in the future. In true neoliberal terms, the cost of implementing these measures will have to be offset against the benefit that can be derived to the state and, in this case, the economy.

I noted in the introduction to this book the potential for tension between my argument for the recruitment of the apparatuses of the state and how this may conflict with alternative readings of Foucault. This is understandable and I acknowledge these tensions openly. After all, Foucault (1998) clearly presents the calculative, manipulative manner in which society can be organised by those in authority. As demonstrated in earlier chapters, Foucault (1998) argues for the regulation of the social body in the interests of government, with society increasingly at the centre of efforts of state administration and regulation. In the era of neoliberal hegemony, these processes of governmental regulation take on a marketised lens evidenced through discourses of efficiencies and performance indicators (Gray 2013). Neoliberal rationalities permeate into all aspects of social life and how to live (Dean 2010). Discourses of efficiency and cost–benefit analyses rule the day with governmental intervention in the social limited by its perceived utility to the advancement of neoliberal ends (Donzelot 2008; Foucault 2010; Giroux 2008).

However, Foucault also provides space for hope as noted above through his concepts of counter conduct (Foucault 1998); and the *'insurrections of subjugated knowledges'* (Foucault 1980a, p. 81; emphasis his). The argument I make here, engaging in a Faustian embrace with the neoliberal state, draws from this space for hope to argue to the apparatuses of the Irish Government the need for a full and proper engagement with anti-Muslim racism; commencing with the collection of data of this phenomenon. In revealing its presence, this book represents an insurrection of the heretofore subjugated knowledges of anti-Muslim racism in Ireland. Using the evocative language of racism we can use the raised knowledges of anti-Muslim racism evidenced here to argue to the state in a form of 'counter-conduct[s] … struggle[s] against the process implemented for conducting' Muslims as 'others' (Foucault 2009, p. 201); de-normalising anti-Muslim racism, turning the 'network of gazes' on those who engage in hostility and discriminatory behaviour towards Muslim communities (Foucault 1991b, p. 171). If the Irish State does not take substantive action we can continue to turn the gaze of those sources of resource-*ful* migrants on to the failure of Ireland to effectively address racism; the knowledges presented in this book play an important role acting as a lens through which this gaze can focus. On the basis of this argument, the state will have to play a central, positive and substantive role in challenging anti-Muslim hostility if it is to be successful in the neoliberal era.

I am not the first to argue for the recruitment of the administrative, regulatory apparatuses of the state to challenge experiences of exclusion and discrimination. Calls have come from various groups at times representing those subjugated knowledges. Moore and Hickman note how calls for the inclusion of an Irish ethnic identifier in the UK Census 'came largely from the Irish community and welfare groups in London … prompted … by the emerging evidence of Irish disadvantage and possible discrimination [inter alia]' (2010, p. 8). The rationale underpinning this argument was that the collection of data on Irish communities in the UK could provide otherwise unknown insights on experiences of exclusion and discrimination. More recently in the UK context, Chris Allen argued in a submission to the UK All Party Parliamentary Group on Islamophobia (APPG), 'there is a desperate need to establish an evidence-base around

Islamophobia. This needs to be addressed and it is something that the APPG should prioritise' (2011a, p. 13). If anti-Muslim hostility and discrimination are to be challenged, we need an evidence base to work from, both in terms of quantitative and qualitative data (Allen 2011, p. 13). Allen (2012, p. 5) reiterated the need to 'collect and collate' data on anti-Muslim sentiment in a submission made to the Cross-Government Working Group on anti-Muslim hatred.

In the Irish context, the mid-90s witnessed representative groups of the Traveller Communities in Ireland, such as Pavee Point, push for the inclusion of a question in the census that would allow for the identification of members of their community (King-O'Riain 2007). Similarly, in the middle part of the last decade representatives from diverse sectors including academia, the Traveller Community, Trades Unions, political parties and the now defunct National Consultative Committee on Racism and Interculturalism, among others, advocated for the inclusion of a question on ethnicity. This was done, as in the UK context, in the belief that the data provided would allow the state to 'track discrimination indirectly' and in doing so inform legislation (King-O'Riain 2007, pp. 524–525).

As stated earlier, the Irish State is not perceived here as a monolithic actor, it is far more layered and multifaceted. As King-O'Riain argues: 'the state ... is a complex actor, fundamentally racialised, but also containing within it ... even through the census, the potential to obstruct racial discrimination' (2007, p. 518). Moreover, data collected by the state through the census 'could be a tool for groups outside [of] the state to challenge institutional racism within state institutions and practices' (King-O'Riain 2007, p. 518). Clearly, then, I am not alone in making an argument to the apparatuses of the state for the collection and analysis of data, in this instance on anti-Muslim racism, in order for this phenomenon to be challenged. Muslim communities themselves have not entirely lost faith in the seeking recourse to apparatuses of the Irish State. The instances of hate mail directed towards Muslim communities in Dublin in late 2013 resulted with some community representatives raising the issue with An Garda Síochána. This is despite the racialised experiences elaborated in this book and offers hope for future community engagement.

While it is beyond the capacity of this study to ascertain the costs of recording anti-Muslim racism as a specific form of racism on the Garda PULSE, for example, the additional cost of collecting data on anti-Muslim racism would be miniscule compared to the economic contribution of resource-*ful* Muslim migrants. Former Minister for Justice and Equality, Alan Shatter, as part of a broader neoliberal governmental campaign of 'downsizing' the public sector, in the process of closing rural Garda stations, championed the need for 'smart policing' approaches (Department of Justice and Equality 2015). Utilising PULSE to capture data on anti-Muslim racism and distribute resources accordingly enables this smarter policing approach. True to the neoliberal zeitgeist there is a strong economic rationale for the Irish State to record of anti-Muslim racism.

The utility of data on anti-Muslim racism is not limited to the area of policing alone but can also be utilised to inform broader policies and practices that challenge historic constructions of Irishness, and of 'otherness'. Foucault (2003a, p. 68) argues that 'history is the discourse of power, the discourse of the obligations power uses to subjugate'. Acknowledgement of anti-Muslim racism by the state can be an aspect of a broader process of recognition of Muslimness in Ireland; part of a 'counterhistory' (Foucault 2003a, p. 69) that targets the 'truth' of how Irishness is constructed in the neoliberal era. There is a need for a new 'truth' of Irishness, one that is not bound by historically informed exclusionary practices of belonging. A counterhistory, whether catalysed by Muslims or non-Muslims, could reveal 'the dazzling effect of power ... [and how it only] illuminates one side of the social body' (Foucault 2003a, p. 70). This in itself constitutes another form of counter conduct that argues that Muslimness and Irishness are not mutually exclusive. Recognition of the experiences of Muslim men, women and children in Ireland, informed by data on anti-Muslim racism, can assist those who wish to challenge historically informed notions of nation, revealing the truth of how some in Irish society are exposed to exclusionary practices on the basis of racialised imaginings. In doing so, a challenge, albeit humble, can also be laid down to the dominant neoliberal regime of 'truth' to demonstrate that Muslimness is not just associated with 'over there' but is also a part of the here, the us.

Learning from best practice: recording of anti-Muslim racism

Data on anti-Muslim racism can provide important insights that inform the aforementioned counter conducts and the construction of a counter-history of Irishness. This requires practical steps in the collection, collation and regular publication of data on anti-Muslim racism. In this section I set out recommendations for positive changes in the reporting and recording of anti-Muslim racism in the Irish context which could also apply to a broader international context given the paucity of data on anti-Muslim racism. These recommendations are informed by the international models of best practice vis-à-vis recording racism elaborated upon in Chapter 4 and the contributions of retired Gardaí in this study. If implemented, these recommendations could create an environment wherein those who live with racism (and other forms of hate crime if similarly addressed) are encouraged to report their experiences to the police. The resultant data could in turn be utilised by state and public actors to challenge the normalcy of anti-Muslim racism.

1 Anti-Muslim racism must be recognised as a specific form of contemporary racism by the state. Recognition is a first step in building trust with Muslim communities as it demonstrates the intent of the state towards challenging this phenomenon.
2 Define anti-Muslim racism. Make clear what constitutes anti-Muslim racism. In terms of policing, states with a singular police force such as Ireland may find this easier to implement than for example in the UK where

43 separate police forces operate. In the case of the latter, uniformity can bring clarity of understanding.

3   Create and implement a specific anti-Muslim racism flag (for crime and non-crime incidents) on police recording mechanisms. In the Irish context, specific 'hate' flags (although underused) are already available on the PULSE system to capture Racism, Xenophobia, Sectarianism, Anti-Semitism and Homophobia. As discussed in Chapter 4, in the UK the facility exists to record hate crime on the basis of race, religion, sexual orientation, disability and transgender. However, a more nuanced understanding of hate crime must be provided for and, as such, a model similar to that utilised in the Netherlands would be more sensitive to the diversity of hate crime.

4   Make the use of such flags obligatory, as in the Swedish 'marker' model. In practical terms this would remind members of the service to be cognisant of the range of motivations underlying a crime/non-crime event. It would also go some way to bringing an anti-racism mentality into the organisational culture.

5   All police staff should receive training on how to record a racist crime/non-crime incident. The policing of racism cannot be left to select 'diversity officers'; policing racisms and broader forms of hate crime has to become cultural in the police force.

6   In relation to both crime and non-crime events, international experience demonstrates the utility of data stored in the narrative reports of crimes/incidents accessed through the application of specific search terms. Narrative reports offer an alternative means to capture those instances of anti-Muslim racism recorded incorrectly or not at all by police. Data derived from narrative reports also provide nuanced insights into how anti-Muslim racism manifests itself, alerting the police in terms of how a particular group is being targeted, where, when, how and by whom. The use of a combination of both flags and narrative is preferred as a means of generating data on anti-Muslim racism than either method in isolation.

7   Construct and implement crime and victimisation surveys that recognise racism as an aggravating factor in experiences of criminality. The crime and victimisation survey model deployed in England and Wales, for example, allows for data on experiences on various forms of hate crime to be identified, as well as providing disaggregated data on which groups are targeted for such offences. As an outlet, surveys such as this allow for a more comprehensive picture of racism to come to the fore.

8   Reporting needs to be encouraged. Members of minority communities in this study evidenced a reluctance to report their experiences to An Garda Síochána on the basis of a fear of self-incrimination or that 'nothing will happen'. Reports of racist crime/non-crime incidents need to be treated professionally and taken seriously by police officers. Consistent policing can encourage reporting, unprofessional policing and racist practices by members of the service must be challenged if reporting is going to be encouraged.

Conclusion

This book provides heretofore unknown insights on the levels and experiences of anti-Muslim racism in the Irish context. As has been demonstrated, the insights derived from the Irish context differ very little from those in the broader international context. Similarities are also in evidence in the manner in which Muslim men and women in Ireland live with their experiences of anti-Muslim racism. In the racism blind, neoliberal era, those who are the target of anti-Muslim racism are directed away from the state as a source of 'care' to either manage their experiences of racism by themselves and/or towards civil society actors who endeavour to fill the space vacated by the state. Ireland is clearly an exemplar of a state intoxicated by neoliberalism and the practices of Irish governmentality strive to fulfil the requirements of neoliberal rationalities as I have pointed out throughout this study. Indeed, as I have argued above, the contemporary ideal type of Irishness is one where neoliberalism pervades and informs how one should be an ideal citizen.

Despite this negativity, this book has succeeded in clearly identifying the manner and space for resistance and change. In line with Foucauldian thought, I have demonstrated the possibility for counter conducts and counter histories in the face of neoliberal regimes of 'truth' that scapegoat Muslims as a threat at home and abroad in the name of neoliberal expansion. I now want to end this book with the voice of one of those who participated in this study, Mona. Throughout this study I have always stated that I undertook this research *with* and not *on* Muslim communities. I feel that it is only fitting that the last words of this study go to a Muslim person sharing her previously subjugated knowledge.

> I experienced an attack with my friend on the bus in 2011, May 2011, basically ... we got on the bus from Ballymun ... we got on top of the bus in the really, really, front of the bus and we sat there just the two of us and then there was about seven girls, they weren't over 18, they were about 16/17, all girls. Seven of them at the back of the bus and they were just you know the normal, so they're screaming whatever, or singing ... [it] was at the time of bin Laden had just been killed not even ... a few days, and then am we hear them screaming things towards us, but ... we weren't really sure if it was to us, or just some general, but obviously ... when they said Muslim we kind of copped on that it was about us.... Then they started saying.... 'Are you upset 'cos bin Laden died? Was he your Da?'.... We just ignored them because I am not going to go down to the same level that they are, anyways, and [to] my friend I was like just leave it, you know, and then they kept saying more and more things, like you f'n this and you f'n that and stuff, because we're Muslim. .... So basically, they started screaming things, like they just started cursing at us and then I'm the type of person that would say something back, I would, but I wouldn't use what they were using, like in language wise, and my friend was about to say something, I said look don't say anything because we're going to be killed and actually, I have never,

I've never, never, ever ... in the 12 years ... I've been here I've never experienced anything like this.... Half way where the bus stops and swaps drivers, they [the gang of girls] started ... my friend said something back to them and that's what kind of sparked it as well, but if she stayed quiet ... then ... they came up to us..... We were laughing first, just by ourselves just me and her.... One of them got paranoid and she was like are you laughing at us and stuff like that ... she just genuinely wanted to say to do something, you know she wanted to get involved in some sort of argument.... We were like we weren't even talking [about you], we didn't even look at you know ... and she kind of like hit my friend's shoulder and then my friend was like, what the hell, so she kind of pushed ... kind of like get away from me like you know, get away from me, and then we came to [a stop] she went back and she started screaming other stuff, so my friend answered her back and then she can't remember, two or three of them came up again and my friend wears glasses ... got up ... took her glasses off and she threw them at me 'cos she just wanted to clear her face.... [One of them] kinda cornered my friend.... I was sitting down ... beside the window, she cornered my friend ... she hit her and the three of them were coming at her, and then the bus driver came up.... They were swapping ... drivers and he came up and he ... told them to get away from us but ... and then one of them ... started blaming us on whatever was happening.... He didn't say get off, he said go down stairs and ... one of them goes to him 'I'm an f'n ginger I'm Irish why are you getting off the bus for ... I'm Irish you shouldn't be getting me down stairs, you should get them downstairs'.... It was shocking, it was funny, it was shocking, it was terrifying because they were three times more than we were, three times, and more because there was 7 and there was 2 of us ... so basically they went down stairs ... but you could still hear them screaming from downstairs and then the bus driver [swapped], but he didn't tell the other bus driver what happened. Initially the problem was he didn't get them off the bus, technically he knew we were in danger and if it wasn't going to happen on the bus it was going to happen outside the bus.... They were screaming you know blah blah blah and they were at the back of the bus downstairs ... they were, just waiting ... they were more annoyed that he got them downstairs to go down stairs and not us.... You could still hear them screaming stuff and then they're wait until we see, that's what they were saying ... giving out and planning ... you know acting all gangster and stuff, you know 'wait til you see', and I was just like, ok and then we went down stairs and ... I realised we're not getting off until the next stop which is here in Dublin City Centre ... We got downstairs ... we were standing beside the driver obviously because we were getting off.... So they came up, they came up beside us and one of them was kind of like pushing off my friend ... one of them, at one stage said I can't wait to take a video of this ... they were giving one of them ... their bags and stuff, their jackets, so they planned it on the bus like they were getting ready on the bus.... And then am as we were getting off the bus, we literally walked no longer than no more than four steps, no exaggeration, I was in front of my friend and they pulled her from her scarf from the back and then and she [the assailant] started cursing how dare you say whatever what was said ... who do you think you are, and stuff like that you f'n this and you f'n that.... They weren't really after me as much as they were after my friend 'cos she's the one who actually said something back.... They pulled her back they got my friend and they actually they were trying to take her scarf off her head and am.... [Mona cries and we break] anyway ... so she approached me, there was about three of them at my friend at the same time and one of them was on the side holding their stuff.... They were kicking, my friend had a red bull can in her hand, they took that off her and they hit her with it on her head, with the can, and it was full like it wasn't open.... The can it actually exploded from the strength of what they did, and they were hitting her head and she got scratches all over here in her hair as well because they had literally pulled her scarf off, am one of them came after me, and for some reason I don't know why, I did but I had my bag on the front, it was like a school bag so I had it in the front and am, from the strength of the pull, the straps broke so one of them pulled it off me ... from the front and it was like the bag ... it wasn't a weak bag, it was a strong bag so you can imagine how strong it was the two straps broke.... I wasn't really concentrating on myself, I was concentrating more on my friend because I know that they want to hurt her you know, so they were kicking ... so her back was bent, actually until now her back is [still] sore ... she was leaned forward because they pulled her from the front and they were kicking her stomach and hurting her back and her head at the same time and at that time ... when she pulled the bag off me, I fell on my knees and but I got back up, I left my bag, I left everything, I went over to my friend and I couldn't actually, I couldn't help her ... [pause] and then a guy, and I can still remember he was Mauritian ... went over and he went in between the girls and he took my friend's head, in like he took her head in between his arms to protect her head because they were hitting her head so hard and she was against the wall and ... they were hitting him for defending her and he just took her away from them.... I knew my friend was really weak like she's very skinny, but she's weak as well, my friend was standing on like the edge of the kerb ... and then, all I see is her collapsing, she like am, she just start, she just collapsed she passed [out] she was hyperventilating as well, but she fell off from the kerb on to the actual road and then I got down on my knees I was trying to get her to get up.... They just, they were walking away ... they looked at her on the floor and ... I just looked up and I said, 'Do you see what you did to her?' and they said, 'We did nothing,' and they walked away they just walked away.

Note

1 I think it is worth reiterating the quote stated earlier:

> Australia's difficulty created by unfavourable media attention around alleged racism towards Indian students in 2009, has lead [*sic*] to a drop of around 30 per cent in applications from Indian students over the last year. This could be Ireland's opportunity.
>
> (Education in Ireland 2014a, p. 19)

Appendix 1
Methodology

Mixed methods research

Mixed Methods Research (MMR) relates to the blending of both qualitative and quantitative research methods at the levels of collection, analysis and interpretation and can span the entire course of a research study (Brewer and Hunter 1989, p. 28; Flick *et al.* 2012, p. 98). MMR developed from the perspective that social inquiry frequently requires more than just 'numbers' or 'words' and the belief that a deeper understanding of social phenomena can emerge by combining both qualitative and quantitative methods (Creswell and Plano-Clark 2011, p. 21). Traditionally, quantitative methods have been perceived as limited because, although they may allow for the generalisable research findings, the insights provided remain distal and superficial. Conversely, qualitative methods do not aim to make generalisable claims, but emphasise gaining a deep understanding of the social world (Archambault 2007, p. 8; Burke-Johnson *et al.* 2007, p. 115; Creswell and Plano-Clark 2011, pp. 9–12; Frankfort-Nachmias and Nachmias 1992, pp. 10–11 and 272).

An MMR strategy was utilised in this study in order to draw on potentially complementary research tools that, together, could provide a deeper understanding of the phenomenon at hand than either method could in isolation. Demonstrating the 'reality' of anti-Muslim racism through statistical findings was deemed vital for providing an evidence base on the effect of anti-Muslim 'truths'. Second, the qualitative aspect of this study develops and adds depth by providing an understanding of the subjective experiences of anti-Muslim racism and the perceptions and practices held by the various participants towards the reporting and recording of this phenomenon. Used together, the various research methods employed in this study, which I now describe, not only complement each other, but also enhance and validate the conclusions of this study.

Accessing the knowledges of anti-Muslim racism

The first phase of this study involved the distribution of a survey amongst Muslim communities across various locations in Ireland. The benefits of deploying a survey among the population of interest include capturing data on a broad range of bases and locations for discrimination. Furthermore, surveys of discrimination/hostility also provide an opportunity to gather data on issues such as racist hostility and/or discrimination that are difficult to capture as they manifest themselves (McGinnity et al. 2012, pp. 2–3). The survey instrument in this study took the form of a self-completion questionnaire.

The rationale for undertaking a survey among Muslim participants was to get a general level of anti-Muslim racism and rates of reporting of these to experiences. The survey was in three parts, the first of which consisted of questions on hostility. The second part of the survey focused on questions of discrimination. Participants were first asked if they had experienced hostility any time from January 2010 in the form of physical assault, theft, graffiti (home or work), damage to property, verbal assault, threats or harassment. Following Sirin and Katsiaficas (2011, p. 1535) emphasis was placed on ascertaining the extent to which people felt that they were or were not targeted/treated '*because they are Muslim*'. Thus, if participants answered 'yes' to any of these options, subsequent questions enquired whether or not they felt that this happened because they were identified as Muslim, and how frequently they had had these types of experiences. Furthermore, participants were also asked to indicate if their skin colour, cultural identity, religious dress, gender, and/or real or perceived status as immigrant were involved in their experience of anti-Muslim hostility.

In relation to discriminatory practices, participants were asked if they had experienced discrimination anytime from January 2010 in the following spheres: at work, looking for work, in/accessing education, accessing health services, restaurants, public transport, obtaining accommodation, accessing financial services. As with questions of hostility, if participants answered 'yes' to any of these options, subsequent questions enquired whether or not they felt that this happened because they were identified as Muslim, how frequently they had had these types of experiences. Participants were also asked to indicate if their skin colour, cultural identity, religious dress, gender, and/or real or perceived status as immigrant were involved in their experience of anti-Muslim discrimination. For both hostility and discrimination, participants were asked if they had reported their experience, and to rate their perception of how this report was received. The majority of questions offered to participants across all sections of the survey were 'closed'. I also included open qualitative comment boxes to provide all participants the opportunity to have their voices heard on their experiences and perceptions of racism and reporting of this phenomenon (similarly see Sheridan 2006, pp. 322–324).

Understanding the impact of 'reality'

There were two main aims for the qualitative phase of this study. The first of these was to add depth in terms of understanding experiences of anti-Muslim racism and practices of and perceptions towards reporting this phenomenon in Ireland. The voices of Muslim participants from a diverse range of backgrounds and personal histories were central to this process. During the qualitative phase I also sought to include additional perspectives to further develop my understanding. These included representatives from national non-governmental organisations that engage with racism as well as retired members of An Garda Síochána. The qualitative methods deployed in this study took the form of semi-structured interviews and focus group discussions. The semi-structured interview can be described as 'a conversation with a purpose', the aim of which is to get some understanding of a particular phenomenon through the participants' insights (Hennink et al. 2011, p. 109). Semi-structured, one-to-one interviews are particularly conducive for the discussion of sensitive issues such as racism as they give the participant an opportunity to share their story in an environment that is secure such as their home (Hennink et al. 2011, pp. 109–110). Focus groups differ from individual interviews in that they follow a format wherein multiple participants can interact in a flexible, moderated discussion on a particular phenomenon of interest. The goal is to elicit multiple perspectives on a given topic, using the group format to stimulate discussion. The interaction between participants can generate nuanced insights and greater depth on a topic than in individual interview methods, albeit contingent on the sensitivity of the issue (Flick 2009, p. 196; Hennink et al. 2011, p. 152).

Building trust with Muslim communities in Ireland

As I am not Muslim, I was very aware from an early stage that I would need to build strong relationships with Muslim communities if this research was to be a success. On this basis I endeavoured to undertake what Bolognani (2007, p. 282) refers to as 'high involvement' with those communities whose insights and experiences I sought. From as early as October 2010, one month into this research, I undertook ethnographic fieldwork to start building rapport with Ireland's Muslim communities. This involved a systematic process of engagement that manifested itself as formal and informal meetings with key stakeholders. All of my introductory meetings were followed by an email detailing the points discussed. The content of these meetings centred upon introducing both my research and I in an effort to build trust and win support for future stages of this study. I did not solicit participation at this early stage, the purpose of meeting was purely introductory, a first effort at getting accepted and reducing suspicion. Like Bolognani (2007, p. 284) 'the fieldwork was built on a series of activities that were not necessarily directly functional to the data collection' but allowed me to get noticed and accepted as a researcher. I attended as many events held by Muslim groups as possible, including visiting mosques during Jumma prayers or other occasions, sharing in *iftar* and participating in *Eid al-fitr* celebrations and less formal communal gatherings.

I did encounter suspicion. At one meeting I was asked if I was 'CIA', at another a person was reluctant to participate because he thought I was from the media (similarly see Dwyer et al. 2008, p. 121). The most unexpected manifestation of this suspicion occurred at a meeting that I had arranged to introduce my research to one particular group. I discovered upon arrival that our discussion was going to be video recorded. A camera was set upon a tripod in a corner of the room and I was asked if I was comfortable with this to which I agreed. I felt that I was being 'scanned' by the potential participants (Bolognani 2007, p. 283). Although initially surprised, given my research ethos of reciprocity I felt it right to participate. I maintained this approach throughout my research and feel that it was vital to building trust and the overall success of the study.

Hearing all voices

Muslim communities in Ireland derive from multifarious ethno-national backgrounds (Scharbrodt and Sakaranaho 2011, p. 474). Participants and key stakeholders in this study were sought on the basis of capturing this diversity as well as other characteristics such as: gender and age; geographic location; urban and rural considerations; aspect of Islam and levels of religiosity; and social class. Contact was initially made with representatives of Sunni, Shi'a, Sufi and Ahmadiyya Muslim communities in the main urban centres of Dublin, Cork, Limerick, Galway and Waterford. These locations were selected because of their geographic spread and the likelihood that they would have a greater Muslim presence (see Central Statistics Office 2013). These locations were added to later to include an even broader geographical range while also offering the opportunity to increase participation. In all, 14 towns and cities were targeted. Key contacts were identified in each through mosques and Islamic student societies and were met[1] with to discuss participation. I was successful in that all contacts agreed to help me with my research. The final full list of towns and cities included: Dublin, Cork, Limerick, Galway, Waterford, Kilkenny, Wexford, Cork City, Killarney, Tralee, Sligo, Ballyhaunis, Portlaoise, Mullingar and Cavan.

In the larger cities such as Dublin, multiple locations were selected in order to encompass the main Muslim sites and aspects of Islam across the city. It was vital that I engaged with representative bodies in order to gain validation for my research (Ryan et al. 2010, p. 8). It was also important that I recognised that not all such bodies are representative of the constituencies they seek to represent (Garland et al. 2006, pp. 427–428). I undertook a process of managing an 'inventory of the voices present in the research' (Bolognani 2007, p. 290) in order to ensure I reached a diverse range of subjectivities. Yet, I faced a dilemma of how to include more voices from Muslim communities without going through mosques and cultural centres. Indeed, it was the recognition of this problem from an early stage that informed the selection of the sampling method (discussed below) that was initially adopted. Thus I also developed contacts within Muslim student societies to include a youth presence; Muslim women's representative bodies to ensure their voices were heard; ethno-national community organisations from Muslim majority societies in order to reach those who may not associate with mosques or Islamic cultural bodies; and unaffiliated individuals known to me were also invited to participate in the research. In addition, I also established an online presence through the social networking site Facebook while also engaging in more traditional methods of raising awareness through the distribution of posters and leaflets that advertised my research in *halal* stores, university campuses and at a conference on Islam in Ireland.

Positionality

Garland *et al.* (2006, p. 433) argue that it is important for the researcher to be reflexive on the multifarious positions they hold in all stages of the research process. The research process necessitated that I, as a non-religious, white, Irish male engage with my own positionality as an 'outsider' and the manner in which this could impact on the research. However, it is important to recognise the fluidity of identities (Dwyer *et al.* 2008, p. 121; Siraj 2011, p. 723). Researchers and those being researched embody multifarious identities and a connection may be made on any of these bases be it gender, age, religion, ethnicity, or being a parent (Bolognani 2007; Garland *et al.* 2006; Ryan *et al.* 2010). I focus here on three particular aspects of my identity that were pertinent to this study: my faith, my gender and my ethno-nationality – albeit remaining cognisant of the fluidity of identity. I will discuss the role each one played in this study in turn.

Garland *et al.* (2006, p. 430) raise the issue of the researchers' faith and the impact it can have when it comes to researching other religious communities. I was raised as a Catholic in a liberal but definitively Catholic home. Over time, and particularly in more recent years, I have moved away from established religion. Nonetheless, like Bolognani (2007, p. 283) I made a conscious efforts to meet the religio-cultural norms of interaction among Muslim communities. Drawing on the ethnographic fieldwork approach I set about interpreting the 'shared and learned patterns of values, behaviours, beliefs, and language' of Muslim communities (Creswell 2007, p. 69). I immersed myself in the various cultural and religious practices among the Muslim communities that I was researching (Creswell 2007, p. 69). Whenever the chance arose I endeavoured to learn some of the broader norms associated with the various Islamic traditions.

Although I am not a theologian I did study the basics of Islam as a faith and gained knowledge of concepts such as *tawhid* (oneness with God) which proved vital for building trust. I was able to demonstrate an awareness of Islam and also to speak the cultural language. Indeed, in the case of the latter I did embrace the use of Islamic phrases such as *Insha'Allah* or *Mash'Allah* to demonstrate my own familiarity with Islamic terms. This was not done in a manner that set out to deceive potential participants into taking part in this research. Participants were never under the illusion that I was Muslim. I was always forthcoming with my religious identity. Instead, the use of the Arabic/Islamic terms mentioned above only ever materialised in a context where there was an established familiarity between myself as a researcher and potential participants. Indeed, I was cautious that the use of such terms with those who did not know me would actually raise suspicion as to my identity and intent to the detriment of my research. The use of these terms demonstrated my respect for religio-cultural norms other than my own, as opposed to manipulating participation or faking friendship. Nonetheless, the fact that I am of no-faith, something I always openly discussed, did not impede my interaction with Muslim participants nor did it restrict their willingness to 'let me in'. This was particularly important in relation to gender.

Siraj (2011, p. 723) posits that her position as a Muslim woman allowed her to gain a deeper understanding of women's perspectives on the concept of *purdah* (being covered) than would be possible for male researchers. For the most part I agree with Siraj (2011), however, her assertions may be somewhat homogenising and possibly restricted in their relevance to more sensitive practices such as covering. My own interactions with Muslim women demonstrated a range of subjective practices vis-á-vis male–female interaction. Given Islamic norms, I was initially unsure of how exactly to proceed in developing trust with Muslim women for this research. This required some learning on my behalf and an ability to understand not only religious norms but the fact that these norms vary between ethnic communities and, of course, between individuals.

In my initial meeting with two female Muslims I was bothered about whether to offer to shake hands at introduction. The women in question were young students and I did not know what to expect as the following vignette from my field notes demonstrates:

> I met the first Muslim woman, she was from the Maghreb and when I put my hand out she shook hands with me. When her friend, a Malaysian, came along I again offered her my hand but she just smiled and put her hand across her chest.

On another occasion I met with a sub-Saharan African Muslim woman who upon introduction instigated a very warm handshake. Over time I learned to allow the woman the opportunity to offer her hand first so as to not make her feel uncomfortable. However, this too could be problematic. In one meeting with an Arabic Muslim woman who did not wear the *hijab* I feel that my reluctance to offer my hand was not taken well and upon leaving we did shake hands. Overall, the meetings I had with Muslim women from diverse backgrounds and the relationships that developed exceeded my expectations. Muslim women's groups and unaffiliated individuals were particularly helpful and willing to meet with me and to distribute my research among other potential female participants. The range of interaction I had with Muslim women was also diverse.

Some met me on their own in cafes or cultural centres, or indeed in university meeting rooms, others met me with friends, at their place of employment and one female Muslim participant met me with her husband. The willingness of Muslim women to contribute to this research, I believe, was premised on the gendered reality of anti-Muslim racism and its significance in the lives of Muslim women. All in all my gender, although an important consideration, was not an 'absolute barrier' to undertaking this research (Bolognani 2007, p. 281).

Hussain and Bagguley (2012, p. 723) contend that 'matching' between the researcher and the researched along gender and ethnic lines can aid in the building of 'cooperation, trust and rapport'. Before going further it is important to remember that Muslim communities in Ireland are very diverse and this makes the possibility of 'matching' along ethnic lines while also capturing a diversity of voices virtually impossible. I engaged in this research fully aware of my positionality as, to quote Hopkins (2004, p. 261) an Irish, 'white, middle-class, non-Muslim male'. Many of my participants were Irish Muslim men and women, some were reverts to Islam, many others were of immigrant origin of different generations. As opposed to being a barrier, I found my ethno-national background to be an advantage given the shared recent histories of Irishness and Muslimness as suspect (see Hickman et al. 2011). This finding was shared by Ryan et al. (2010, p. 9) in their research among Muslim communities in the UK where they felt that a shared history as a 'suspect' created a platform of shared identity and served to benefit their study. This underscores the fluid character of identity and how the researcher may be read by participants; while some saw me as Catholic, some saw me as a member of a community that has being exposed to racialised constructions of the threatening 'other'. Overall, I acknowledged my 'outsider' status, particularly in relation to religion and gender, but it is important to note that I did not feel that I was always on the 'outside' but that my position as researcher was more fluid and contingent upon the participant and the research context.

Sampling methods: respondent driven sampling

I initially employed a Respondent Driven Sampling (RDS) method to recruit research participants. RDS enables researchers to gain access to 'hard to reach' populations by dispersing the research throughout broader reaches of the communities (Heckathorn 1997, p. 174; Ramirez-Valles et al. 2005; Salganik and Heckathorn 2004). Theoretically, it is argued that RDS provides the researcher with a sample upon which investigations of statistical probability can be applied. This sample is achieved through multiple waves of recruitment. All of these waves are tracked with all new participants being traceable back to the original recruiter or 'seed' that started the recruitment chain. This allows the researcher to compare differences in characteristics such as ethnicity and/or gender from the seed to the final recruit for statistical purposes (Ramirez-Valles et al. 2005, pp. 388–389). All new participants are asked go on to be recruiters for the study and are incentivised, normally monetarily, to participate *and* recruit (Heckathorn 1997, p. 178; Ramirez-Valles et al. 2005, pp. 393–394). RDS is similar to a snowball sampling method but the problem of bias in the selection of the original participant or seed by the researcher is removed, resulting in a sample that should reflect the diversity of the population in question (Heckathorn 1997, p. 178; Salganik and Heckathorn 2004, pp. 205–206). The main advantage and attraction of RDS for this study was the ability to reach diverse participants and locations in order to gain insights on the effects of 'truth' on Muslim communities. However, there were disadvantages.[2]

From deployment in September 2011, RDS had limited success in recruiting participants. Although strong relationships facilitated the distribution of the survey, the response rate did not surpass 30 per cent. Furthermore, recruitment failed to surpass two 'waves' and I realised that the RDS model was not delivering on the diversity I had hoped for. I feel that the overriding reason for failing to develop beyond two waves is due to the lack of an incentive to encourage participation, as is usually deployed in the RDS approach. Discussions with university colleagues who have recently employed RDS noted the importance of utilising an incentive to stimulate recruitment and participation. The reason for not utilising an incentive in this study centred predominantly on research ethics, resource limitations and cultural sensitivities. I did not have access to the kinds of monetary resources larger studies can offer to recruit participants. I was concerned that the use of an incentive could result in the coercion of participants. On the other hand, I felt that it would be culturally inappropriate to offer some form of lottery ticket for assistance in recruiting participants. Gambling is forbidden in Islam and on that basis I refused to entertain any thought of offering this form of incentive. The fact that RDS was not working necessitated that I move my sampling to a contingency strategy.

Snowball sampling

From January 2012, a conventional snowball sampling method was employed. According to Hennink *et al.* (2011, p. 100) snowball sampling is advantageous as, like RDS it 'is a method of recruitment particularly suitable for identifying ... "hidden" population groups'. Unlike RDS, snowball sampling can be problematic in that it may lead to the amplification of one group of similar voices from within a community(ies). However, I overcame this problem by having already gained access to a diverse range of contacts with Muslim communities for the deployment of RDS. The diversity of Muslim communities in Ireland necessitated that I recruit a diverse range of seeds so that no one voice would dominate. Muslims from South-Asian, South Asian–British, Sub-Saharan African, North-African, Middle Eastern Arab, Malaysian, and Irish all acted as seeds. This diverse group included not only Muslim men but also Muslim women, and representatives from all aspects of Islam in Ireland were represented including Sunni, Shi'a, Sufi and also the Ahamdiyya.

On the basis of maintaining ethical principles of confidentiality and voluntarism, I did not conduct a standard snowball method where participants would provide details of potential new contacts (see Siraj 2011). Instead I continued with the model I used in RDS and asked existing seeds to distribute the research instrument among friends. The move to a more traditional form of snowball sampling facilitated distribution of the research instrument online among seeds' email lists. The move to snowball sampling proved successful. In December 2011, 124 people had completed the survey via RDS and new participants were not forthcoming. By the end of June 2012, 323 people had taken part. The composition of the final survey sample was very diverse and included participants from 51 different countries of birth with multifarious national and ethnic identities.[34] In terms of gender, 49 per cent of participants were female and 51 per cent male, remarkably close to the gender distribution of the last Census (Central

Appendix 1 159

Statistics Office 2012). Finally, in terms of age, there was a relatively even representation from each of the categories provided in the survey. The highest represented age group was that of the 25 to 35 year old category.[5]

Purposive sampling

The findings from the first phase of fieldwork, in keeping with the MMR design, informed the sampling decisions for the predominantly qualitative phase (Burke-Johnson *et al.* 2007, p. 115). Purposive sampling directs the researcher towards recruiting participants that hold a particular relevance to the study, be it identity, personal experiences and/or geographical location (Creswell 2007, p. 125; Mythen *et al.* 2009, p. 741; Silverman 2001, p. 250). The sampling of Muslim participants was informed by three issues in particular. First, I wanted to elucidate the differences in experiences of anti-Muslim racism and reporting perceptions/practices between Muslim women and Muslim men. Second, the experiences of Irish Muslims were also of particular interest given their place somewhere between two communities in the public mind-set. Third, some particular individuals of interest who participated in the study or who became known to me in the course of my research were asked to take part. For example, I became aware of a Sikh male and two Muslim women in different parts of the country who had experienced particularly insightful instances of anti-Muslim racism and I felt it was important to hear their voices.

Upon commencing the qualitative phase I also moved to include members of An Garda Síochána who, it was envisaged, would allow the emergence of new insights on the recording of anti-Muslim racism by the state. A formal request for access to serving Gardaí was submitted in June 2012 but this was subsequently denied for reasons unknown. This was a setback but it was not insurmountable. I decided not to reapply for research access to the Gardaí and an alternative plan was devised which would involve recruiting recently retired members of An Garda Síochána. Additionally, I decided to approach representatives of selected Non-Governmental Organisations (NGOs) operating in the field of anti-racism who also liaise with members of the Garda service. In both cases a purposive sampling method was deployed. Retired Gardaí from various ranks were identified through third parties. Based on established contacts I was also able to interview representatives from five different NGOs based in Ireland and one former representative of a Muslim NGO in the UK. The representatives of these NGOs know the workings of the state vis-á-vis racism and I felt that interviewing representatives of such groups, in addition to the former Gardaí, would provide the next best thing to gaining direct access to Garda systems.

Phase one: self-completion questionnaire

The first phase of this study involved the distribution of a self-completion questionnaire amongst Muslim communities across various locations in Ireland. The distribution of the questionnaire commenced in September 2011. In keeping with the RDS sampling method each seed participant was given a limited number (seven) of questionnaires in order to help generate a more diverse sample. Each seed was asked to complete one questionnaire themselves and distribute the remainder among their social circle (to men and women) who in turn were directed on how to contact me in order to become seeds themselves. By the end of December 2011, just over 120 people had taken part in the survey; in January 2012 I decided to implement a conventional snowball sampling method in order to increase participation as detailed above.

In addition to changing the sampling method I also placed a greater emphasis on the use of the online version of the self-completion questionnaire. The online survey was identical to the hardcopy distributed earlier and existing contacts agreed to distribute this electronic version via a specially constructed email that I forwarded on to them. Distributing a survey online is not without its disadvantages. To begin with, not everyone will have access to the internet and of those who are online, they may simply choose to ignore the email containing the link to the survey. There is also the risk that some participants may make multiple replies (Bryman 2012, p. 677). I was cognisant of these limitations throughout this phase of the study. In particular, I monitored online responses in terms of personal characteristics, types of experiences and Internet Service Provider addresses of participants taking part to ensure, as much as possible, that no one was completing the survey on multiple occasions; I am confident that this did not occur.

The disadvantages of online distribution were offset by the advantages, especially for studies such as this that were limited in resources. Some of the key advantages of distributing a survey online include: lower costs; potentially faster response turnaround times; and the possibility for broader distribution (Bryman 2012, p. 676). Each of these advantages encouraged me to distribute the survey online. The results of doing so were very positive. By June 2012, 323 Muslim men and women had taken part in the study. The levels of experience and reporting of anti-Muslim racism, combined with the qualitative insights from the first phase of fieldwork, informed the next stage.

Phase two: discussions with a purpose

The second phase of fieldwork commenced in June 2012. In keeping with the MMR design of this study, qualitative methods were deployed to complement and develop the findings from the previous primarily quantitative stage (Creswell and Plano-Clark 2011, p. 12; Greene *et al.* 1989, p. 256; Jick 2008, pp. 108–110). Initially, the focus of this second phase was premised on working with Muslim communities in order to elaborate their experiences of anti-Muslim racism, and practices and perceptions towards reporting these experiences to the state. However, I also sought to gain an understanding of state practices through the perspectives of retired Gardaí and NGO representatives. Overall 34 people took part in this phase of the study, including NGO representatives and retired Gardaí. These participants were spread across focus groups (three) and semi-structured interviews (19). Focus groups and interviews lasted between 30 minutes and over two hours depending on the participant. All interviews were recorded with one exception, where written notes were taken instead. This interview was 'member checked' in order to ensure that I had captured the participant's perspective accurately (Creswell 2007, pp. 208–209).

There were different rationales for the two groups that participated in the qualitative phase of this study. My discussions with Muslim men (six plus one Sikh male) and women (16) were conducted with the purpose of deepening my understanding of anti-Muslim racism in Ireland and, in particular, experiences of and perceptions toward reporting this phenomenon to the state. The points of interest I had prepared for my initial aide-memoire were derived from the analysis of the first phase of this study (Bryman 2012, p. 471). Of particular interest were the experiences and perceptions of Muslim women and also of Irish reverts to Islam (six reverts took part). My initial aide-memoire gradually developed over time to include more nuanced points that were raised by participants. I ceased the qualitative phase with Muslim participants when I felt I had reached 'saturation' (Hennink *et al.* 2011, pp. 88–90). The rationale for interviewing retired members of An Garda Síochána and representatives from NGOs was essentially to get an 'insiders' perspective on how racism, including anti-Muslim racism, is recorded by the state. The content of my discussions with retired Gardaí was premised on their knowledge and experiences of anti-racism policing within the Garda organisation. The ranks of the retired Gardaí that participated varied to include: one who left the service within his first year of service as a probationer; a retired local Garda in charge of Community Policing for his district; and a retired Garda Inspector; and one very senior officer who chose not to reveal his rank. The three latter retirees had over 30 years service each. The insights they provided were incredibly valuable for this study. The contributions of NGO representatives were also of tremendous value as they provided an almost 'fly on the wall' perspective of Garda practice. The content of the discussions with NGO representatives focused on their interactions with members of An Garda Síochána and the services' approach, or lack thereof, towards tackling racism.

Notes

1 The Muslim contact in Cavan discussed the research with me over the telephone and was not met in person. This was based on his insistence that I not travel during late winter.
2 For a brief discussion of statistical theoretical disadvantages see Salganik and Heckathorn 2004, p. 230.
3 Participants were asked to self-identify their ethnic identity in the following open question: 'How would you describe your cultural identity? (For example your nationality may be Pakistani but your cultural identity may be Pashtun)'.
4 Participants were also asked to self-identify their nationality through an open question: 'What is your nationality? (include dual nationalities).'
5 Participants were offered the following age group choices: 18–24; 25–35; 36–45; 46–55; 56–65; 66–75; 76 and over.

Appendix 2

Hate mail sent to Muslim communities in Dublin, November 2013

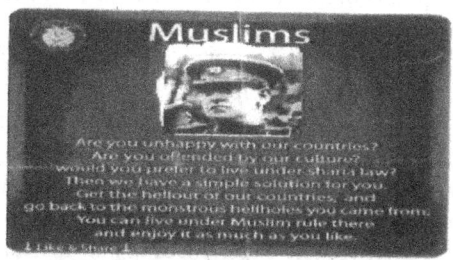

WE ARE THE DEFENDERS OF IRELAND AND WE TAKE OFFENCE OF MUSLIMS IN OUR COUNTRY , WE WILL DEFEND THIS COUNTRY BY ANY MEANS AGAINST THE EXPANSION OF THE MUSLIM FAITH .
WE ARE READY AS THE TRUE HOLDERS OF THE IRISH PEOPLES HERITAGE AND HISTORY TO USE WHATEVER POWERS WE NEED TO STOP YOU THE MUSLIM PEOPLE WHO HAVE NO RIGHT TO BE ON OUR ISLAND .
WE WILL ATTACK ANY MUSLIM MAN WOMEN AND CHILD THAT ENTERS ANY MOSQUE IN IRELAND AND ESPECIALLY IF THE NEW LARGER MOSQUE IS BUILT IN NORTH DUBLIN AND OUR CHILDREN WILL ATTACK YOURS IN SCHOOLS , MUSLIMS HAVE NO RIGHT TO REMAIN IN IRELAND , THE IRISH PEOPLE ARE NOT HAPPY WITH YOUR PRESENCE IN THIS COUNTRY WHICH BELONGS TO THE TRUE IRISH PEOPLE.
JUST BECAUSE SOME SAD POLITICIONS BACK YOU BEING HERE THEY HAVE NEVER SPOKEN FOR THE MAJORITY OF IRISH PEOPLE , ALL THE LEADERS CAN SHAKE HANDS AS MUCH AS THEY WANT BUT THE TRUE FACT REMAINS THE IRISH PEOPLE DO NOT WANT YOU HERE AND WE ARE NOW TASKED TO MAKE SURE YOU AND YOUR CHILDREN BECOME AWARE HOW LITTLE WE WANT YOU HERE .
YOU HAVE NEVER SHOWN ANY INTEGRATION IN ANY COUNTRY AND THIS IS EVIDENT BY HUGE WALLS AND GATES AROUND THE MOSQUES .
MUSLIM TAXI DRIVERS ARE BEING ATTACKED NOT FOR MONEY BUT BECAUSE THEY COMPLAINED ABOUT CHRISTIAN STATUES AT TAXI RANKS UP AND DOWN THE COUNTRY .
HOW DARE MUSLIMS COMPLAIN IN THIS COUNTRY THAT IS NOT THEIRS , HOW DARE YOU MAKE HOSPITALS REMOVE CHRISTIAN STATUES , YOU TELL US IN OUR OWN COUNTRY THAT IT IS US WHO NEEDS TO DO MORE ON INTEGRATION WHEN IT IS THE MUSLIM PEOPLE WHO ARE IN OUR COUNTRY .
WE WILL DEFEND OUR CULTURE AT ANY COST , WILL WILL DEFEND OUR CHRISTIAN FAITH AT ANY COST AND WILL WILL ATTACK ANY MUSLIM OR PERSON WE FEEL IS MUSLIM .
YOUR TIME HERE WILL NOW BECOME DANGERIOUS AND ALL BECAUSE YOU ARE TRYING TO CHANGE US .
YOUR VERY PRESENCE IN OUR COUNTRY IS DESTROYING OUR HERITAGE AND CULTURE AND WE ARE CALLING ON OUR COUNTRIES PEOPLE TO ATTACK ANY MUSLIM THEY COME ACROSS IN SHOPS ,TAXI'S , AT MOSQUES OR ANY OTHER PLACE THEY COME ACROSS THEM.
ANYONE SEEN WEARING A VAIL OR HIJAAB WILL BE SEVERLY DELT WITH .
OUR GOVERNMENT ARE ACTING DUMB TO THE TRUE INTENTIONS OF MUSLIMS BUT MANY IRISH PEOPLE TO WHICH MUSLIMS ARE NOT ARE FULLY AWARE OF WHAT YOU ARE AIMING FOR .
THIS LAND BELONGS TO THE CHRISTIAN FAITH AND WE WILL NOT ALLOW YOU TO TURN IT INTO A MUSLIM COUNTRY .
PEOPLE WHO HAVE BEEN MADE A CITIZEN ARE NOT IRISH , THEY HAVENT PLAID ANY PART OF OUR HISTORY , THEY WERE NOT HERE IN THE 1920'S , 1916 OR EVENTS SUCH AS THE FAMINE.
OUR GOVERNMENT IS INTENT ON FORCING IRISH PEOPLE TO LEAVE THE COUNTRY AND ALLOWING IT TO BE FILLED BY SCUM SUCH AS MUSLIMS BUT NOW WE ARE READY TO DEFEND OUR COUNTRY FOR THE MEN WHO DIED FIGHTING FOR OUR FREEDOM , WHERE WERE ANY MUSLIMS PRIOR TO 1959 ? THEY WERE NOT HERE HELPING US THE IRISH PEOPLE , YOU ARE HEREBY WARNED WE WILL ATTACK ALL MUSLIMS AND IF SOME DIE WE HOPE YOU BURN IN HELL .
WE KNOW THAT THERE IS NOTHING THE GOVERNMENT OR GARDAI CAN DO TO STOP US NOMATTER HOW MUCH YOU GO RATTING TO THEM , WE TRUSTED OUR GOVERNMENT TO STRENGTHEN OUR BOARDERS BUT THEY FAILED THE IRISH PEOPLE .
JUST REMEMBER THERE ARE MORE OF US AND WE HAVE MORE GUNS THAN YOU WILL EVER SEE.
A MOSQUE AND MUSLIMS ARE THE DEVIL AND A LEGITIMATE TARGET AND WE WILL ATTACK .
WE WILL NOT ALLOW YOU TO TAKE OVER AREAS LIKE YOU HAVE IN THE UK , FRANCE, GERMANY .

Bibliography

Abbas, T. (2011) 'Islamophobia in the United Kingdom: Historical and contemporary political and media discourses in the framing of 21 century anti-Muslim racism', in Esposito, J.L. and Kalin, I. (eds) *Islamophobia: The Challenge of Pluralism in the 21 Century*, Oxford and New York: Oxford University Press, 63–77.

Agresti, A. and Finlay, B. (2009) *Statistical Methods for the Social Sciences*, 4th edn, Upper Saddle River New Jersey: Pearson Prentice Hill.

Ahluwalia, M.K. and Pellettiere, L. (2010) 'Sikh Men Post-9/11: Misidentification, discrimination, and "coping"', *Asian American Journal of Psychology*, 1(4), 303–314.

Al-Amoudi, I. (2007) 'Reviewing Foucault's Social Onotology', *Organisation*, 14(4), 543–563.

Al-Amoudi, I. and Willmott, H. (2011) 'Where Constructionism and Critical Realism Converge: Interrogating the domain of epistemological relativism', *Organisation Studies*, 32(1), 27–46.

Allen, C. (2010) *Islamophobia*, Farnham: Ashgate Publishing.

Allen, C. (2010a) 'Fear and Loathing: The political discourse in relation to Muslims and Islam in the British contemporary setting', *Politics and Religion*, 4(2), 221–235.

Allen, C. (2011) *Written Submission to the re-launched All Party Parliamentary Group on Islamophobia*, available online at http://wallscometumblingdown.files.wordpress.com/2012/10/chrisallen-written-evidence-appg-launch-nov-2011.pdf (accessed 2 April 2014).

Allen, C. (2012) *Cross-Government Working Group on anti-Muslim Hatred: Scoping Exercise Submission*, available online at http://wallscometumblingdown.files.wordpress.com/2012/10/chrisallen-cgwgscopingexercise-feb2012.pdf (accessed 2 April 2014).

Allen, C. (2013) 'Passing the Dinner Table Test: Retrospective and prospective approaches to tackling Islamophobia in Britain', *Sage Open*; 3, 1–10.

Allen, C. (2014) 'New Labour Governmental Policies to Influence and Challenge Islam in Contemporary Britain: A Case Study on the National Muslim Women's Advisory Group's Theology Project', *Social Sciences Directory*, 3(1).

Allen, C. and Nielsen, J. (2002) 'Summary Report on Islamophobia in the EU after 11 September 2001', available online at http://fra.europa.eu/fraWebsite/attachments/Synthesis-report_en.pdf (accessed 10 September 2010).

Allen, K. (2009) *Ireland's Economic Crash: A radical agenda for change*, Dublin: The Liffey Press.

Ameli, S.R., Merali, A. and Shahghasemi, E. (2012) *France and the Hated Society: Muslim experiences*, Wembley: Islamic Human Rights Commission.

An Garda Síochána (2003) 'Annual Report of An Garda Síochána 2003', available online at

http://garda.ie/Documents/User/Annual%20Report%202003%20-Part%201.pdf (accessed 11 September 2013).
An Garda Síochana (2009) 'An Garda Síochána National Model of Community Policing', available online at www.garda.ie/Documents/User/national%20model%20of%20community%20policing%20-%20jan%2026%202009.pdf (accessed 28 September 2013).
An Garda Síochana (2009a) 'Diversity Strategy 2009–2012', available online at www.garda.ie/Documents/User/DiversityStrat.pdf (accessed 28 September 2013).
An Garda Síochána (2012) 'About us' [online], available at: www.garda.ie/Controller.aspx?Page=5416&Lang=1 (accessed 15 March 2012).
An Garda Síochána (2012a) 'Information Services', available online at www.garda.ie/Controller.aspx?Page=65 (accessed 10 March 2012).
An Garda Síochána (2013) 'Your Police Service in Intercultural Ireland', available online at www.garda.ie/Documents/User/racial%20and%20intercultural%20english.pdf (accessed 18 September 2012).
Archambault, H. (2007) 'A Community United? Going in search of community with Edinburgh Muslims', Edinburgh Papers in South Asian Studies, available online at www.csas.ed.ac.uk/__data/assets/pdf_file/0007/38536/WP23_Hannah_Archambault.pdf (accessed 27 September 2013).
Armstrong, K. (1988) *Holy Wars: The Crusades and Their Impact on Today's World*, London: MacMillan.
Arnold, S.K. (2012) *State Sanctioned Child Poverty and Exclusion: The case of children in state accommodation for asylum seekers*, available online at www.irishrefugeecouncil.ie/wp-content/uploads/2011/08/State-Sanctioned-Child-Poverty-and-Exclusion-The-case-of-children-in-state-accomodation-for-asylum-seekers.pdf (accessed 7 February 2014).
Associated Press (2014) 'End of NYPD Muslim Surveillance Program Applauded', available online at http://hosted.ap.org/dynamic/stories/U/US_NYPD_INTELLIGENCE?SITE=AP&SECTION=HOME&TEMPLATE=DEFAULT (accessed 16 April 2014).
Association of Chief Police Officers (2015) 'Truevision', available online at http://report-it.org.uk/report_a_hate_crime (accessed 5 February 2015).
Baker, P. (2010) 'Representations of Islam in British Broadsheet and Tabloid Newspapers 1999–2005', *Journal of Language and Politics*, 9(2), 310–338.
Balibar, E. and Wallerstein, I. (1991) *Race, Nation, Class: Ambiguous identities*, London: Verso.
Barker, M. (1981) *The New Racism: Conservatives and the ideology of the tribe*, London: Junction Books.
Barrett, A. and Kelly, E. (2008) 'How Reliable is the Quarterly National Household Survey for Migration Research?' *The Economic and Social Review*, 39(3), 191–205.
Bastalich, W. (2009) 'Reading Foucault: Genealogy and Social Science Research Methodology and Ethics', *Sociological Research Online*, 14(2), available online at www.socresonline.org.uk/14/2/3.html (accessed 15 August 2013).
Batty, D. (2011) 'Lady Warsi claims Islamophobia is now socially acceptable in Britain', *Guardian*, 20 January 2011, available online at www.theguardian.com/uk/2011/jan/20/lady-warsi-islamophobia-muslims-prejudice (accessed 27 September 2013).
Bauman, M. (2009) 'Anxieties, banning minarets and populist politics in Switzerland – a preliminary analysis', Universität Luzern, available online at http://pluralism.org/files/spotlight/Baumann_Swiss-ban-on-minarets_Nov09.pdf (accessed 23 February 2015).
BBC News (2014) 'The Islamic Veil Across Europe', available online at www.bbc.com/news/world-europe-13038095 (accessed 23 February 2015).
BBC News Europe (2015) 'UKIP's Nigel Farage urges "Judeo-Christian" defence after

Paris attacks', available online at www.bbc.com/news/world-europe-30776186 (accessed 14 January 2015).

Bennetto, J. (2009) 'Police and Racism: What has been achieved 10 years after the Stephen Lawrence Inquiry report', available online at www.equalityhumanrights.com/uploaded_files/raceinbritain/policeandracism.pdf (accessed 20 April 2012).

Bhaskar, R. (1989) *Reclaiming Reality: A critical introduction to contemporary philosophy*, London: Verso.

Bhaskar, R. (1989a), *The Possibility of Naturalism: A philosophical critique of the contemporary human sciences*, 2nd edn, London and New York: Harvester Wheatsheaf.

Bhattacharyya, G. (2006) 'Wars on our doorstep: Islamicising "race" and militarising everyday life', in Lentin, A. and Lentin, R. (eds) *Race and State*, Newcastle: Cambridge Scholars Press, 138–150.

Bilge, S. (2010) 'Beyond Subordination vs. Resistance: An intersectional approach to the agency of veiled women', *Journal of Intercultural Studies*, 31(1), 9–28.

Bolognani, M. (2007) 'Islam, Ethnography and Politics: Methodological issues in researching amongst West Yorkshire Pakistanis in 2005', *International Journal of Social Research Methodology*, 10(4), 279–293.

Bonilla-Silva, E. (19970 'Rethinking Racism: Toward a structural interpretation', *American Sociological Review*, 62(3), 465–480.

Bord Bia (2013) Speech by the Taoiseach, Mr. Enda Kenny, T.D., at the Bord Bia 'Pathways for Growth' – Food and Drink Summit, 27 May 2011, available online at www.bordbia.ie/eventsnews/ConferencePresentations/2011/PathwaysForGrowthReviewOutlookMay2011/Pathways%20for%20Growth,%20Food%20and%20Drink%20Summit%20(Presentation%20text)%20Taoiseach,%20Mr%20Enda%20Kenny,%20TD.pdf (accessed 6 September 2013).

Brå (2010) 'The Swedish Crime Survey 2009: Victimisation, fear of crime and public confidence in the criminal justice system', available online at www.bra.se/download/18.cba82f7130f475a2f1800022472/2010_swedish_crime_survey_2009.pdf (accessed 18 September 2012).

Brå (2011) 'Hate Crimes 2010: Statistics relating to offences reported to the police with an identified hate crime motive', available online at www.red-network.eu/resources/toolip/doc/2012/01/14/hate-crimes-in-sweden-2010.pdf (accessed 18 September 2012).

Brå (2011a) 'The Swedish Crime Survey 2010: Victimisation, fear of crime and public confidence in the criminal justice system', available online at www.bra.se/download/18.cba82f7130f475a2f1800021921/2011_1_swedish_crime_survey_2010.pdf (accessed 18 September 2012).

Brå (2012) 'About Brå', available online at www.bra.se/bra/bra-in-english/home/about-bra.html (accessed 18 September 2012).

Brå (2012a) 'Hate Crime', available online at www.bra.se/bra/bra-in-english/home/crime-and-statistics/hate-crime.html (accessed 18 September 2012).

Brå (2013) *The Swedish Crime Survey 2012: Victimisation, fear of crime and public confidence in the criminal justice system*, available online at www.bra.se/download/18.421a6a7d13def01048a80006535/1380267567631/2013_summary_the_swedish_crime_survey_NTU_2012.pdf (accessed 5 January 2015).

Brå (2014) *Hate Crime 2013: Statistics on police reports with identified hate crime motives and self-reported exposure to hate crime*, available online at www.bra.se/download/18.626651b0148b20bd39c87f/1413792518477/2014_hatecrime_2013_summary.pdf (accessed 6 January 2015).

Brå (2014a) *The Swedish Crime Survey 2013: Comparing exposure to crime, insecurity*

Bibliography

and confidence; Summary, available online at https://www.bra.se/bra/bra-in-english/home/publications/archive/publications/2014-04-29-the-swedish-crime-survey-2013.html (accessed 6 January 2015).

Brå (2015) *Reported Hate Crimes*, available online at www.bra.se/bra/bra-in-english/home/crime-and-statistics/crime-statistics/reported-hate-crimes.html (accessed 6 January 2015).

Brå (2015a) 'Hate Crime', available online at www.bra.se/bra/bra-in-english/home/crime-and-statistics/hate-crime.html (accessed 5 February 2015).

Brady, T. (2010) 'Three Freed in Death Plot Probe: Gardaí confirm prime suspect had online link with Jihad Janes', *The Irish Independent*, 13th March 2010, available online at www.independent.ie/irish-news/three-freed-in-death-plot-probe-26640359.html (accessed 28 September 2013).

Brewer, J. and Hunter, A. (1989) *Multimethod Research: A synthesis of styles*, Newbury Park, California: Sage.

Britain First (2014) Videos, available online at www.liveleak.com/c/BRITAIN-FIRSTVIDEOS (accessed 22 December 2014).

Bryan, A. (2012) '"You've Got to Teach People That Racism is Wrong and Then They Won't Be Racist": Curricular representations and young people's understandings of 'race'and racism', *Journal of Curriculum Studies*, 44(5), 599–629.

Bryan, A. and Bracken, M. (2011) 'They Think the Book is Right and I am Wrong', in Darmody, M., Tyrell, N. and Song, S. (eds) *The Changing Faces of Ireland*, Rotterdam, Boston, Taipei: Sense Publishers, 105–123.

Bryman, A. (2012) *Social Research Methods*, 4th edn, Oxford: Oxford University Press.

Brown, K. 2008 'The promise and perils of women's participation in UK mosques: The impact of securitisation agendas on identity, gender and community', *The British Journal of Politics & International Relations*, 10(3), 472–491.

Brown, K.E. and Saeed, T. (2014) 'Radicalisation and counter-radicalisation at British universities: Muslim encounters and alternatives', *Ethnic and Racial Studies*, published online, DOI: 10.1080/01419870.2014.911343

Browne, C. (2008) 'Garda Public Attitudes Survey 2008', available online at www.garda.ie/Documents/User/24.%20GARDA%20PUBLIC%20ATTITUDES%20-%202008.pdf (accessed 1 September 2012).

Bunzl, M. (2005) 'Between anti-Semitism and Islamophobia: Some thoughts on the new Europe', *American Ethnologist*, 32(4), 499–508.

Burke-Johnson, R., Onwuegbuzie, A.J. and Turner, Lisa A. (2007) 'Toward a Definition of Mixed Methods Research', *Journal of Mixed Methods Research*, 1(2), 112–133.

Campbell, P. and Cadogan, G. (2013) *Experience of Crime: Findings from the 2012/13 Northern Ireland Crime Survey* available online at www.dojni.gov.uk/index/statistics-research/stats-research-publications/northern-ireland-crime-survey-s-r/nics-2012-13-experience-bulletin.pdf (accessed 6 of January 2015).

Carey, S. (2008) 'Crime and Justice Statistics in Ireland', United Nations Expert Group Meeting on The Scope and Content of Social Statistics, available online at http://unstats.un.org/unsd/demographic/meetings/egm/NewYork_8-12Sep.2008/EGM%20Papers/Ireland%20-%20Crime%20and%20Justice.pdf (accessed 18 September 2012).

Carmichael, S. and Hamilton, C.V. (1967) *Black Power: The politics of liberation in America*, New York: Vintage Books.

Carr, J. (2009) 'Measuring Islamophobia', *Socheolas: Limerick Student Journal of Sociology*, 2 (2), 39–57.

Carr, J. (2011) 'Regulating Islamophobia: The need for collecting disaggregated data on racism in Ireland', *Journal of Muslim Minority Affairs; Special Issue on Islam in Ireland,* 31(4), 574–593.

Carr, J. and Haynes, A. (2013) 'A Clash of Racialisations: The policing of 'race' and of anti-Muslim racism in Ireland', *Critical Sociology,* 1–20.

Carr, N. (2008) '*Minorities and Youth Justice: An Irish concern?*' in Association for Criminal Justice Research and Development; *11 Annual Conference Report, Minorities, Crime and Justice,* available online at www.acjrd.ie/reports/11/AnnualConferenceReport.pdf (accessed 11 November 2009), 33–41.

Carter, B. (2000) *Realism and Racism: Concepts or race in sociological research,* London: Routledge.

Centraal Bureau de Statistiek (2013) 'Veiligheidsmonitor 2012', available online at www.cbs.nl/nl-NL/menu/themas/veiligheid-recht/publicaties/publicaties/archief/2013/2013-veiligheidsmonitor-2012-pub.htm (accessed 14 September 2013).

Central Statistics Office (2004) 'Quarterly National Household Survey: Crime and Victimisation, Quarter 4, 1998 and 2003', available online at www.cso.ie/en/media/csoie/newsevents/documents/qnhscrimeandvictimisation.pdf (accessed 30 August 2012).

Central Statistics Office (2005) 'Quarterly National Household Survey: Equality, Q4 2004', available online at www.cso.ie/en/media/csoie/releasespublications/documents/labourmarket/current/equality.pdf (accessed 30 August 2012).

Central Statistics Office (2007) 'Interpreting Crime Statistics', available online at www.cso.ie/en/media/csoie/releasespublications/documents/crimejustice/current/interpretingcrimestats.pdf (accessed 18 September 2012).

Central Statistics Office (2008) 'Irish Crime Classification System', available online at www.cso.ie/en/media/csoie/releasespublications/documents/crimejustice/current/crimeclassification.pdf (accessed 21 August 2013).

Central Statistics Office (2009) 'Standard Report on Methods and Quality (v1) for Recorded Crime', available online at www.cso.ie/en/media/csoie/surveysandmethodologies/documents/pdfdocs/quarterly_crime_quality_report.pdf (accessed 18 September 2012).

Central Statistics Office (2010) 'Crime and Victimisation: Quarterly National Household Survey, 2010', available online at www.cso.ie/en/media/csoie/releasespublications/documents/crimejustice/current/crimeandvictimisation_qnhs2010.pdf (accessed 30 August 2012).

Central Statistics Office (2011) 'Quarterly National Household Survey: Equality, Q4 2010', available online at www.cso.ie/en/media/csoie/releasespublications/documents/labourmarket/2010/qnhs_equalityq42010.pdf (accessed 29 December 2011).

Central Statistics Office (2012) 'Census 2011: This is Ireland (Part 1)', available online at www.cso.ie/en/census/census2011reports/census2011isisirelandpart1/ (accessed 29 March 2012).

Central Statistics Office (2013) 'Census 2006 Reports', available online at www.cso.ie/en/census/census2006reports/ (accessed 31 August 2013).

Cesari, J. (2011) 'Islamophobia in the West: A Comparison between Europe and the United States', in Esposito, J.L. and Kalin, I. (eds) *Islamophobia: The Challenge of Pluralism in the 21 Century,* Oxford and New York: Oxford University Press, 21–47.

Chakraborti, N., Garland, J. and Hardy, S.J. (2014) *Leicester Hate Crime Project: Findings and Conclusions, Report,* available online at www2.le.ac.uk/departments/criminology/research/current-projects/hate-crime/documents-and-images/findings-and-conclusions-full-report (accessed 3 February 2015).

Ciciora, A.C. (2010) 'Integrating Ireland's Muslims: Attitudes of Muslim and Irish elites towards value compatibility and mainstreaming Islam', *Journal of Muslim Minority Affairs*, 30(2), 199–216.

Cincotta, T. (2011) 'Manufacturing the Muslim Menace: Private firms, public servants and the threat to rights and security', available online at www.publiceye.org/liberty/training/Muslim_Menace_Complete.pdf (accessed 2 April 2011).

Clarke, H. (2013) 'Recording Racism in Ireland', available online at www.integrationcentre.ie/getattachment/d70f7539-ce06-403d-98d7-da21f7d46426/Recording-Racism-in-Ireland.aspx (accessed 27 September 2013).

Clifford, M. (2015) 'Godfather of social partnership believes it is time for its rebirth', *The Irish Times*, available online at www.irishexaminer.com/viewpoints/analysis/godfather-of-social-partnership-believes-it-is-time-for-its-rebirth-305022.html (accessed 9 February 2015).

Cole, M. (1998) 'Racism, reconstructed multiculturalism and antiracist education', *Cambridge Journal of Education*, 28(1), 37–48.

Cole, M. (2004) '"Brutal and Stinking" and "Difficult to Handle": The historical and contemporary manifestations of racialisation, institutional racism, and schooling in Britain', *Race Ethnicity and Education*, 7(1), 35–56.

Cole, M. (2009) 'A plethora of "suitable enemies": British racism at the dawn of the twenty-first century', *Ethnic and Racial Studies*, 32(9), 1671–1685.

Cole, J. (2011) 'Islamophobia and American Foreign Policy: A comparison between Europe and the United States', in Esposito, J.L. and Kalin, I. (eds) *Islamophobia: The Challenge of Pluralism in the 21 Century*, Oxford and New York: Oxford University Press, 127–143.

College of Policing (2014) *Hate Crime Operational Guidance*, available online at www.report-it.org.uk/files/hate_crime_operational_guidance.pdf (accessed 10 January 2015).

Coolahan, J., Hussey, C, and Kilfeather, F. (2012) 'The Forum on Patronage and Pluralism in the Primary Sector: Report of the forum's advisory group', available online at www.education.ie/en/Publications/Policy-Reports/fpp_report_advisory_group.pdf (accessed 27 September 2013).

Connolly, P. (2006) '"It Goes Without Saying (Well Sometimes)": Racism, whiteness and identity in Northern Ireland', in Neal, S. and Agyeman, J. (eds) *The New Countryside? Ethnicity, nation, and exclusion in temporary rural Britain*, Bristol: The Policy Press, 21–46

Cotter, E. (2012) 'Woman Beaten and Taunted as She Wore a Hijab', *The Herald,*, available online at www.herald.ie/news/courts/woman-beaten-and-taunted-as-she-wore-a-hijab-28002686.html (accessed 26 September 2013).

Council on American-Islamic Relations (2010) 'Same Hate, New target', available online at www.cair.com/Portals/0/islamophobia2010.pdf (accessed 30 August 2012).

Creese, B. and Lader, D. (2014) *Hate Crimes, England and Wales, 2013/14,* available online at www.gov.uk/government/uploads/system/uploads/attachment_data/file/364198/hosb0214.pdf (accessed 10 January 2015).

Crenshaw, K. (1991) 'Mapping the Margins: Intersectionality, identity politics, and violence against women of colour', *Stanford Law Review*, 43(6), 1241–1299.

Creswell, J. (2007) *Qualitative Inquiry and Research Design: Choosing among five approaches*, 2nd edn, Thousand Oaks: Sage.

Creswell, J.W. and Plano-Clark, V. (2011) *Designing and Conducting Mixed Methods Research*, London: Sage.

Crosbie, J. (2013) 'Winding down of philanthropic organisations to create €50 funding void', *The Irish Times*, 9 May 2013, available online at www.irishtimes.com/news/social-affairs/winding-down-of-philanthropic-organisations-to-create-50m-funding-void-1.1386681 (accessed 20 September 2013).

Crowley, U. and Kitchin, R. (2007) 'Paradoxical Spaces of Traveller Citizenship in Contemporary Ireland', *Irish Geography*, 40(2) 128–145.

Crown Office Procurator Fiscal Services (2014) *Hate Crime in Scotland 2013–2014*, available online at www.copfs.gov.uk/images/Documents/Equality_Diversity/Hate%20Crime%20in%20Scotland%202013-14.pdf (accessed 9 January 2015).

Crown Prosecution Service (2014) *Hate crime and crimes against older people report 2013–2014*, available online at www.cps.gov.uk/publications/docs/cps_hate_crime_report_2014.pdf (accessed 9 January 2015).

Davis, D.A. (2007) 'Narrating the Mute: Racialising and racism in a neoliberal moment', in *Souls: A Critical Journal of Black Politics, Culture, and Society*, 9(4), 346–360.

Dean, M. (2010) *Governmentality: power and rule in modern society*, 2nd edn, Los Angeles, London, New Delhi, Singapore, Washington DC: Sage.

Dean, M. (2010a). 'A response to the questions what is neoliberalism? Contesting neoliberalism and its future', Workshop, University of Sydney, available online at http://sydney.edu.au/arts/political_economy/downloads/Mitchell_Dean.pdf (accessed 20 August 2013).

Deflem, M. (1997) 'Surveillance and Criminal Statistics: Historical foundations of governmentality', available online at www.cas.sc.edu/socy/faculty/deflem/zcrist.htm (accessed 22 June 2011).

Department of Jobs, Enterprise and Innovation (2013) 'Public Consultation: A national entrepreneurship policy statement for Ireland', available online at www.djei.ie/publications/enterprise/2013/Public_Consultation_A_National_Entrepreneurship_Policy_Statement_for_Ireland.pdf (accessed 6 September 2013).

Department of Justice Equality and Law Reform (2005) 'Planning for Diversity: National action plan against racism 2005–2008', available online at www.nccri.ie/pdf/ActionPlan.pdf ('accessed 14 January 2012).

Department of Justice and Equality (2013) 'Shatter announces publication of General Scheme of Irish Human Rights and Equality Commission Bill', available online at www.justice.ie/en/JELR/Pages/PR12000155 (accessed 16 September 2013).

Department of Justice and Equality (2014) 'Shatter publishes the Irish Human Rights and Equality Commission Bill 2014', available online at www.justice.ie/en/JELR/Pages/PR14000083 (accessed 9 April 2014).

Department of Justice and Equality (2014a) Minister Fitzgerald addresses European colleagues on issues relating to foreign fighters and organised crime', available online at www.justice.ie/en/JELR/Pages/PR14000276 (accessed 22 December 2014).

Department of Justice and Equality (2015) 'Equality', available online at www.justice.ie/en/JELR/Pages/Equality_FAQ (accessed 5 February 2015).

Department of the Taoiseach (2003) 'Sustaining Progress: Social Partnership Agreement 2003–2005', available online at www.taoiseach.gov.ie/upload/SustProgagri.pdf (accessed 5 September 2013).

Devine, D. and Kelly, M. (2006) '"I Just Don't Want to Get Picked on by Anybody": Dynamics of Inclusion and Exclusion in a Newly Multi-Ethnic Irish Primary School', *Children & Society*, 20(2), 128–139.

Devine, D., Kenny, M. and Macneela, E. (2008) 'Naming the "Other": Children's construction and experience of racisms in Irish primary schools', *Race Ethnicity and Education*, 11(4), 369–385.

Dinsbach, W., Walz, G. and Boog, I. (2009) 'ENAR Shadow Report 2008: Racism in the Netherlands', available online at http://cms.horus.be/files/99935/MediaArchive/national/Netherlands%20-%20SR%202008.pdf (accessed 12 September 2013).

Donegal Democrat (2014) 'Ballyshannon Traveller Family Torn Apart by Fire and Comments', available online at www.donegaldemocrat.ie/news/donegal-news/ballyshannon-traveller-family-torn-apart-by-fire-and-comments-1-4810609 (accessed 7 February 2014).

Donzelot, J. (2008) 'Michel Foucault and Liberal Intelligence', *Economy and Society*, 37(1), 115–134).

Duncombe, J. and Jessop, J. (2002) '"Doing Rapport" and the Ethics of "Faking Friendship"', in Mauthner, M., Birch, M., Jessop, J. and Miller, T. *Ethics in Qualitative Research*, 107–123.

Dunn, K.M., Klocker, N. and Salabay, T. (2007) 'Contemporary Racism and Islamophobia in Australia: Racialising religion', *Ethnicities*, 7(4), 564–589.

Dwyer, C. (1999) 'Veiled Meanings: Young British Muslim women and the negotiation of differences', *Gender, Place and Culture: A Journal of Feminist Geography*, 6(1), 5–26.

Dwyer, C., Shah, B. and Sanghera, G. (2008) '"From Cricket Lover to Terror Suspect" – Challenging representations of young British Muslim men', *Gender, Place and Culture: A Journal of Feminist Geography*, 15(2), 117–136.

Education in Ireland (2014) 'Why study in Ireland?' available online at www.educationinireland.com/en/Why-Study-in-Ireland-/ (accessed 2 April 2014).

Education in Ireland (2014a) *International Students in Higher education in Ireland 2009/10*, available online at www.educationinireland.com/en/publications/international-students-in-higher-education-in-ireland-2010-.pdf (accessed 2 April 2014).

Elliot, J. (2007) *Using Narrative in Social Research: qualitative and quantitative approaches*, London: Sage.

Engage (2012) 'Police and Crime Commissioner Elections: Engage briefing', available online at www.iengage.org.uk/images/stories/pccmanifesto2012.pdf (accessed 7 September 2013).

English Defence League (2014) Homepage, available online at www.englishdefenceleague.org/ (accessed 20 February 2014).

Enterprise Ireland (2014) 'Ministers Quinn and Bruton Launch new International Brand for Education in Ireland', available online at www.enterprise-ireland.com/en/News/PressReleases/2011-Press-Releases/Overseas-Marketing-Drive-to-Double-the-Number-of-International-Students-Choosing-to-Study-in-Ireland.html (accessed 2 April 2014).

Equality Authority (2006) 'Discrimination Against Travellers Highlighted in Traveller Focus Week – Pub Apologises for Discrimination Against Travellers', Equality Authority Press Release – 7 December 2006, available online at www.equality.ie/en/Press-Office/Discrimination-Against-Travellers-Highlighted-in-Traveller-Focus-Week-Pub-Apologises-for-Discrimination-Against-Travellers.html (accessed 18 September 2013).

Equality and Rights Alliance (2012) 'Submission to the heads of Irish Human Rights and Equality Commission Bill 2012 to the Oireachtas Committee on Justice, Equality and Defence', available online at http://tinyurl.com/brgyv62 (accessed 30 August 2012).

Equality and Rights Alliance (2014) 'A difficult beginning for the Irish Human Rights and Equality Commission', available online at www.eracampaign.org/uploads/Article%20for%20CWC%20%20Equality%20and%20Rights%20Alliance%20Feb%202014.pdf (accessed 5 February 2015).

Esposito, J.L. (2011) 'Introduction', in Esposito, J.L. and Kalin, I. (eds) *Islamophobia: The Challenge of Pluralism in the 21 Century*, Oxford and New York: Oxford University Press, xxi–xxxv.
Essed P (2002) 'Everyday Racism: A new approach to the study of racism', in Essed P. and Goldberg D.T. (eds) *Race Critical Theories*, Malden, Oxford, Carlton: Blackwell Publishing, 176–195.
Europa (2013) 'Framework Decision on Combating Racism and Xenophobia', available online at http://europa.eu/legislation_summaries/justice_freedom_security/combating_discrimination/l33178_en.htm (accessed 20 July 2013).
European Network Against Racism (Ireland) (2013) 'Reports of racism flood in in 4 weeks since iReport.ie launch', available online at http://enarireland.org/reports-of-racism-flood-in-in-4-weeks-since-ireport-ie-launch/ (accessed 11 September 2013).
European Monitoring Centre on Racism and Xenophobia (2006) 'Muslims in the European Union: Discrimination and Islamophobia', available online at http://fra.europa.eu/fraWebsite/attachments/Manifestations_EN.pdf (accessed 30 August 2012).
European Monitoring Centre on Racism and Xenophobia (2006a) 'Perceptions of Discrimination and Islamophobia: Voices from members of Muslim communities in the European Union', available online at http://fra.europa.eu/sites/default/files/fra_uploads/182-Perceptions_EN.pdf (accessed 27 September 2013).
European Network Against Racism (Ireland) (2015) 'About iReport.ie', available online at http://enarireland.org/ireport/?page_id=15 (accessed 5 February 2015).
European Network Against Racism (Ireland) (2015a) *iReport Quarterly*, available online at http://enarireland.org/ireport-quartertly/ (accessed 5 February 2015).
European Union Agency for Fundamental Rights (2009) 'EU-MIDIS European Union Minorities and Discrimination Survey: Main Results Report', available online at http://fra.europa.eu/sites/default/files/fra_uploads/664-eumidis_mainreport_conference-edition_en_.pdf (accessed 20 September 2013).
European Union Agency for Fundamental Rights (2009a) 'EU-MIDIS Data in Focus Report 2: Muslims', available online at http://fra.europa.eu/fraWebsite/research/publications/publications_per_year/2009/pub_dif2_en.htm (accessed 10 January 2010).
European Union Agency for Fundamental Rights (2011) 'Data in Focus Report 5: Multiple discrimination', available online at http://fra.europa.eu/fraWebsite/attachments/EU_MIDIS_DiF5-multiple-discrimination_EN.pdf (accessed 14 February 2011).
European Union Agency for Fundamental Rights (2012) 'Making Hate Crimes Visible in the European Union: Acknowledging victim's rights', available online at http://fra.europa.eu/en/publication/2012/making-hate-crime-visible-european-union-acknowledging-victims-rights (accessed 20 July 2013).
European Union Agency for Fundamental Rights (2013) 'Annual Report 2012 Chapter Six', available online at http://fra.europa.eu/sites/default/files/annual-report-2012-chapter-6_en.pdf (accessed 20 July 2013).
Fanning, B. (2002) *Racism and social change in the Republic of Ireland*, Manchester and New York: Manchester University Press.
Fanning, B. (2011) *Immigration and Social Cohesion in the Republic of Ireland*, Manchester: Manchester University Press.
Fanning, B. (2012) *Racism and social change in the Republic of Ireland*, 2nd edn, Manchester and New York: Manchester University Press.
Fanning, B., Killoran, B., Ní Bhroin, S. and McEvoy, G. (2011) 'Taking Racism Seriously: Migrant's experiences of violence, harassment and anti-Social behaviour in the Dublin area', available online at www.immigrantcouncil.ie/research-publications/2010/

499-taking-racism-seriously-migrants-experiences-of-violence-harassment-and-antisocial-behaviour-in-the-dublin-area (accessed 14 April 2012).
Fekete, L. (2004) 'Anti-Muslim Racism and the European Security State', *Race and Class*, 46(3), 3–29.
Fekete, L. (2009) *A Suitable Enemy: Racism, migration and Islamophobia in Europe*, London and New York: Pluto Press.
Fekete, L. (2015) 'Where Monoculturalism Leads', Institute of Race Relations, available online at www.irr.org.uk/news/where-monoculturalism-leads/ (accessed 14 January 2015).
Feldman, M. and Littler, M. (2014) *Tell MAMA Reporting 2013/14 Anti-Muslim Overview, Analysis and 'Cumulative Extremism'* available online at http://tellmamauk.org/wp-content/uploads/2014/07/finalreport.pdf (accessed 24 February 2015).
Fianna Fáil (2013) 'History of Fianna Fáil', available online at www.fiannafail.ie/content/pages/5098/ (accessed 16 September 2013).
Flick, U. (2009) *An Introduction to Qualitative Research*, 4th edn, Los Angeles, London, New Delhi, Singapore and Washington DC: Sage.
Flick, U., Garms-Homolvá, V., Hermann, W., Kuck, J. and Rohnsch, G. (2012) '"I Can't Prescribe Something Just Because Someone Asks for It ..." Using mixed methods in the framework of triangulation', *Journal of Mixed Methods Research*, 6(2), 97–110.
Flynn, K. (2006) 'Understanding Islam in Ireland', *Islam and Christian–Muslim Relations*, 17 (2), 223–238.
Foucault, M. (1980) 'Truth and Power', in Gordon, C. (ed.) *Michel Foucault Power/Knowledge: selected interviews and other writings 1972–1977 by Michel Foucault*, Edinburgh: Pearson, 109–134.
Foucault, M. (1980a) 'Two Lectures', in Gordon, C. (ed.) Michel Foucault *Power/Knowledge: selected interviews and other writings 1972–1977* by Michel Foucault, Edinburgh: Pearson, 78–109.
Foucault, M. (1991) 'Governmentality', in Burchell, G., Gordon, C. and Miller, P. (eds) *The Foucault Effect: studies in governmentality*, Chicago: University of Chicago Press, 87–105.
Foucault, M. (1991b) *Discipline and Punish: The birth of the prison*, London: Penguin.
Foucault, M. (1991c) 'Questions of Method', in Burchell, G., Gordon, C. and Miller, P. (eds) *The Foucault Effect: studies in governmentality*, Chicago: University of Chicago Press, 73–87.
Foucault, M. (1998) *The Will to Knowledge: The History of Sexuality: Volume One*, London: Penguin.
Foucault, M. (2000) 'The Subject and Power' in Faubion, J.D. (ed.) *Power: Michel Foucault essential works of Foucault 1954: 1984*, London: Penguin, 326–349.
Foucault, M. (2000a) 'Truth and Power', in Faubion, J.D. (ed.) *Power: Michel Foucault essential works of Foucault 1954: 1984*, London: Penguin, 111–134.
Foucault, M. (2000b) 'Confronting Governments: Human Rights', in Faubion, J.D. (ed.) *Power: Michel Foucault essential works of Foucault 1954: 1984*, London: Penguin, 474–477.
Foucault, M. (2003) 'Lecture 11, 17 March 1976', in Bertani, M. and Fontana, A. (eds) *Michel Foucault: Society Must Be Defended; Lectures at the Collége de France 1975–76*, London: Penguin, 239–265.
Foucault, M. (2003a) 'Lecture 4, 28 January 1976', in Bertani, M. and Fontana, A. (eds) *Michel Foucault: Society Must Be Defended; Lectures at the Collége de France 1975–76*, London: Penguin, 65–87.

Foucault, M. (2009) Lecture 4, 1 February 1978, in Senellart, M. (ed.) *Michel Foucault: Security, Territory, Population; Lectures at the Collége de France 1977–78;* Basingstoke, New York: Palgrave Macmillan, 87–115.

Foucault, M. (2009a) 'Lecture 8, 1 March 1978', in Senellart, M. (ed.) *Michel Foucault: Security, Territory, Population; Lectures at the Collége de France 1977–78;* Basingstoke, New York: Palgrave Macmillan, 191–227.

Foucault, M. (2009b) 'Lecture 5, 8 February 1978', in Senellart, M. (ed.) *Michel Foucault: Security, Territory, Population; Lectures at the Collége de France 1977–78;* Basingstoke, New York: Palgrave Macmillan, 115–135.

Foucault, M. (2010) 'Lecture 10, 21 March 1979', in Senellart, M. (ed.) *Michel Foucault: The Birth of Biopolitics; Lectures at the Collége de France 1978–79;* Basingstoke, New York: Palgrave Macmillan, 239–267.

Foucault, M. (2010a) 'Lecture 9, 14 March 1979', in Senellart, M. (ed.) *Michel Foucault: The Birth of Biopolitics; Lectures at the Collége de France 1978–79;* Basingstoke, New York: Palgrave Macmillan, 215–239.

Frankfort-Nachmias, C. and Nachmias, D. (1992) *Research methods in the Social Sciences*, 4th edn, London, Melbourne and Auckland: Edward Arnold.

Frost, D. (2008) 'Islamophobia: Examining causal links between the state and "race hate" from "below"', *International Journal of Sociology and Social Policy*, 28(11), 546–563.

Frost, D. (2008a) Islamophobia: Examining causal links between the media and 'race hate' from 'below', *International Journal of Sociology and Social Policy* 28(11), 564–578.

Garner, S. (2009) 'Ireland: From racism without "race" to racism without racists', *Radical History Review*, 2009(104), 41–56.

Garner, S. (2010) *Racisms: An introduction*, Los Angeles, London, New Delhi, Singapore and Washington DC: Sage.

Garland, J., Spalek, B. and Chakraborti, N. (2006) 'Hearing Lost Voices: Issues in researching minority ethnic communities', *British Journal of Criminology*, 46(3), 423–437.

Gest, J. (2010) *Apart. Alienated and Engaged Muslims in the West*, London: Hurst and Company.

Ghatak, S. (2008) 'The Whole Extent of the Evil: origin of crime statistics in the United States, 1880–1930', *Journal of Historical Sociology*, 21(1), 30–54.

Giroux, H.A., (2008) 'Beyond the Biopolitics of Disposability: Rethinking neoliberalism in the New Gilded Age', *Social Identities*, 14(5), 587–620.

Goffman, E. (1968) *Stigma: notes on the management of spoiled identity*, London and New York: Penguin.

Goldberg, D.T. (2002) *The Racial State*, Malden, MA: Blackwell Publishers.

Goldberg, D.T. (2009) *The Threat of Race: Reflections on racial neoliberalism*, Malden, Oxford and Victoria: Blackwell Publishing.

Goldstone, K. (2002) 'Christianity, conversion and the tricky business of names: Images of Jews and Blacks in nationalist Irish Catholic discourse', in Lentin, R. and McVeigh, R. (eds) *Racism and Anti-Racism in Ireland*, Belfast: Beyond the Pale, 167–177.

Gramsci, A. (1971) *Selections from the Prison Notebooks of Antonio Gramsci*, Hoare, Q. and Nowell Smith, G. (eds) London: Lawrence and Wishart.

Gray, B. (2011) 'Governing Integration', in Fanning, B. and Munck, R. (eds) *Globalisation, Migration and Social Transformation: Ireland in Europe and the World*, Farnham: Ashgate, 93–105.

Gray, B. (2013) 'Catholic Church Civil Society Activism and the Neoliberal Governmental Project of Migrant Integration in Ireland', in Martikainen, T. and Gauthier, F. (eds) *Religion in the Neoliberal Age: Political Economy and Modes of Governance*, Farnham: Ashgate, 69–91.

Grbich, C. (2007) *Qualitative data analysis: an introduction*, London, Thousand Oaks, New Delhi: Sage.

Greene, J.C., Caracelli, V.J. and Graham, W.F. (1989) 'Toward a Conceptual Framework for Mixed Method Evaluation Design', *Educational Evaluation and Policy Analysis*, 11(3), 255–274.

Greene, J.R. (2000) 'Community policing in America: Changing the nature, structure, and function of the police', *Criminal Justice*, 3, 299–370.

Guerin, P. (2002) 'Racism and the media in Ireland: Setting the anti-immigration agenda', in Lentin, R. and McVeigh, R. (eds) *Racism and Anti-Racism in Ireland*, Belfast: Beyond the Pale, 91–102.

Gündüz, Z.Y. (2010) 'The European Union at 50 – Xenophobia, Islamophobia and the rise of the radical Right', *Journal of Muslim Minority Affairs*, 30(1), 35–47.

Hacking, I. (1991) 'How Should We Do The History of Statistics?' in Burchell, G., Gordon, C. and Miller, P. (eds) *The Foucault Effect: studies in governmentality*, Chicago: University of Chicago Press, 181–197.

Hafez, F. (2014) 'Shifting borders: Islamophobia as common ground for building pan-European right-wing unity', *Patterns of Prejudice*, 48(5), 479–499.

Hall, N. (2013) *Hate Crime*, 2nd edn, London and New York: Routledge.

Halliday, F. (2003) *Islam and the Myth of Confrontation: Religion and politics in the Middle East*, 2nd edn, London and New York: I.B. Tauris.

Hannimann, W. (2008) 'Canadian Muslims, Islamophobia and National Security', *International Journal of Law, Crime and Justice*, 36, 271–285.

Hartman, A. (2000) 'In Search of Subjugated Knowledge', *Journal of Feminist Family Therapy*, 11(4), 19–23.

Harvey, D. (2005) *A Brief History of Neoliberalism*, Oxford and New York: Oxford University Press.

Hassan, M. (2015) 'As a Muslim, I'm fed up with the hypocrisy of the free speech fundamentalists', *Huffington Post*, 13 January 2015, available online at www.huffingtonpost.co.uk/mehdi-hasan/charlie-hebdo-free-speech_b_6462584.html?ncid=tweetlnkukhpmg00000008 (accessed 14 January 2015).

Haynes, A., Devereux, E. and Breen, M. (2006) 'Fear, framing and foreigners: The Othering of immigrants in the Irish print media', *Critical Psychology*, 16, 100–121.

Haynes, A., Power, M.J. and Devereux, E. (2010) *How Irish Politicians Construct Transnational EU Migrants*, available online at http://ulir.ul.ie/bitstream/handle/10344/2635/Haynes%2c%20Power%2c%20%26%20Devereux%20-%20Doras%20Report%20Nov%202010.pdf?sequence=2 (accessed 2 April 2014).

Heckathorn, D.D. (1997) 'Respondent-Driven Sampling: A new approach to the study of hidden populations', *Social Problems*, 44(2), 174–199.

Hellyer, H. (2009) *Muslims of Europe: The 'other' Europeans*, Edinburgh: Edinburgh University Press.

Hennessey, M. (2014) 'Tallaght Roma Girl's Family Victims of Racist Attacks', available online at www.thejournal.ie/roma-tallaght-racist-1144134-Oct2013/ (accessed 7 February 2014).

Hennink, M., Hutter, I. and Bailey, A. (2011) *Qualitative Research Methods*, Los Angeles, London, New Delhi, Singapore and Washington: Sage.

Herek, G.M., Cogan, J.C. and Gillis, J.R. (2002) 'Victim Experiences in Hate Crimes Based on Sexual Orientation', *Journal of Social Issues*, 58(2), 319–339.

Herbert, J., May, J., Wills, J., Datta, K., Evans, Y. and McIlwaine, C. (2008) 'Multicultural Living? Experiences of everyday racism among Ghanaian migrants in London', *European Urban and Regional Studies*, 15(2), 103–117.

Hewer, C.T.R (2006) *Understanding Islam: The first ten steps*, London: SCM Press.

Hickman, M., Thomas, L., Silvestri, S. and Nickels, Henri (2011) 'Suspect Communities'? Counter-terrorism policy, the press, and the impact on Irish and Muslim communities in Britain', London Metropolitan University, available online at www.statewatch.org/news/2011/jul/uk-london-met-suspect-communities-findings.pdf (accessed 29 July 2011).

Hickman, M.J. (1998) 'Reconstructing deconstructing "race": British political discourses about the Irish in Britain', *Ethnic and Racial Studies*, 21(2), 288–307.

High-level Group on International Education (2010) *Investing in Global Relationships: Ireland's International Education Strategy 2010–15, Report of the High-level Group on International Education to the Tánaiste and Minister for Education and Skills*, available online at www.educationinireland.com/en/publications/full-report-education-global-strategy.pdf (accessed 2 April 2014).

Hillyard, P. (1994) 'Irish People and the British Criminal Justice System', *Justice Law & Society*, 21, 39–56.

HM Government UK (2012) 'Challenge it, Report it, Stop it: The government's plan to tackle hate crime', available online at www.suffolkhatecrime.org.uk/assets/Gallery-1/govt-action-plan.pdf (accessed 18 September 2012).

Hogan, C. (2011) 'Accommodating Islam in the Denominational Irish Education System: Religious freedom and education in the Republic of Ireland', *Journal of Muslim Minority Affairs*, 31(4), 554–573.

Holt, E. (2009) *Stick to the Budget Minister, Irish Central*, available online at www.irishcentral.com/opinion/letat-cest-moi-45399237-237642981.html# (accessed 5 February 2015).

Home Office (2010) 'Crime in England and Wales 2009/10: An overview of the findings', available online at www.homeoffice.gov.uk/publications/science-research-statistics/research-statistics/crime-research/hosb1210/hosb1210-chap1?view=Binary (accessed 18 September 2012).

Home Office UK (2011) 'Prevent Strategy', available online at www.gov.uk/government/uploads/system/uploads/attachment_data/file/97976/prevent-strategy-review.pdf (accessed 27 September 2013).

Home Office UK (2011a) 'User Guide to Home Office Crime Statistics', available online at www.homeoffice.gov.uk/publications/science-research-statistics/research-statistics/crime-research/user-guide-crime-statistics/user-guide-crime-statistics?view=Binary (accessed 18 September 2012).

Home Office UK (2012) 'Statistical News Release: Racist incidents, England and Wales, 2011/2012', available online at www.homeoffice.gov.uk/publications/science-research-statistics/research-statistics/crime-research/racist-incidents-1112/racist-incidents-1112-snr?view=Binary (accessed 18 September 2012).

Home Office UK (2015) *National Crime Recording Standard*, available online at www.gov.uk/government/uploads/system/uploads/attachment_data/file/116269/ncrs.pdf (accessed 10 January 2015).

Home Office, Office for National Statistics, and Ministry for Justice (2013) *An Overview of Hate Crime in England and Wales*, available online at www.gov.uk/government/

uploads/system/uploads/attachment_data/file/266358/hate-crime-2013.pdf (accessed 6 January 2015).

Hoodfar, H. (1993) 'The Veil in Their Minds and on Our Heads: The persistence of colonial images of Muslim women', *Resources for Feminist Research*, 22(3/4), 5–18.

Hopkins, P.E. (2004) 'Young Muslim Men in Scotland: Inclusions and exclusions', *Children's Geographies*, 2(2), 257–272.

Hopkins, P.E. (2006) 'Youthful Muslim masculinities: gender and generational relations', *Transactions of the Institute of British Geographers*, 31(3), 337–352.

Hosford, P. (2014) 'Racist Graffiti Painted Outside Immigrant Council Offices', available online at www.thejournal.ie/graffiti-painted-across-from-immigrant-council-offices-1301926-Feb2014/ (accessed 7 February 2014).

Human Rights First (2008) 'Violence Against Muslims: 2008 Hate Crime Survey', available online at www.oic-oci.org/uploads/File/humanrightsfirst-fd-080924-muslims-web.pdf (accessed 21 November 2010).

Human Rights First (2013) 'Hate Crime Report Card – The Netherlands', available online at www.humanrightsfirst.org/our-work/fighting-discrimination/hate-crime-report-card/hate-crime-report-card-the-netherlands/ (accessed 12 September 2013).

Human Rights First (2014) *Illusions of Justice: Human Rights Abuses in US Terrorism Prosecutions*, available online at www.hrw.org/sites/default/files/reports/usterrorism0714_ForUpload_0_0_0.pdf (accessed 23 February 2015).

Hussain, D. (2014) 'Theresa May exiled me to Pakistan via a "secret court"', *Huffington Post*, 22 December 2014 [online] available: www.huffingtonpost.co.uk/dilly-hussain/theresa-may-pakistan_b_6363868.html?utm_hp_ref=tw (accessed 22 December 2014).

Hussain, M. (2000) 'Islam, Media, and Minorities in Denmark', *Current Sociology*, 48(4), 95–116.

Hussain, Y. and Bagguley, P. (2012) 'Securitised citizens: Islamophobia, racism and the 7/7 London bombings', *The Sociological Review*, 60, 715–734.

Ibec (2014) 'About Us', available online at www.ibec.ie/IBEC/IBEC.nsf/vPages/About_Us~about-us?OpenDocument (accessed 2 April 2014).

Iganski, P. (2001) 'Hate Crimes Hurt More', *American Behavioural Scientist*, 45(4), 626–638.

Iganski, P. (2008) *Hate Crime and the City*, Bristol: Policy Press.

Ignatiev, N. (1995) *How the Irish Became White*, Abingdon: Routledge.

Immigrant Council of Ireland (2013) '50 Serious racist incidents reported in 10 weeks', available online at www.immigrantcouncil.ie/media/press-releases/703-50-serious-racist-incidents-reported-in-10-weeks (accessed 11 September 2013).

Immigrant Council of Ireland (2015) 'Report a Racist Incident', available online at www.immigrantcouncil.ie/component/content/article/243 (accessed 5 February 2015).

Immigrant Council of Ireland (2015a) 'Over 5,000 Calls for Help Answered in 2014', Press Release, available online at www.immigrantcouncil.ie/media/press-releases/918-over-5-000-calls-for-help-answered-in-2014 (accessed 5 February 2015).

Inspired by Muhammad (2013) 'YouGov Poll', available online at www.inspiredbymuhammad.com/yougov.php (accessed 27 September 2013).

Ionann Management Consultants (2004) 'Garda Human Rights Audit', available online at www.cilevics.eu/minelres/reports/ireland/PDF_Ireland)Comhlamh_GardaHRreport.pdf (accessed 18 September 2012).

Iordanou, G. (2013) 'Golden Dawn is Growing – Europe must help curb the rise of the far right', *Guardian*, 19 September 2013, available online at www.theguardian.com/

commentisfree/2013/sep/19/golden-dawn-europe-greek-cypriot (accessed 27 September 2013).
Iqbal, Z. (2010) 'Understanding Islamophobia: Conceptualising and Measuring the Construct', *European Journal of Social Sciences*, 13(4), 574–590.
Irish Council for Civil Liberties (2012) 'Know Your Rights: Gardaí', available online at www.iccl.ie/garda%C3%AD-2.html (accessed 18 September 2012).
Irish Times (2013) 'Two for Court Over 'Murder Plot'', *The Irish Times*, 15 March 2010, available online at www.irishtimes.com/news/two-for-court-over-murder-plot-1.854679 (accessed 28 September 2013).
Islamic Foundation of Ireland (2014) 'Who Lives Here Belongs Here', available online at www.islaminireland.com/news/who-lives-here-belongs-here/#Comment357 (accessed 20 February 2014).
Jansson, K., Budd, S., Lovbakke, J., Moley, S. and Thorpe, K. (2007) 'Attitudes, Perceptions and Risks of Crime: Supplementary volume 1 to Crime in England and Wales 2006/7', 2nd edn, available online at http://webarchive.nationalarchives.gov.uk/20110218135832/rds.homeoffice.gov.uk/rds/pdfs07/hosb1907.pdf (accessed 18 September 2012).
Jick, T.D. (2008 [1979]) 'Mixing Qualitative and Quantitative Methods: Triangulation in action', in Plano-Clark, V.L. and Creswell, J.W. (eds) *The Mixed Methods Reader*, Thousand Oaks and London: Sage, 107–120.
Jones, S.H. (2013) 'New Labour and the re-making of British Islam: The case of the radical middle way and the "reclamation" of the classical Islamic tradition', *Religions*, 4(4), 550–566.
Joyce, C. and Quinn, E. (2014) *The Organisation of Reception Facilities for Asylum Seekers in Ireland, European Migration Network Report*, available online at http://emn.ie/files/p_20140211023423The%20Organisation%20of%20Reception%20Facilities%20for%20Asylum%20Seekers.pdf (accessed 20 February 2014).
Kääriäinen, J. and Ellonen, N. (2008) 'The Finnish Racist Crime Monitoring System', in Goodey, J. and Aromaa, K. (eds) *Hate Crime: papers from the 2006 and 2007 Stockholm Criminology Symposiums*, available online at www.middlebury.edu/media/view/147451/original/Hate_Crime.pdf (accessed 10 January 2015), 56–67.
Kääriäinen, J. and Niemi, J. (2014) 'Distrust of the Police in a Nordic Welfare State: Victimisation, discrimination, and trust in the police by Russian and Somali minorities in Helsinki', *Journal of Ethnicity in Criminal Justice*, 12(1), 4–24.
Kapoor, N. (2013) 'The Advancement of Racial Neoliberalism in Britain', *Ethnic and Racial Studies*, 36(6), 1028–1046.
Kaya, A. (2011) 'Islamophobia as a Form of Governmentality: Unbearable weightness of the politics of fear', Willy Brandt Series of Working Papers in *International Centre for the Study of Radicalisation* (2014) ICSR Insight – Offering Foreign Fighters in Syria and Iraq a Way Out, available online at http://icsr.info/2014/08/icsr-insight-offering-foreign-fighters-syria-iraq-way/ (accessed 5 February 2015).
Kelly, F. and Ní Bhraonain, E. (2012) 'Hogan Request to Council Not to House Traveller family Ignored', available online at www.independent.ie/irish-news/hogan-request-to-council-not-to-house-traveller-family-ignored-28814075.html (accessed 7 February 2014).
Keohane, K. and Kuhling, C. (2014) *The Domestic, Moral and Political Economies of Post-Celtic Tiger Ireland: What rough beast?*, Manchester: Manchester University Press.
Khan, A.H. (2011) 'Transnational Influences on Irish Muslim Networks: From local to global perspectives', *Journal of Muslim Minority Affairs*, 31(4), 486–502.

Khiabany, G. and Williamson, M. (2008) 'Veiled bodies – Naked Racism: culture, politics and race in the Sun', *Race & Class*, 50(2), 69–88.

Kielinger, V. and Paterson, S. (2007) 'Policing Hate Crime in London', *American Behavioral Scientist*, 51(2), 196–204.

Kilpatrick, C. and Farrell, N. (2013) 'Derryman's journey from disillousioned teen to Syrian jihadist leaves neighbours at compete loss', *Belfast Telegraph*, 23 August 2014, available online at www.belfasttelegraph.co.uk/news/local-national/northern-ireland/derrymans-journey-from-disillusioned-teen-to-syrian-jihadist-leaves-neighbours-at-complete-loss-30529893.html (accessed 22 December 2014).

King-O'Riain, R.C. (2007) 'Counting on the "Celtic Tiger": Adding ethnic census categories in the Republic of Ireland', *Ethnicities*, 7(4), 516–542.

Kitching, K. (2010) 'An Excavation of the Racialised Politics of Viability Underpinning Education Policy in Ireland', *Irish Educational Studies*, 29(3), 213–229.

Klingspor, K. (2008) 'The Challenges of Collecting Statistical Data in the Field of Hate Crime: The case of Sweden', in Goodey, J. and Aromaa, K. (eds) *Hate Crime: papers from the 2006 and 2007 Stockholm Criminology Symposiums*, available online at www.middlebury.edu/media/view/147451/original/Hate_Crime.pdf (accessed 10 January 2015), 40–56.

Kumar, D. (2012) *Islamophobia and the Politics of Empire*, Chicago: Haymarket Books.

Kundnani, A. (2009) 'Spooked: How not to prevent violent extremism', available online at www.irr.org.uk/publications/issues/spooked-how-not-to-prevent-violent-extremism/ (accessed 14 February 2012).

Kundnani, A. (2014) *The Muslims are Coming: Islamophobia, Extremism and the Domestic War on Terror*, London: Verso.

Lally, C. and Kelly, F. (2014) 'Jihadist suspects passing through Ireland monitored: National Security Agency passes information about named suspects to Garda [sic]', *The Irish Times*, 5 September 2014, available online at www.irishtimes.com/news/crime-and-law/jihadist-suspects-passing-through-ireland-monitored-1.1918234 (accessed 22 December 2014).

Lemke, T. (2001) '"The Birth of Biopolitics": Michel Foucault's lecture at the College de France on neo-liberal governmentality', *Economy and Society*, 30(2), 190–207.

Lentin, A. (2008) *Racism: A Beginner's Guide*, Oxford: Oneworld.

Lentin, A. and Lentin, R. (2006) 'Speaking of Racism', in Lentin, A. and Lentin, R. (eds), *Race and State*, Newcastle: Cambridge Scholars Press, 1–14.

Lentin, A. and Titley, G. (2011) *The Crises of Multiculturalism: Racism in a neoliberal age*, London and New York: Zed Books.

Lentin, R. (2002) 'Who ever heard of an Irish Jew? The intersection of "Irishness" and "Jewishness"', in Lentin, R. and McVeigh, R. (eds) *Racism and Anti-Racism in Ireland*, Belfast: Beyond the Pale, 153–167

Lentin, R. and McVeigh, R. (2006) *After Optimism? Ireland, Racism and Globalisation*, Dublin: Metro Éireann Publications

Lewis, J., Mason, P. and Moore, K. (2011) 'Images of Islam in the UK: The representation of British Muslims in the national press 2000–8', in Petley, J. and Richardson, R. (eds), *Pointing the Finger: Islam and Muslims in the British Media*, Oxford: Oneworld, 40–66.

Limerick Leader (2014) 'Home Destined for Traveller Family is Gutted', available online at www.limerickleader.ie/news/local-news/home-destined-for-traveller-family-is-gutted-1-2189506 (accessed 7 February 2014).

Lincoln, Y.S. and Guba, E.G. (1986) 'But is it rigorous? Trustworthiness and authenticity in naturalistic evaluation', *New Directions for Program Evaluation*, 30, 73–84.

Lynch, C. (2009) 'Racism in Ireland. European Network Against Racism Shadow Report, Ireland, 2008', available online at http://enarireland.org/enar-ireland-shadow-reports/enar-ireland-shadow-reports-2003-2008/ (accessed 30 August 2012).

Lynch, C. (2011) *Putting Racism on the Record: a framework for monitoring racist incidents*, Dublin: Irish Network Against Racism (ENAR Ireland).

London Metropolitan Police Service (2014) *Freedom of Information Response*, available online at www.met.police.uk/foi/pdfs/disclosure_2014/june_2014/2013030001613.pdf (accessed 10 January 2015).

Mac An Ghaill, M. (1999) *Contemporary Racisms and Ethnicities: Social and cultural transformations*, Buckingham and Philadelphia: Open University Press.

MacDonald, H. (2011) 'Irish Coalition Government Formed Between Fine Gael and Labour', *Guardian*, Sunday, 6 March, available online at www.theguardian.com/world/2011/mar/06/irish-coalition-government-fine-labour (accessed 16 September 2013).

Mac Éinri, P. (2007) 'The Challenge of Migrant Integration in Ireland', *Evidence from New Countries of Immigration*, 9(1), 75–90.

Mac Gréil, M. (1977) *Prejudice and Tolerance in Ireland: Based on a survey of intergroup attitudes of Dublin adults and other sources*, Dublin: College of Industrial Relations

Maher, S. and Neumann, P. (2014) 'ICSR Insight – Offering Foreign Fighters in Syria and Iraq a Way Out', available online at http://icsr.info/2014/08/icsr-insight-offering-foreign-fighters-syria-iraq-way/ (accessed 7 May 2015).

Malik, K. (2005) 'The Islamophobia Myth', available online at www.kenanmalik.com/essays/prospect_islamophobia.html (accessed 30 August 2013).

McClintock, M. (2006) 'Statement by Michael McClintock, Director of Research, Human Rights First', November 9, 2006, available online at www.humanrightsfirst.org/wp-content/uploads/pdf/061130-discrim-hrf-vienna-dcm.pdf (accessed 18 September 2012).

McDevitt, J., Balboni, J., Garcia, L. and Gu, J. (2001) 'Consequences for Victims: A comparison of bias and non-bias-mitivated assaults', *American Behavioural Scientist*, 45(4), 697–713.

McDonald, H. (2010) '"Jihad Jane" Met Islamists Plotting to Kill Cartoonist, Irish Police Say: Accused US Islamist Colleen Renee LaRose "discussed plan" to kill Swedish artist Lars Vilks over Muhammad cartoon', *Guardian*, 11 March 2010, available online at www.theguardian.com/world/2010/mar/11/jihad-jane-muhammed-cartoon-plot (accessed 28 September 2013).

McDonald, H. (2013) 'Blonde girl, 7, removed from Roma family in Ireland: tipoff leads to removal of seven-year-old girl in Dublin following case in Greece where four-year-old Maria was allegedly abducted', available online at www.theguardian.com/world/2013/oct/22/irish-police-remove-blonde-child-roma-family, available online at (accessed 7 February 2014).

McDonald, H. (2013a) 'Child taken from second Roma family in Ireland by police returned to parents: DNA samples taken from Athlone boy of two and his parents, while family await results of tests on girl seven', available online at www.theguardian.com/world/2013/oct/23/second-child-roma-ireland-returned-athlone-dna (accessed 7 February 2014).

McElgunn, J. (2011) 'Al-Qaeda's Irish Terror Cell: Jihad fanatics hiding out amongst us', *The Irish Sun*, 5 May 2011.

McGinnity, F., O'Connell, P., Quinn, E. and Williams, E.J. (2006) *Migrants' Experience of Racism and Discrimination in Ireland*, Dublin: The Economic and Social Research Inistitute in association with the Equality Authority.

McGinnity, F., Watson, D. and Kingston, G. (2012) 'Analysing the Experience of Discrimination in Ireland: Evidence from the QNHS Equality Module 2010', available online at www.equality.ie/Files/Analysing-the-Experience-of-discrimination-in-Ireland.pdf (accessed 27 September 2013).

McNay, L. (2009) 'Self as Enterprise: Dilemmas of Control and Resistance in Foucault's The Birth of Biopolitics', *Theory Culture Society*, 26(6), 55–77.

McVeigh, R. (2002) 'Nick, Nack, Paddywhack: Anti-Irish racism and the racialisation of Irishness' in Lentin, R. and McVeigh, R. (eds) *Racism and Anti-Racism in Ireland*, Belfast: Beyond the Pale, 136–153.

McVeigh, R. (2007) 'Ethnicity Denial and Racism: The Case of the Government of Ireland Against Irish Travellers', *Translocations* 2(1), 90–133.

Meagher, J. (2014) 'Lifting the veil on Ireland's fastest growing religion', *The Irish Independent*, 21 September 2014, available online at www.independent.ie/life/lifting-the-veil-on-irelands-fastestgrowing-religion-30600549.html (accessed 7 May 2015).

Medina, J. (2011) 'Toward a Foucaultian Epistemology of Resistance: Counter-Memory, Epistemic Friction, and *Guerilla* Pluralism', *Foucault Studies*, (12), 9–35.

Meer, N. and Nayak, A. (2013) 'Race ends where? Race, racism and contemporary sociology', *Sociology*, Special E-Issue, 1–18.

Migrant's Rights Centre Ireland (2011) 'Singled Out: Exploratory study on ethnic profiling in Ireland and its impact on migrant workers and their families', available online at http://mrci.ie/wp-content/uploads/2011/03/Singled_Out.pdf (accessed 27 September 2013).

Miles, R. and Brown, M. (2003) *Racism*, 2nd edn, London and New York: Routledge.

Miller, P. and Rose, N. (2008) *Governing the Present*, Cambridge and Malden: Polity.

Ministry for Justice UK (2011) 'Statistics on Race and the Criminal Justice System 2010: A Ministry of Justice publication under Section 95 of the Criminal Justice Act 1991', available online at www.justice.gov.uk/downloads/statistics/mojstats/stats-race-cjs-2010.pdf (accessed 18 September 2012).

Mock, V. and Lichfield, J. (2010) 'Belgium passes Europe's first ban on wearing burka in public', *The Independent Online*, available online at www.independent.co.uk/news/world/europe/belgium-passes-europes-first-ban-on-wearing-burka-in-public-1959626.html (accessed 23 February 2015).

Modood, T. (1997) 'Difference, Cultural Racism and Anti-Racism', in Werbner, P. and Modood, T. (eds) *Debating Cultural Hybridity: Multi-cultural Identities and the Politics of Racism*, London: Zed Books, 154–172.

Modood, T. (2005) *Multicultural Politics: Racism, Ethnicity and Muslims in Britain*, Edinburgh: Edinburgh University Press.

Modood, T. and Meer, N. (2010) 'The Racialisation of Muslims', in Sayyid, S. and Vakil, A. (eds), *Thinking Through Islamophobia: Global perspectives*, London: Hurst, 69–85.

Modood, T., Berthoud, R. and Nazroo, J. (2002) '"Race", Racism and Ethnicity: A response to Ken Smith', *Sociology*, 36(2), 419–427.

Moore, R. and Hickman, M.J. (2010) *Changing and Claiming Ethnic Identities in the 1991 and 2001 Censuses*, Institute for the Study of European Transformations, available online at https://metranet.londonmet.ac.uk/fms/MRSite/Research/iset/Working%20Paper%20Series/WP20%20M%20Hickman.pdf (accessed 2 April 2014).

Morse, J.M. and Richards, L. (2002) *Read Me First for a User's Guide to Qualitative Research*, Thousand Oaks, London and New Delhi: Sage.

Muir, H. and Smith, L. (2004) *Islamophobia: Issues, challenges and action. A Report by the Commission on British Muslims and Islamophobia*, Stoke on Trent: Trentham Books.

Murphy, M. (2012) 'Interests, Institutions and Ideas: Explaining the Irish social security solicy', *Policy and Politics*, 40(3), 347–365.

Mythen, G., Walklate, S. and Khan, F. (2009) '"I'm a Muslim but I'm Not a Terrorist": Victimisation, risky identities and the performance of safety', *British Journal of Criminology*, 49, 736–754.

Najjair, S. (2013) *Soldier for a Summer: One Irishman's part in Gadaffi's downfall*, Dublin: Hachette Books.

Nasc (2011) 'Submission on the Merger of Irish Human Rights Commission (IHRC) and the Equality Authority: A service provider's perspective', available online at www.upr.ie/website/upr/uprweb.nsf/page/BEHO-8RXK8W14412629-en/$file/Submission%20Nov2011%20NASC.pdf (accessed 27 September 2013).

Nasc (2013) 'In From the Margins: Roma in Ireland', available online at www.nascireland.org/wp-content/uploads/2013/05/NASC-ROMA-REPORT.pdf (accessed 28 September 2013).

National Focal Point (2002) 'Analytical Study on Racist Violence EUMC RAXEN3 Report on Ireland', available online at www.nccri.ie/pdf/RacialViolence_RAXEN3.pdf (accessed 18 September 2012).

National Focal Point (2004) 'National Analytical Study on Racist Violence and Crime', available online at http://fra.europa.eu/fraWebsite/attachments/CS-RV-NR-IE.pdf (accessed 18 September 2012).

National Consultative Committee on Racism and Interculturalism (2002) 'Racial Violence and Related Crime in Ireland: Submission to the National Crime Council Re. the underlying causes of crime', available online at www.nccri.ie/submissions/02NovCrime.pdf (accessed 11 September 2013).

National Consultative Committee on Racism and Interculturalism (2007) 'The Muslim Community in Ireland: Challenging so of myths [sic] and misinformation', available online at www.nccri.ie/pdf/ChallengingMyths-Muslims.pdf (accessed 27 September 2013).

National Consultative Committee on Racism and Interculturalism (2013) 'Racist Incidents', available online at www.nccri.ie/incidents2001.html (accessed 27 September 2013).

National Consultative Committee on Racism and Interculturalism (2013a) 'Recent newspaper articles and letters related to the dissolution of NCCRI' [sic], available online at www.nccri.ie/pdf/recent_coverage_about_nccri.pdf (accessed 27 September 2013).

National Consultative Committee on Racism and Interculturalism (2013b) 'NCCRI Six-Monthly Racist Incidents Reports', available online at www.nccri.ie/incidents-reports.html (accessed 27 September 2013).

National Crime Council (2004) 'Report of the Expert Group on Crime Statistics', available online at www.crimecouncil.gov.ie/downloads/ExpertGroupStats.pdf (accessed 18 September 2012).

National Policing Improvement Agency (2011) 'The National Standard for Incident Recording', available online at www.homeoffice.gov.uk/publications/science-research-statistics/research-statistics/crime-research/count-nsir11?view=Binary (accessed 18 September 2012).

Neumann, P. (2014) *The New Jihadism: A global snapshot; The International Centre for the Study of Radicalisation and Political Violence*, available online at http://icsr.info/

wp-content/uploads/2014/12/ICSR-REPORT-The-New-Jihadism-A-Global-Snapshot. pdf (accessed 23 February 2015).

NGO Alliance Against Racism (2011) 'Shadow Report: In response to the third and fourth periodic reports of Ireland under the UN International Convention on the Elimination of All Forms of Racial Discrimination', available online at www.immigrant-council.ie/images/stories/NAAR_Shadow_Report_to_CERD_final.pdf (accessed 10 February 2012).

Nickels, H.C., Thomas, L., Hickman, M.J. and Silvestri, S. (2012) 'Constructing "suspect" communities and Britishness: Mapping British press coverage of Irish and Muslim communities, 1974–2007', *European Journal of Communication,* 27(2), 135–151.

Ní Chatháin, S. (2011) 'Transnational Migrants' Negotiations of Formal and Cultural Citizenship', *Irish Journal of Sociology,* 19 (2), 27–42.

Niemi, J. (2011) 'Poliisin Tietoon Tullut Viharikollisuus Suomessa 2010', available online at www.poliisiammattikorkeakoulu.fi/poliisi/poliisioppilaitos/home.nsf/files/DB 54AA1FE9A222B9C2257925004A8CDA/$file/Raportteja95_Niemi_web.pdf (accessed 18 September 2012).

Ní Laoire, C. (2007) 'The "Green Green Grass of home"? Return migration to rural Ireland', *Journal of Rural Studies,* 23(3), 332–344.

Ni Shúinéar, S. (2002) 'Other the Irish (Travellers)', in Lentin, R. and McVeigh, R. (eds) *Racism and Anti-Racism in Ireland,* Belfast: Beyond the Pale, 177–193

Nocon, A., Iganski, P. and Lagou, S. (2011) 'Disabled People's Experiences and Concerns About Crime: Analysis of the British Crime Survey 2007–8, 2008–9 and 2009–10', available online at http://eprints.lancs.ac.uk/54416/1/EHRC_briefing_paper_3.pdf (accessed 20 September 2013).

Nolan, J. (2006) 'Tolerance Implementation Meeting: Addressing the Hate Crime Data Deficit', Keynote Address, available online at http://tandis.odihr.pl/documents/03034. pdf (accessed 18 September 2012).

O'Carroll, S. (2013) 'Racist Graffiti Scrawled On Walls During Halal Store Ransacking', available online at www.thejournal.ie/halal-store-trashed-graffiti-dublin-1171599-Nov2013/ (accessed 7 February 2014).

O'Connell, J. (2002) 'Travellers in Ireland: An examination of discrimination and racism', in Lentin, R. and McVeigh, R. (eds) *Racism and Anti-Racism in Ireland,* Belfast: Beyond the Pale, 49–63.

O'Connell, P.J. and McGinnity F. (2008) 'Immigrants at Work: Ethnicity and Nationality in the Irish Labour Market', available online at www.equality.ie/Files/Immigrants%20 at%20Work%20-%20Ethnicity%20and%20Nationality%20in%20e%20Irish%20 Labour%20Market.pdf (accessed 18 September 2012).

O'Connor, S. (2011) *Impact of the Transfer System in Direct Provision: 'It was sleepless nights, to be honest, then the letter came a few days later' – Direct Provision and Asylum in Ireland: The transfer system and its consequences,* available online at http://dorasluimni.org/wp-content/uploads/pdf/publications/transfersystemimpact.pdf (accessed 7 February 2014).

O'Curry, S. and Michael, L. (2013) *Reports of Racism in Ireland: 1 quarterly report of ireport.ie,* available online at http://enarireland.org/wp-content/uploads/2013/12/iReport_QR_2013_3mb.pdf (accessed 20 January 2014).

Office for the Press Ombudsman (2014) 'European Network Against Racism Ireland and the Irish Independent', available online at www.pressombudsman.ie/decided-by-press-ombudsman/european-network-against-racism-ireland-and-the-irish-independent.2356. html (accessed 20 February 2014).

Office for the Promotion of Migrant Integration (2015) 'Reported Racist Crime', available online at www.integration.ie/website/omi/omiwebv6.nsf/page/statistics-RacistIncidentsstatisticscrime-en (accessed 5 February 2015).

Office of the Minister for Integration (2008) 'Migration Nation: Statement on integration strategy and diversity management', available online at www.integration.ie/website/omi/omiwebv6.nsf/page/AXBN-7SQDF91044205-en/$File/Migration%20Nation.pdf (accessed 27 September 2013).

Office of the Refugee Applications Commissioner (2014) 'Statistics', available online at www.orac.ie/website/orac/oracwebsite.nsf/page/orac-stats-en (accessed 7 February 2014).

Oksala, J. (2011) 'Violence and Neoliberal Governmentality', *Constellations*, 18(3), 474–486.

Omi, M. and Winant, H. (2002) 'Racial Formation', in Essed P. and Goldberg D.T. (eds) *Race Critical Theories*, Malden, Oxford and Carlton: Blackwell Publishing, 123–146.

Onwuegbuzie, A.J. and Johnson, R.B. (2008 [2006]) 'The Validity Issue in Mixed Research', in Plano-Clark, V.L. and Creswell, J.W. (eds), *The Mixed Methods Reader*, Thousand Oaks and London: Sage, 273–298.

Open Society (2010) *Muslims in Europe, At Home in Europe: A report on 11 EU Cities*, available online at www.sv.uio.no/iss/english/research/projects/eumargins/news/documents/muslims%20in%20europe-osi.pdf (accessed 17 January 2015).

Open Society (2011) 'Unveiling the Truth: Why 32 Muslim Women Wear the Full Face Veil in France', available online at www.soros.org/initiatives/home/articles_publications/publications/unveiling-the-truth-20110411 (accessed 12 April 2011).

Open Society (2011a) *Muslims in Marseille, At Home in Europe Project*, available online at www.opensocietyfoundations.org/sites/default/files/a-muslims-marseille-en-20110920.pdf (accessed 17 January 2015).

Organisation for Security and Cooperation in Europe (2011) 'Hate Crimes in the OSCE Region – Incidents and responses', *Office for Democratic Institutions and Human Rights*, Annual Report for 2010, available online at http://tandis.odihr.pl/hcr2010/pdf/Hate_Crime_Report_full_version.pdf (accessed 30 November 2011).

Organisation for Security and Cooperation in Europe (2012) 'Hate Crimes in the OSCE Region – Incidents and Responses', *Office for Democratic Institutions and Human Rights*, Annual Report for 2011, available online at www.osce.org/ru/odihr/102100 (accessed 23 September 2013).

Organisation for Security and Cooperation in Europe (2015) *Hate Crime Reporting*, available online at http://hatecrime.osce.org/ (accessed 9 February 2015).

O'Riordan, S. (2011) 'Cork City Councillor Calls for Ban on Burka and Hoodies', *The Irish Examiner*, 19 August 2011, available online at www.irishexaminer.com/ireland/cork-city-councillor-calls-for-ban-on-burkas-and-hoodies-164769.html (accessed 27 September 2013).

Pantazis, C. and Pemberton, S. (2009) 'From the "Old" to the "New" Suspect Community: Examining the impacts of recent UK counter-terrorist legislation', *British Journal of Criminology*, 49(5), 646–666.

Parliament UK (2012) 'Register Of All-Party Groups', available online at www.publications.parliament.uk/pa/cm/cmallparty/register/islamophobia.htm (accessed 1 September 2012).

Pasquino, P. (1991) 'Crimnology: The birth of special knowledge' in Burchell, G., Gordon, C. and Miller, P. (eds) *The Foucault Effect: studies in governmentality*, Chicago: University of Chicago Press, 105–119.

Bibliography

Pavee Point (2010) *All Ireland Traveller Health Study: Our Geels*, available online at www.paveepoint.ie/tempsite3/wp-content/uploads/2013/10/AITHS-Summary-of-Findings.pdf (accessed 5 February 2014).

Peachy, P. (2014) 'Police racism: Top forces in the dock over failure of 94 discrimination inquiries', *Guardian*, available online at www.independent.co.uk/news/uk/crime/police-racism-top-forces-in-the-dock-over-failure-of-94-discrimination-inquiries-9488243.html (accessed 9 February 2015).

Perry, B. (2001) *In the Name of Hate: Understanding hate crimes*, New York and London: Routledge.

Perry, B. (2009) 'Counting and Countering Hate Crime', available online at www.osce.org/odihr/39220 (accessed 18 September 2012).

Peutere, L. (2009) 'Hate Crimes Reported to the Police in Finland, 2008: Reports of the Police College of Finland 85/2009', available online at www.poliisiammattikorkeakoulu.fi/poliisi/poliisioppilaitos/home.nsf/files/raportti_85_en/$file/raportti_85_en.pdf (accessed 18 September 2012).

Pew Research (2011) *The Future of the Global Muslim Population. Region: Europe*, available online at www.pewforum.org/2011/01/27/future-of-the-global-muslim-population-regional-europe/ (accessed 15 February 2015).

Phelan, S. (2007) 'The Discourses of Neoliberal Hegemony: The case of the Irish Republic', *Critical Discourse Studies*, 4(1), 29–48.

Phillips, C. and Bowling, B. (2003) 'Racism, Ethnicity and Criminology: Developing minority perspectives', *British Journal of Criminology*, 43(2), 269–290.

Police Service of Northern Ireland (2014) *Incidents and Crimes with a Hate Motivation Recorded by the Police in Northern Ireland: Quarterly Update to 31 March 2014* (Providing final figures for 1 April 2013 to 31 March 2014), available online at www.psni.police.uk/quarterly_hate_motivations_bulletin_period_ending_sep14.pdf (accessed 9 January 2015).

Porter, S. (1993) 'Critical Realist Ethnography: The case of racism and professionalism in a medical setting', *Sociology*, 27(4), 591–609.

Power, M.J., Haynes, A. and Devereux, E. (2012) 'From the Mouths of Janus: Irish politicians' constructions of transnational EU migrants in Ireland', available online at www.dit.ie/icr/media/diticr/documents/1%20Power.pdf (accessed 28 September 2013).

Poynting, S. and Noble, G. (2004) *Living with Racism: The experience and reporting by Arab and Muslim Australians of discrimination, abuse and violence since 11 September 2001*, Report to the Human Rights and Equal Opportunity Commission available online at www.stepone.org.au/media/1712/living%20with%20racism.pdf (accessed 20 September 2013).

Poynting, S. and Perry, B. (2007) 'Climates of hate: Media and state inspired victimisation of Muslims in Canada and Australia since 9/11', *Current Issues in Criminal Justice*, 19, 151–171.

Public Prosecution Service of Northern Ireland (2014) *Statistical Bulletin: Cases Involving Hate Crime 2013/14 1 April to 31 March*, available online at www.ppsni.gov.uk/Branches/PPSNI/PPSNI/Files/Documents/Stats%20and%20Research/Statistical%20Bulletin%20on%20Cases%20Involving%20Hate%20Crime%202013-14.pdf (accessed 9 January 2015).

Raidió Teilifís Éireann (2013) 'Now it's Personal', available online at www.rte.ie/tv/programmes/now_its_personal.html (accessed 27 September 2013).

Ramadan, T. 2015 'The Paris Attackers hijacked Islam but there is no war between Islam and the west', *Guardian*, 9 January 2015, available online at www.theguardian.com/

commentisfree/2015/jan/09/paris-hijackers-hijacked-islam-no-war-between-islam-west (accessed 14 January 2015).

Ramirez-Valles, J., Heckathorn, D.D., Vázquez, R., Diaz, R.M. and Campbell, R.T. (2005) 'From Networks to Populations: the development and application of respondent-driven sampling among IDUs and Latino gay men', *AIDS and Behavior*, 9(4), 387–402.

Rana, J. (2007) 'The Story of Islamophobia', *Souls: A Critical Journal of Black Politics, Culture, and Society*, 9(2), 148–161.

Rattansi, A. (2005) 'The Uses of Racialisation: The time-spaces and subject-objects of the raced body', in Murji, K. and Solomos, J. (eds), *Racialisation: Studies in Theory and Practice*, 271–303.

Rattansi, A. (2007) *Racism: A Very Short Introduction*, Oxford: Oxford University Press.

Razack, S.H. (2004) 'Imperilled Muslim Women, Dangerous Muslim Men and Civilised Europeans: Legal and social responses to forced marriages', *Feminist Legal Studies* 12(2), 129–174.

Razack, S.H. (2008) *Casting Out: The eviction of Muslims from western law and politics*, Toronto, Buffalo and London: University of Toronto Press.

Reception and Integration Agency (2014) 'Direct Provision', available online at www.ria. gov.ie/en/RIA/Pages/Direct_Provision_FAQs (accessed 7 February 2014).

Redclift, V. (2014) 'New Racisms, new racial subjects? The neo-liberal moment and the racial landscape of contemporary Britain', *Ethnic and Racial Studies*, 37(4), 577–288.

Richards, L. (2005) *Handling Qualitative Data: A practical guide*, London, Thousand Oaks and New Delhi: Sage.

Richardson, E. (2011) 'Islamic Finance for Consumers in Ireland: A comparative study of the position of retail-level Islamic finance in Ireland', *Journal of Muslim Minority Affairs*, 31(4), 534–553.

Richardson, R. (2009) 'Islamophobia or anti-Muslim Racism – or What? Concepts and terms revisited', Paper given at Islamophobia and Religious Discrimination: new perspectives, policies and practices, University of Birmingham, 9 December 2009, available online at www.insted.co.uk/anti-muslim-racism.pdf (accessed 4 January 2012).

Riley-Smith, J. (2010) 'Islamophobia and the Crusades', in Sayyid, S. and Vakil, A. (eds), *Thinking Through Islamophobia: Global perspectives*, London: Hurst, 19–23.

Riessman, C.K. (2005) 'Narrative Analysis', University of Huddersfield Repository, available online at http://eprints.hud.ac.uk/4920/2/Chapter_1_-_Catherine_Kohler_ Riessman.pdf (accessed 27 September 2013).

Roberts, D.J. and Mahtani, M. (2010) 'Neoliberalizing Race, Racing Neoliberalism: Placing 'race' in neoliberal discourses', *Antipode*, 42(2), 248–257.

Rolston, B. and Shannon, M. (2002) *Encounters: How racism came to Ireland*, Belfast: Beyond the Pale.

Rose, N., O'Malley, P. and Valverde, M. (2006) 'Governmentality', in *Annual Review of Law Soc. Sci.*, 2, 83–104.

Roy, O. (2008) *Islamic terrorist radicalisation in Europe. European Islam. Challenges for public policy and society*, Brussels: Centre for European Policy Studies.

Runnymede Trust (1997) *Islamophobia: A challenge to us all*, available online at www. runnymedetrust.org/publications/17/32.html (accessed 1 August 2010).

Russell, H. (2010) 'Inequality and Discrimination in the Irish Labour Market' in *Equality in a Time of Change: Mainstreaming equality in further education, training and labour market programmes*, Conference Papers 2007–2009, available online at www.equality. ie/Files/Equality%20in%20a%20Time%20of%20Change.pdf (accessed 18 September 2012).

Russell, H., Quinn, E., King O'Riain, R. and McGinnity, F. (2008) 'The Experience of Discrimination in Ireland: Analysis of the QNHS Equality Module', available online at www.equality.ie/Files/The%20Experience%20of%20Discrimination%20in%20 Ireland.pdf (accessed 18 September 2012).

Ryan, L., Kofman, E. and Aaron, P. (2010) 'Insiders and Outsiders: Working with peer researchers in researching Muslim communities', *International Journal of Social Research Methodology*, 14(1), 49–60.

Ryan, O. (2013) 'Alan Shatter Condemns Racist Vandalism in Dublin', *The Irish Times*, 6 June 2013, available online at www.irishtimes.com/alan-shatter-condemns-racist-vandalism-in-dublin-1.1418241 (accessed 28 September 2013).

Ryan, P. (2015) 'Unit aims to "build bridges" with Muslim community in Ireland', *The Irish Independent*, available online at www.independent.ie/irish-news/unit-aims-to-build-bridges-with-muslim-community-in-ireland-30973270.html (accessed 9 February 2015).

Rydgren, J. (2008) 'Immigration Sceptics, Xenophobes or racists? Radical right-wing voting in six west European countries', *European Journal of Political Research*, 47(6), 737–738.

Sahramäki, I., Niemi, J. and Kääriäinen, J. (2014) 'Racist Crime Reported to the Police in Finland', *European Journal of Crime, Criminal Law and Criminal Justice*, 22, 59–78.

Said, E. (2003 [1985]) *Orientalism*, London: Penguin.

Sakaranaho, T. (2006) *Religious Freedom, Multiculturalism, Islam: Cross-reading Finland and Ireland*, Leiden and Boston: Brill.

Salganik, M.J. and Heckathorn, D.D. (2004) 'Sampling and Estimation in Hidden Populations Using Respondent-driven Sampling', *Sociological Methodology*, 34(1), 193–240.

Sapsted, D. (2010) 'Irish Police Hold Four Allegedly for Links with Jihad Jane', *The National*, 14 March 2010, available online at www.thenational.ae/news/world/europe/irish-police-hold-four-allegedly-for-links-with-jihad-jane (accessed 28 September 2013).

Saul, H. (2014) 'Britain First picture: Photographer "horrified" after Afghan policewoman killed by Taliban used for "ban the burka" campaign', *The Independent Online*, available online at www.independent.co.uk/news/world/australasia/photographer-horrified-after-claims-britain-first-used-picture-of-first-afghan-policewoman-killed-by-taliban-for-ban-the-burka-campaign-9745959.html (accessed 23 February 2015).

Sayyid, S. (2010) 'Thinking Through Islamophobia', in Sayyid, S. and Vakil, A. (eds) *Thinking Through Islamophobia: Global perspectives*, London: Hurst, 1–5.

Scharbrodt, O. (2011) 'Islam in Ireland: Organising a migrant religion', in Cosgrove, O., Cox, L., Kuhling, C. and Mulholland, P. (eds), *Ireland's New Religious Movements*, Newcastle-Upon-Tyne: Cambridge Scholars Publishing, 318–337.

Scharbrodt, O. (2012) 'Muslim Immigration to the Republic of Ireland: Trajectories and dynamics since World War II', *Éire-Ireland: A Journal of Irish Studies*, 47 (1 and 2), 221–243.

Scharbrodt, O. and Sakaranaho, T. (2011) 'Islam and Muslims in the Republic of Ireland: An Introduction to the Special Issue', *Journal of Muslim Minority Affairs*, 31(4), 469–485.

Schweppe, J. and Walsh, D. (2008) 'Combating Racism and Xenophobia through the Criminal Law', available online at www.integration.ie/website/omi/omiwebv6.nsf/page/AXBN-7UPE6D1121207-en/$File/Combating%20Racism%20with%20e%20 Criminal%20Law.pdf (accessed 23 September 2013).

Schweppe, J., Haynes, A. and Carr, J. (2014) 'A Life Free From Fear. Legislating for Hate Crime in Ireland: An NGO Perspective', University of Limerick, available online at www.ul.ie/emotions/publications [accessed:24 February 2015).

Schiffer, S. and Wagner, C. (2011) 'Anti-Semitism and Islamophobia – New enemies, old patterns', *Race and Class*, 52(3), 77–84.

Secretary of State for the Communities and Local Government UK (2010) 'All-party Inquiry into Anti-Semitism: Government response', available online at www.communities.gov.uk/documents/communities/pdf/1798120.pdf (accessed 18 September 2012).

Sending, O.J. and Neumann, I.B. (2006) 'Governance to governmentality: analyzing NGOs, states, and power', *International Studies Quarterly*, 50(3), 651–672.

Semati, M. (2010) 'Islamophobia, Culture and Race in the Age of Empire', *Cultural Studies*, 24(2), 256–275.

Shanneik, Y. (2011) 'Conversion and Religious Habitus: The experiences of Irish women converts to Islam in the pre-Celtic Tiger era', *Journal of Muslim Minority Affairs*, 31(4), 503–517.

Sharp, D. and Atherton, S. (2007) 'To Serve and Protect? The experiences of policing in the community of young people from Black and other ethnic minority groups', *British Journal of Criminology*, 47(5), 746–763.

Sheehan, M. (2011) '"Jihad Jane" to Testify Here in Terror Trial', *Independent*, 6 February 2011, available online at www.independent.ie/irish-news/jihad-jane-to-testify-here-in-terror-trial-26658104.html (accessed 28 September 2013).

Sheehi, S. (2011) *Islamophobia: The ideological campaign against Muslims*, Atlanta: Clarity Press.

Sheridan, L. (2006) 'Islamophobia Pre-and Post-September 11, 2001', *Journal of Interpersonal Violence*, 21(3), 317–336.

Silverman, D. (2001) *Interpreting Qualitative Data: Methods for analysing talk, text and interaction*, 2nd edn, London, Thousand Oaks and New Delhi: Sage.

Silverman, D. (2010) *Doing Qualitative Research*, 3rd edn, London, Thousand Oaks, New Delhi and Washington DC: Sage.

Sinha, S. (2002) 'Generating awareness for the experiences of women of colour in Ireland', in Lentin, R. and McVeigh, R. (eds) *Racism and Anti-Racism in Ireland*, Belfast: Beyond the Pale, 116–129

Siraj, A. (2011) 'Meanings of modesty and the hijab amongst Muslim women in Glasgow, Scotland', *Gender, Place & Culture*, (6), 716–731.

Sirin, S.R. and Katsiaficas, D. (2011) 'Religiosity, Discrimination, and Community Engagement: Gendered pathways of Muslim American emerging adults', *Youth and Society*, 43(4) 1528–1546.

Skeggs, B. (1997) *Formations of Class and Gender: Becoming Respectable*, London: Sage.

Skogan, W.G. (2006) 'Asymmetry in the impact of encounters with police', *Policing and Society*, 16(2), 99–126.

Smith, C.P. (2000) 'Content Analysis and Narrative Analysis', available online at http://faculty.fuqua.duke.edu/~jglynch/Ba591/Session02/Smith%202000%20Handbook%20Content%20Analysis.pdf (accessed 12 June 2012).

Smith, K., Lader, D., Hoare, J and Lau, I. (2012) 'Hate Crime, Cyber Security and the Experience of Crime among Children: Findings from the 2010/11 British Crime Survey. Supplementary Volume 3 to Crime in England and Wales 2010/11', available online at www.homeoffice.gov.uk/publications/science-research-statistics/research-statistics/crime-research/hosb0612/hosb0612?view=Binary (accessed 18 September 2012).

Spalek, B. (2002) *Islam, Crime and Criminal Justice*, Cullompton: Willan.

Spalek, B. (2010) 'Community Policing, Trust, and Muslim Communities in Relation to "New Terrorism"', *Politics and Policy*, 38(4), 789–815.

Spalek, B. (2011) 'A Top Down Approach', *Soundings: Policy Matters for Muslims in Britain*, available online at http://soundings.mcb.org.uk/?p=29 (accessed 27 September 2013).

Sparks, C. (2006) 'The Production of the Imaginary Terrorist as an Object of Fear: Orientalism in the twenty first century', in Lentin, A. and Lentin, R. (eds) *Race and State*, Newcastle: Cambridge Scholars Press, 152–168.

Special Group on Public Service Numbers and Expenditure Programmes (2009) *Report of the Special Group on Public Service Numbers and Expenditure Programmes*, available online at www.google.ie/url?sa=t&rct=j&q=&esrc=s&source=web&cd=1&sqi=2&ved=0CCwQFjAA&url=http%3A%2F%2Fper.gov.ie%2Fwp-content%2Fuploads%2FBord_Snip_Nua_Volume_I.pdf&ei=dYdOU_ScJe2B7Qa6sYHICA&usg=AFQjCNGmssJKSwoU_MVSglhPhWqwoTdQLw&sig2=RzamRFrNUgjzJwko1s5BgQ&bvm=bv.64764171,d.ZGU (accessed 20 February 2014).

Spiegel (2014) 'The End of Tolerance? Anti-Muslim Movement Rattles Germany', available online at www.spiegel.de/international/germany/anti-muslim-pegida-movement-rattles-germany-a-1009245.html (accessed 22 December 2014).

Spiegel (2015) 'Prying into PEGIDA: Where did Germany's Islamophobes come from?' available online at www.spiegel.de/international/germany/origins-of-german-anti-muslim-group-pegida-a-1012522.html (accessed 14 January 2015).

Stevens, P.E. and Doerr, B.T. (1997) 'Trauma of Discovery: Women's narratives of being informed they are HIV-infected', *AIDS care*, 9(5), 523–538.

Strabac, Z. and Listhaug, O. (2008) 'Anti-Muslim prejudice in Europe: A multilevel analysis of survey data from 30 countries', *Social Science Research*, 37(1), 268–286.

Taylor, S. (2010) 'Responding to Racist Incidents and Racist Crimes in Ireland', available online at www.equality.ie/en/Publications/Policy-Publications/Responding-to-Racist-Incidents-And-Racist-Crimes-in-Ireland.html (accessed 18 April 2012).

Tell MAMA (2015) 'Measuring anti-Muslim Attacks', available online at http://tell-MAMAuk.org/ (accessed 5 February 2015).

Tell MAMA (2015a) '51 Anti-Muslim Incidents in France, mapper by Tell MAMA', available online at http://tellmamauk.org/tag/anti-muslim/ (accessed 6 February 2015).

Tell MAMA (2015b) 'More Rotherham Racial and Religious Hate Crimes in the City as Extremist Far Right Groups Agitate', available online at http://tellmamauk.org/rotherham-racial-religious-hate-crimes-city-extremist-far-right-groups-agitate/ (accessed 6 February 2015).

The Scottish Government (2014) *Religiously Aggravated Offending in Scotland 2012–13*, available online at www.scotland.gov.uk/Resource/0042/00424865.pdf (accessed 9 January 2015).

The Scottish Government (2014a) *Scottish Crime and Justice Survey 2012/13: Main Findings*, available online at www.scotland.gov.uk/Publications/2014/03/9823 (accessed 9 January 2015).

Thompson, G. (2007) 'Responsibility and neo-liberalism', available online at www.opendemocracy.net/article/responsibility_and_neo_liberalism (accessed 5 February 2015).

Tracey, M. (2000) 'Racism and Immigration in Ireland: A comparative analysis', MPhil Thesis, Trinity College Dublin, Ireland, available online at www.tcd.ie/sociology/ethnicracialstudies/assets/documents/Marshall_01.pdf (accessed 1 September 2012).

Triandafyllidou, A. and Gropas, R. (2009) 'Constructing Difference: The mosque debates on Greece', *Journal of Ethnic and Migration Studies*, 35(6), 957–975.

True Vision (2012) 'True Vision Stop Hate Crime', available online at http://report-it.org.uk/home (accessed 17 June 2012).

University of Limerick (2013) 'Faculty of Arts, Humanities and Social Sciences: Ethical guidelines', available online at www.artsoc.ul.ie/faculty-of-arts-humanities-and-social-sciences-ethics-guidelines.php (accessed 22 August 2013).

Vakil, A. (2010) 'Is the Islam in Islamophobia the same as the Islam in Anti-Islam; or when is it Islamophobia time?', in Sayyid, S. and Vakil, A. (eds) *Thinking Through Islamophobia: Global perspectives*, London: Hurst, 23–45.

Vakil, A. (2014) *British values and British Muslims*, Open Democracy, available online at www.opendemocracy.net/ourkingdom/abdoolkarim-vakil/british-values-and-british-muslims (accessed 15 February 2015).

Vale, P. (2014) 'Bill Maher, Ben Affleck And Sam Harris in Heated Row About Islamophobia And Radical Islam', *Huffington Post*, available online at www.huffingtonpost.co.uk/2014/10/04/bill-maher-ben-affleck-and-sam-harris-in-heated-row-about-islam_n_5931284.html (accessed 4 December 2014).

van der Valk, I. (2012) *Islamophobia in the Netherlands*, Amsterdam: Amsterdam University Press.

van der Veen, G. (2011) 'Fear of Crime: Its social construction in the Netherlands', *Criminology* (Special Issue), 44–49.

van Donselaar, J. and Rodrigues, P.R. (2008) 'Racism and Extremism Monitor Eight Report', available online at www.annefrank.org/ImageVaultFiles/id_12121/cf_21/Monitor8UK.PDF (accessed 12 September 2013).

van Nieuwkerk, K. (2004) 'Veils and Wooden Clogs Don't Go Together', *Ethnos*, 69(2), 229–246.

Venkatesh, S. (2006) 'Research: The Researcher's Dilemma', *Law & Social Inquiry*, 24(4), 987–991.

Walsh, D.P.J. (2009) *Human Rights and Policing in Ireland: Law, policy and practice*, Dublin: Clarus.

Werbner, P. (1997) 'Essentialisng Silence: Ambivalence and multiplicity in the constructions of racism and ethnicity', in Werbner, P. and Modood, T. (eds) *Debating Cultural Hybridity: Multi-cultural identities and the politics of racism*, London: Zed Books, 226–257.

White, E.J. (2002) 'The new Irish storytelling: Media, representations and racialised identities', in Lentin, R. and McVeigh, R. (eds) *Racism and Anti-Racism in Ireland*, Belfast: Beyond the Pale, 102–116

Wieviorka, M. (1997) 'Essentialism Versus Hybridity, Negotiating Difference: Is it so difficult to be anti-racist?', in Werbner, P. and Modood, T. (eds) *Debating Cultural Hybridity: Multi-cultural identities and the politics of racism*, London: Zed Books, 139–153.

Younge, G. (2015) 'Charlie Hebdo: the danger of polarised debate', *Guardian*, 11 January 2015, available online at www.theguardian.com/commentisfree/2015/jan/11/charie-hebdo-danger-polarised-debate-paris-attacks (accessed 14 January 2015).

Your Rights Right Now (2013) 'Video of Ireland's Appearance at the UN Human Rights Council – 15 March 2012 Geneva', available online at www.rightsnow.ie/ (accessed 11 September 2013).

Zappone, K. (2003) 'Rethinking Identity: The challenge of diversity', available online at www.ihrc.ie/download/pdf/rethinking_identity_the_challenge_of_diversity.pdf (accessed 27 September 2013).

Zempi, I. and Chakraborti, N. (2014) *Islamophobia, Victimisation and the Veil*, Basingstoke and New York: Palgrave MacMillan.

Zhao, J., Thurman, Q.C. and Lovrich, N.P. (1995) 'Community-oriented Policing across the US: Facilitators and impediments to implementation', *American Journal of Police* 14(1), 11–28.

Ziemer, U. (2011) 'Minority Youth, Everyday Racism and Public Spaces in Contemporary Russia', *European Journal of Cultural Studies*, 14(2), 229–242.

Index

Page numbers in **bold** denote figures.

agency 30, 50, 51, 90, 93
Al-Minnah Foods incident 40–1
Ali, Azad 10–11
All Party Parliamentary Group on Islamophobia 143–4
Allen, Chris 3, 6, 10, 34, 35, 40, 41, 42, 44–5, 48–9, 51, 52, 53, 78, 143–4
Ameli, S.R. 3–4
An Garda Siochána *see* police
anti-Muslim racism: accessing the knowledges of anti-Muslim racism 151–2; anti-Muslim sentiment 44–5, 46; coping strategies for dealing with racism 120, 125–7; as cultural racism 42; defining anti-Muslim racism as anti-Muslim *racism* 37–44; denormalisation of 30; discrimination 66–7, 75–6, 87; hegemonic Irishness 76–7; image of Muslims as traitors 80–1; in Ireland 74–6; lack of data on 1, 2, 10–11, 30–1, 55–6, 143–4; lack of recognition in Ireland 10; 'liberation' of women 92–6; Muslimness outside the 'norm' of Irishness 79, 134–5; in the neoliberal era 2–4; and neoliberal Ireland 135–9; neoliberal Irishness 77–81; and the neoliberal state 8–11, 74–98; normalised acceptance of racism 97, 120–1; and organisational blindness 109–12; physical assault 1, 75, 89, 92, 135, 148–9; police recognition of 140; property damage 75; proposed definition 52–3; random security checks 84–6; recognition as a distinct form of racism 33–4; recording of 7, 145–6; reporting of 7, 10, 137–9; resisting anti-Muslim racism in the neoliberal era 140–5;

resisting racelessness and anti-Muslim racism 29–31; right wing groups 50–1; subjugated knowledge 5, 13–14, 14n1, 33–4, 135, 140, 143, 147–9; suspect communities 77, 82–6; suspicious communities 86–8; verbal abuse 1, 74, 80–1, 86–7, 92, 135, 147–8
anti-racism 101–4; rhetorical anti-racism 104–12, 139–40
anti-Semitism 39, 60, 63, 71n9, 77
Associated Press 47
Association of Chief Police Officers (UK) 60
Atherton, S. 138
Australia 3, 7, 120, 142, 150n1
auto-racialisation 37

Bagguley, P. 156–7
belonging 2, 37, 38, 74; hegemonic Irishness 76–7; historical notions of 8, 13, 39; national belonging 5, 7, 78
bin Laden, Osama 86, 87
bio-power 16–17, 26
Bolognani, M. 153, 155
Bonilla-Silva, E. 50
Brå 63, 64
Brady, T. 118
Brown, M. 33, 35, 36–7, 37–8, 39–40, 43, 52

Cannon, Matt 105
Carr, Nicola 55
Catholic-ness 39, 76, 77, 81; White, Heterosexual, Irish, Sedentary and Catholic (WHISC) 77, 78, 89, 96–7, 98n5, 100–1, 125, 126, 135
census data 8, 31, 143–4, 158–9

Index

Central Statistical Office (Ireland) 10, 65, 67, 70
Chador case (France) 49
Chakraborti, N. 43, 79, 88, 125–6, 131
citizenship 101, 118, 122–3, 137
Clarke, H. 58, 63, 68–9, 111
clothing 3, 41, 48–9, 81, 89, 91, 93, 95–6, 110, 136, 156
Cole, M. 42, 52
colonialism 8, 76
conduct 22, 23–4, 134; counter conduct 13–14, 29–30, 53, 140, 141, 143, 145
Corr, Gerard 59
criminality 23, 63, 65, 67, 77, 110, 146
Crowley, U. 100
cultural racism 42

Damache, Ali Charaf 118
data on racism, lack of 1, 2, 10–11, 30–1, 55–6, 69, 70–1; *see also* recording racism
de Wan, Jennifer 103–4, 105, 106, 122, 130
Dean, M. 5, 7, 20, 21, 22, 30, 82
Dinsbach, W. 62
discrimination 66–7, 75–6, 136, 152; employment discrimination 90–2, 121–2, 136; public service 88–9; on public transport 87
diversity 27–8
Diversity Consultations 68, 69, 107–9, 139
Dunn, K.M. 38
Dwyer, C. 93

education 78, 141–2
employment discrimination 90–2, 121–2, 136
English Defence League 43
Equality Authority 32n3, 127
'Ethnic Liaison/Diversity Officers' 68, 69, 105–6
ethnic profiling 84
EUFRA (European Union Agency for Fundamental Rights) 69
European Monitoring Centre for Racism and Xenophobia 55
European Network Against Racism (Ireland) 58, 127–8
European Union Agency for Fundamental Rights 59
European Union Framework Decision on Combating Racism and Xenophobia 28, 56

European Union Minorities and Discrimination Survey 120
European Values Survey (EVS) 74
exclusion 7, 26, 35, 53; exclusionary practices 36

Fanning, B. 7, 55, 67–8, 106, 107, 108, 109, 114
Fekete, L. 3, 47
Fianna Fáil 101
Finland 61, 63–4
'foreign fighters' 47–8
Foucault, Michel 4–6, 7–8, 11–12, 15, 22, 133, 140, 143; counter conduct 29–30; disciplinary power and the norm 17–18, 29; governmentality concept 15, 18–19; *homo-œconomicus* 24, 133, 138; on racism 26; sovereign and discipline power 16–17; 'truth' 19–20
France 3–4, 49

Garda Human Rights Audit 2004 58, 117
Garda National Consultation Day 107–9
Garda Public Attitude Surveys 67
Garda Racial Intercultural and Diversity Office (GRIDO) 67–8, 100, 102, 103–4, 104–5, 106, 108, 139
Gardaí *see* police
Garland, J. 155
Garner, S. 7, 34, 39, 43
Germany 49
Giroux, H.J. 135
'global war on terror' 1, 46, 48
Goldberg, D.T. 7–8, 27, 28, 30–1, 45, 134
government/state: anti-Muslim racism and the neoliberal state 8–11; confidence/trust in 67, 70, 115–19, 131, 138; denial of the salience of race 8, 53, 58–9; disciplinary power and the norm 17–18; Foucauldian theories 11–12; government rationalities and truth 4–6; governmentality concept of Foucault 15, 18–19; governmentality studies 7, 8; Ireland and post-racial neoliberal governmentality 137; privatising care 25–6, 28, 123, 124, 125, 127–30, 138–9; race, racism and the post-racial neoliberal 'moment' 26–9; resisting anti-Muslim racism in the neoliberal era 140–5; resisting racelessness and anti-Muslim racism 29–31; self-care 23–5, 125–7; sovereign and discipline power 16–17; 'truth'/rationalities of neoliberal governmentality 4–6, 21–6, 133–5

Gray, B. 25–6
Greater London Authority 51–2
Greene, J.R. 108

Harvey, David 8, 21, 77
hate 8; hate crime 60–3, 63–4, 65, 70, 137, 146; hate mail 41, 142, 144, **162**; normalised hate 120
Hennink, M. 158
Herek, G.M. 120
hetero-racialisation 37
Hickman, M. 3, 143
hijab 3, 41, 48–9, 81, 91, 93, 95–6, 135, 136
History of Sexuality: Volume One (Foucault) 16
homo-œconomicus 24, 133, 138
Hopkins, P.E. 157
Hussain, Y. 156–7

identities 7, 27, 32, 35, 39, 77, 110, 155; Catholic-ness 39, 76, 77, 81; communal identities 78–9; cultural identity 38–9; group-based identities 49; hegemonic Irishness 76–7; Muslim reverts 80–1, 81–2, 93–4, 110, 116–17, 117–18, 121, 124; religious identifiability and 'selective invisibility' 88–92; visual identifiers of Muslimness 2–3, 41, 79, 81, 84, 88, 89; White, Heterosexual, Irish, Sedentary and Catholic (WHISC) 77, 78, 89, 96–7, 98n5, 100–1, 125, 126, 135
Iganski, Paul 30, 120
Immigrant Council of Ireland (ICI) 58, 68, 103, 128
Incitement to Hatred Act (1989) 56
individualism 22, 23–4, 29, 31, 78–9, 134
International Association of Chiefs of Police 70
International Education Strategy 141
iReport.ie 58, 127–8
Irish Human Rights Commission 127
Irish state: anti-Muslim racism 7, 9, 12–13, 74–6; anti-Muslim racism and neoliberal Ireland 135–9; anti-racism and the Irish state 101–4; criminal legislation 56; equality legislation 56; facade of 'care' 69, 100, 101, 104, 106–7, 114, 139; as a neoliberal state 8; organisational blindness and anti-Muslim racism 109–12; and post-racial neoliberal governmentality 137; privatising care 25–6, 28, 123, 124, 125, 127–30, 138–9;

racism blindness 9–10, 12, 67; resisting anti-Muslim racism in the neoliberal era 140–5; rhetorical anti-racism and the Irish state 104–12, 139–40
Irish Sun newspaper 86
Irishness 125, 145; hegemonic Irishness 76–7; Muslimness outside the 'norm' of Irishness 79, 134–5; neoliberal Irishness 77–81; White, Heterosexual, Irish, Sedentary and Catholic (WHISC) 77, 78, 89, 96–7, 98n5, 100–1, 125, 126, 135
ISIS 3, 4, 48
Islam 4, 8–9, 34, 35, 43, 45, 51–2, 54n1, 87, 94, 155
Islamophilia 34
Islamophobia 6–7, 12; anti-Muslim sentiment 44–5, 46; as a conceptual term 42–3, 44, 53; de-construction of 33–54; defining anti-Muslim racism as anti-Muslim *racism* 37–44; defining racism 36–7; definitions of Islamophobia 34–6, 37–8; denial of the salience of race 8, 53, 58–9; double truths of problematic communities 46–8; neoliberalism and efficient racialised 'truths' of the Muslim as 'other' 44–53; proposed definition for anti-Muslim racism 52–3; purveyors of racialised 'truths' 51–2; right wing groups 50–1; saving Muslim women 48–50
Islamophobia: A Challenge for us all (Runnymede Trust) 2, 34–5

Jewish people 39, 77
'Jihad Jane' affair 118
Jones, S.H. 47

Katsiaficas, D. 152
Kaya, A. 46
Keohane, K. 78
Kilkenny Integration Forum 68
Killoran, Brian 103, 105, 107
King-O'Riain, R.C. 144
Kitchin, R. 100
'Know Racism' campaign 100
Kuhling, C. 78
Kumar, D. 6, 46
Kundnani, A. 46

LaRose, Colleen 118
Lawrence Stephen 8, 57, 70
Leicester Hate Crime Project 120
Lentin, A. 8, 44

Lewis, J. 51, 52
Listhaug, O. 74
Lynch, Catherine 68, 111–12, 122, 131

Mac Gréil, M. 39, 77
McCue, Ken 107
McGinnity, F. 66
Machiavelli, Niccolo 18
McInerney, Dave (police officer) 57, 58, 69, 138
McNay, L. 22
Macpherson report 57, 58, 60, 70
McVeigh, R. 36
Maher, S. 47
Mahtani, M. 27
media 51–2; sensationalist reports 86–7
Meer, N. 35, 38, 39, 42
migrant integration 2–3, 26, 39–40
Migrant Rights' Centre Ireland 84, 116, 123
Migration Nation (Office of the Minister for Integration) 127
Miles, R. 33, 35, 36–7, 37–8, 38, 39–40, 43, 52
mixed methods research (MMR) 151
Modood, T. 35, 38, 39, 42
Moore, R. 143
Muir, H. 45
Muslim communities: *Al-Minnah Foods* incident 40–1; alleged failure to integrate 2–3, 39–40; anti-Muslim sentiment 44–5, 46; discrimination 66–7; double truths of problematic communities 46–8; effect of racialised discourses, policies and practices 3–4; exclusion 7, 26, 35, 36, 53; growth of 2; hate mail 41, 142, 144, **162**; image of 2; in Ireland 8–9; as suspect communities 82–6, 136; suspicious communities 86–8; view of, as an enemy within 3, 46–7, 52
Muslimness 6, 35, 53; Muslim reverts 80–1, 81–2, 93–4, 110, 116–17, 117–18, 121, 124; Muslimness outside the 'norm' of Irishness 79, 134–5; religious identifiability and 'selective invisibility' 88–92; visual identifiers of 2–3, 41, 79, 81, 84, 88, 89

narrative reports 63–4
Nasc 115–16
National Action Plan Against Racism 9, 55, 65, 100
National Consultative Committee on Racism and Interculturalism (NCCRI) 1, 26, 32n3, 86, 100, 127, 129, 137, 144

neoliberalism 5, 11, 15, 31–2, 139–40; anti-Muslim racism and the neoliberal state 8–11, 74–98; anti-racism and the Irish state 101–4; double truths of problematic communities 46–8; and efficient racialised 'truths' of the Muslim as 'other' 44–53; Ireland and post-racial neoliberal governmentality 137; neoliberal governmentalities of 'care' 99–113, 139–40; neoliberal Irishness 77–81; neoliberal (non)racial republic 99–101; organisational blindness and anti-Muslim racism 109–12; privatising care 25–6, 28, 123, 124, 125, 127–30, 138–9; proposed definition for anti-Muslim racism 52–3; purveyors of racialised 'truths' 51–2; 'race' racism and the post-racial neoliberal 'moment' 26–9; as a regime of 'truth' 21; resisting anti-Muslim racism in the neoliberal era 140–5; resisting racelessness and anti-Muslim racism 29–31; rhetorical anti-racism and the Irish state 104–12, 139–40; right wing groups 50–1; saving Muslim women 48–50; self-care 23–5; 'truth'/ rationalities of neoliberal governmentality 4–6, 21–6, 133–5
Netherlands 62–3, 81
Neumann, P. 47
NGO NASC 68
Nickels, H.C. 82
Nielsen, J. 3, 41, 48–9
niqab 3, 89, 95–6, 135
Noble, G. 3, 120, 126
Nocon, A. 110
non-governmental organisations (NGOs) 25–6, 58, 61, 68, 127–30, 131, 138–9, 159, 160–1

Office for the Promotion of Migrant Integration (OPMI) 69, 137
Oksala, J. 29
Open Society Institute 4
Organisation for Security and Cooperation in Europe 55–6
'other', the 6, 7, 12, 15, 26–7, 28, 29, 30, 32, 36–7; double truths of problematic communities 46–8; Muslims as the 'other' 35, 134–5, 136; neoliberalism and efficient racialised 'truths' of the Muslim as 'other' 44–53; proposed definition for anti-Muslim racism 52–3; purveyors of racialised 'truths' 51–2; religion and

Index   195

defining the 'other' 38–9; right wing groups 50–1; saving Muslim women 48–50; and statistical knowledge 31

Perry, B. 85, 86
personal failures 24, 27
Peuteure, L. 63
phenotype 33, 36, 37–8, 39
physical assault 1, 75, 89, 92, 135, 148–9
police 10, 129–30, 144, 159, 160–1; alternative and complementary data on racism 64–7; community policing 102–4, 106, 108–9, 112, 139; confidence/trust in 67, 70, 115–19, 131, 138; 'Ethnic Liaison/ Diversity Officers' 68, 69, 105–6; Finland 61, 63; Garda Human Rights Audit 2004 58, 67, 117; Garda National Consultation Day 107–9; Garda Public Attitude Surveys 67; Garda Racial Intercultural and Diversity Office (GRIDO) 67–8, 69, 100, 102, 103–4, 104–5, 106, 108, 139; identifying racism through narrative reports 63–4; inconsistent policing methods 68, 108–9, 138; lack of understanding of racist crime 110–11; need for recognition of anti-Muslim racism 140; Netherlands 62–3; profiling practices 82–6, 115–16, 132n3; Sweden 61–2, 63–4; United Kingdom (UK) 60–1; *see also* recording racism; reporting racism
Police College of Finland 61
Police Using Leading Systems Effectively (PULSE) 56–7, 58, 64, 111, 144, 146
population management 16–17, 18–19
power 5, 26; disciplinary power and the norm 17–18, 29–30; and resistance 140; sovereign and discipline power 16–17
Poynting, S. 3, 85, 86, 120, 126
Prevent (Home Office) 46
Prince, The (Machiavelli) 18
privatisation 25–6, 28, 123, 124, 125, 127–30, 138–9
profiling practices 82–6, 115–16, 132n3
Prohibition of the Incitement to Hatred Act (1989) 71n3
property damage 75
Protestants 76–7
purposive sampling 159

Quarterly National Household Survey Equality Module 66–7, 75

racelessness 27, 29–31
racialisation 7, 27, 33, 36–7, 38, 50, 136–7

racism 133, 134; anti-racism and the Irish state 101–4; biological/cultural racism 42; care of victims of 26; defining anti-Muslim racism as anti-Muslim *racism* 37–44; definitions 36–7; and neoliberalism 15, 23; and the post-racial neoliberal 'moment' 26–9; 'race' 11–12; rhetorical anti-racism and the Irish state 104–12, 139–40; risks of exposure to 24–5; theories of 'race' and *racism-lessness* 6–8; *see also* recording racism; reporting racism
racism blindness 9–10, 12, 25, 27–8, 31; organisational blindness and anti-Muslim racism 109–12
Rana, J. 38
random checks 84–6
Rational Reporting Routine (RAR) (Sweden) 61–2
Razack, S.H. 93, 137
recording racism 7, 12, 55–73, 137, 139–40, 144; alternative and complementary data 64–7; best practice on recording anti-Muslim racism, 145–6; discrimination 66–7; encouraging reporting 67–9, 146; Finland 61; international best practice: flags, markers and codes 59–63, 146; Ireland and the international context 56–64; lack of data on anti-Muslim racism 1, 2, 10–11, 30–1, 55–6, 143–4; narrative reports 63–4; Netherlands 62–3; police 55, 56–9, 111–12; search terms 63–4; surveys 64–5; Sweden 61–2; United Kingdom (UK) 60–1
religion 136; and defining the 'other' 38–9; religious identifiability and 'selective invisibility' 88–92, 136; religiously aggravated crime 60
reporting racism 13; coping strategies for dealing with racism 120, 125–7; encouraging reporting 67–9, 102–4, 146; erosion of trust 115–19; fear of 121–3, 138; feelings of futility 123–5, 138; managing care 127–30; normalised acceptance of racism 97, 120–1, 138; underreporting of anti-Muslim racism 137–9; underreporting of racism 114–15
respondent driven sampling (RDS) 157–8
Rigby, Lee 4
right wing groups 50–1
risk management 24–5
Roberts, D.J. 27
Rose, N. 15

Roy, O. 47
Runnymede Trust 2, 34–5
Russell, H. 66
Ryan, L. 157

Saudi Arabian Cultural Attaché to Ireland 142
Sayyid, S. 45
securitisation 3, 13, 46–7, 48, 51; random checks 84–6
'selective invisibility' 88–92
self-care 23–5, 125–7
Semati, M. 38
Sharp, D. 138
Shatter, Alan 144
Sheehi, S. 48
Siraj, A. 156
Sirin, S.R. 152
Smith, L. 45
snowball sampling 158–9
social care 22–3, 31, 134; facade of 'care' 69, 100, 101, 104, 106–7, 114, 139; neoliberal governmentalities of 'care' 99–113; neoliberal (non)racial republic 99–101; privatising care 25–6, 28, 123, 124, 125, 127–30, 138–9; self-care 23–5, 125–7
statistical knowledge 16–17, 19; of anti-Muslim racism 1, 2, 10–11, 30–1, 53, 143–4; census data 143–4
stereotypical imagery 51–2
Strabac, Z. 74
students 141–2, 150n1
study methodology: accessing the knowledges of anti-Muslim racism 151–2; building trust with Irish Muslim communities 153–4; diversity 154–5; interviews 153; mixed methods research (MMR) 151; phase one: self-completion questionnaire 159–60; phase two: purposeful discussions 160–1; positionality 155–7; purposive sampling 159; respondent driven sampling (RDS) 157–8; snowball sampling 158–9; understanding the impact of 'reality' 152–3
subjugated knowledge 5, 13–14, 14n1, 33–4, 135, 140, 143, 147–9
surveillance 17–18, 47, 48, 81–2
surveys 64–5, 146, 151–2; European Values Survey (EVS) 74; Quarterly National Household Survey Equality Module 66–7
suspect communities 77, 82–6; random security checks 84–6

suspicious communities 86–8
Sweden 61–2, 63, 65
Swedish Crime Survey (SCS) 65

Taylor, S. 57
telos 134
Tell MAMA (Measuring Anti-Muslim Attacks) 61
terrorism 3, 44, 46, 47, 52, 74–5, 81, 82, 84, 86–7, 88, 116
Thatcher, Margaret 23
Thompson, Graham 8, 13, 21, 141
Titley, G. 8
Traveller Community 31, 37, 39, 42, 69, 77, 100–1, 117, 137, 144
'True vision' (website) 60
'truth' 19–20, 74; double truths of problematic communities 46–8; and neoliberalism 21, 29, 30; neoliberalism and efficient racialised 'truths' of the Muslim as 'other' 44–53; privatising care 25–6; proposed definition for anti-Muslim racism 52–3; purveyors of racialised 'truths' 51–2; and rationalities of neoliberal governmentality 4–6, 21–6, 133–5; right wing groups 50–1; saving Muslim women 48–50; self-care 23–5

United Kingdom (UK) 4, 10; census data 31, 143; recording racism 60–1; surveys 65
United Nations Convention on the Elimination of All Forms of Racial Discrimination (CERD) 28, 100
United Nations Universal Periodic Review 2011 59
Urban, Pope 45

Vakil, A. 42–3
Van Nieuwkerk, K. 81
verbal abuse 1, 74, 75, 80–1, 86–7, 92, 135, 147–8
Vilks, Lars 118

Walsh, D. 70
'war on terror' 1, 46, 48, 52, 74–5, 86
women 3, 4, 24, 84, 93–4, 110, 136, 156; employment discrimination 90–2; frustration about the oppression myth 93–4; lack of trust in the police 115–16; 'liberation' of
women: as passive victims of oppressive cultures 93; religious identifiability and 'selective invisibility' 88–92

Zempi, I. 43, 79, 88, 125–6